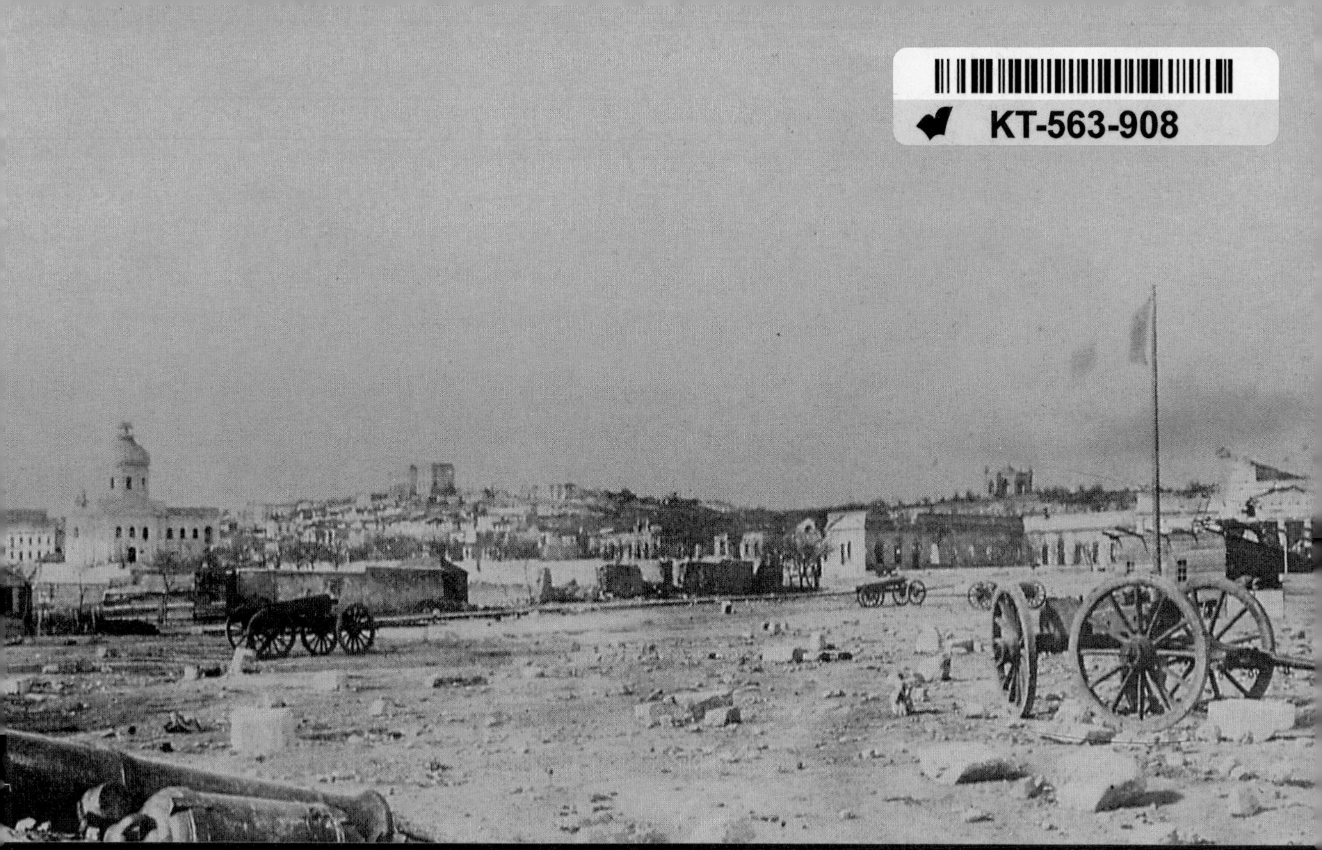

THE CRIMEAN WAR

PAUL KERR, GEORGINA PYE, TERESA CHERFAS, MICK GOLD
AND MARGARET MULVIHILL

First published in Great Britain in hardback in 1997 by Boxtree

This edition published in 1998 by Boxtree
an imprint of Macmillan Publishers Ltd
25 Eccleston Place, London SW1W 9NF and Basingstoke

Associated companies throughout the world

ISBN 07522 1184 6

1 3 5 7 9 8 6 4 2

A CIP catalogue entry for this book is available from the British Library.

Designed by Hammond Hammond
Jacket design: Hammond Hammond

Printed and bound in Italy by New Inter Litho

PREVIOUS PAGE: SEBASTOPOLN (PHOTO BY LEON-EUGENE MÉHÉDIN).
FRONT JACKET PHOTOGRAPH: THE CAPTURE OF SEBASTOPOLN A FRENCH VIEW (UNATTRIBUTED).
COURTESY OF MARY EVANS/EXPLORER/DESMARTEAU.
BACK JACKET PHOTOGRAPH: ISMAIL PASHA AND ATTENDANTS (ROGER FENTON, 1855).

THE CRIMEAN WAR

Paul Kerr is the Series Producer of *The Crimean War*. He has worked in television, for both the BBC and Channel 4, since 1984, specialising in arts and history programmes, most recently as Series Editor of BBC2's award-winning cinema series *Moving Pictures*. He has edited two previous books about film and television.

Mick Gold is the Series Director of *The Crimean War*. He has directed many film and TV documentaries, including *Death of Apartheid* (BBC2), *Victorian Values* (Granada TV) and the Emmy award-winning series *Watergate* (BBC2).

Teresa Cherfas is Assistant Producer of *The Crimean War*. She has an M.Phil. in Russian Studies and has worked in the former Soviet Union where she researched and produced several historical documentaries for UK and US television including *Stalin* (Thames TV), *Messengers from Moscow* (BBC2 and WNET) and *Last of the Czars* (The Discovery Channel).

Georgina Pye is Researcher of *The Crimean War*. She graduated in French and Italian in 1994 and has done the development research which led to the commissioning of this Channel 4 series.

Margaret Mulvihill is a novelist and historian. She has published three novels, most recently *St Patrick's Daughter*, many general history books and a biography of Charlotte Despard.

The Crimean War accompanies the major television series on Channel 4 produced by Mentorn Barraclough Carey Productions Limited.

CONTENTS

INTRODUCTION

In December 1854 Captain Henry Clifford, of the Rifle Brigade, was reading the latest Dickens novel, *Hard Times*, in his tent outside Sebastopol. He put the book to one side and jotted down a note in his journal:

> **I wish he could sit, with my pen and paper, and write a book, '*Hard Times* in the Crimea'. Only just what is passing in front of my comfortable little tent, would give him plenty of matter.**

Charles Dickens was in England of course, but he did feel strongly about what he heard from the Crimea, and found time to make speeches and write articles denouncing the mismanagement of the war while working on his next novel. *Little Dorritt* turned out to be an acerbic attack on Britain's seemingly endemic bureaucracy; in fact, its anger was fuelled by the notorious mishandling of the war effort. Dickens' foreword to the first edition explains the book's venom by referring to the 'Russian war' and in one of *Little Dorrit*'s most celebrated chapters, on the 'Circumlocution Office', the author creates a wonderful parody of civil service inertia. The civil service, in the form of the Treasury, contributed a great deal to the British army's legendary Commissariat difficulties in the Crimea.

While Captain Clifford was reading *Hard Times*, an artillery ensign in the Russian army was enjoying a translation of Dickens' *Bleak House*, which was being serialized that year in the Russian literary journal, *The Contemporary*. Within a year that ensign, Leo Tolstoy, had written and published an account of life inside Sebastopol during the siege in the same journal. Tolstoy fought on all three fronts of the land war – the Caucasus, the Danube and the Crimea; he wrote letters, diaries and much of his early fiction about his experiences while serving there. In December 1853, Leo Tolstoy wrote in his diary, 'Every historical fact needs to be explained in human terms...' This compilation of the images and words of eye witnesses is an attempt to reinsert those human stories back into history.

There was no shortage of 'Dickenses' at the front. Besides 'official' on-the-spot historians like Britain's A.W. Kinglake and France's César de Bazancourt, and war correspondents such as *The Times'* William Howard Russell, there were prolific and powerful diarists and letter-writers.

And just as there were writers of note among the eye-witnesses of the campaign there were also pioneering war photographers like Britain's Roger Fenton and James Robertson, and war artists such as France's Constantin Guys, Britain's William Simpson and Russia's Vasili Timm. The first ever war photographer was a little-known Rumanian, Karol de Szathmari, who took some 200 pictures of the campaign on the Danube in the spring of 1854 – a full year before Fenton arrived in the Crimea. As well as the professionals, there were also gifted amateur artists, nurses such as Ann Morton and soldiers like Captain Henry Clifford, who painted some of the most extraordinary images of the war.

This first-person approach to the war shifts the emphasis of history from the words of ministers, diplomats and military commanders to those of ordinary soldiers and sailors, doctors and nurses, artists and reporters, tourists and clergymen. Furthermore, these eye-witness accounts from the front line and the field hospital are not only British - they are also French, Russian, Turkish and Sardinian. In taking such an approach this book cannot hope to equal the detailed descriptions of diplomacy and strategy that the best books on the war already offer. A bibliography at the end of the book lists some further reading in this vein.

The very term 'Crimean' is something of a misnomer. Known at the time as 'the Russian War', the historian Kinglake was the first to make the Crimea the war's titular centre. Kinglake's eight-volume 1877 account, *The Invasion of the Crimea*, only takes the story up to the death of Lord Raglan, following the Homeric model of the death of Achilles in *The Iliad.* And yet Raglan died three months before the fall of Sebastopol and another six before the end of the war. William Howard Russell, whose contemporary accounts of the conflict are among the best known, still entitled his 1895 retrospective volume *The Great War with Russia*, and was with the Allies in Bulgaria and on board ship in the attacks on both Kertch in the Sea of Azov and Kinburn on the mouth of the Dniepr. But the Crimean War it remains – to the extent that even dissenting perspectives are obliged to borrow the phrase – if only for recognition value.

The Crimean War was, in many ways, not only the last of the old wars but also the first of the modern ones. It was the first to use railways, iron-clad steamships, mines and the telegraph; and it foreshadowed the end of outmoded military traditions, epitomized on the British side by nepotism and the buying of commissions, on the French by the reward of senior posts to officers who had supported Napoleon III's coup, and on both the Russian and Ottoman sides by serfdom. It even offered a glimpse of trench warfare more than half a century before the First World War.

Nor was the Crimean War simply the succession of politically inconsequential military catastrophes of popular memory. There were more casualties than in the American Civil War, but like that war, the Crimean conflict transformed the balance of power of a continent. Indeed, the war can be seen as the crucible of modern Europe – the only major military conflict involving the great powers in the hundred years between Waterloo and the Somme. It changed Russia forever, resulting in the freeing of the serfs and the first revolutionary stirrings; it reformed the medical establishment, transformed the British army and destroyed a British government; it left a power vacuum at the heart of Europe that Prussia swiftly exploited with the creation of a unified Germany; it destroyed the Holy Alliance, weakening Austria and resulting in a new kingdom of Italy. Nascent Balkan nationalism led to the independence of Rumania. French military prestige, shattered by Waterloo, was recovered. Nothing would ever be quite the same again.

The Crimean War has left evocations of the past in the legendary heroics of the Light Brigade and the 'Lady with the Lamp', made mythic by Alfred Lord Tennyson and Hollywood. It has left its mark on the language too, inspiring the remarks 'C'est magnifique, mais c'est n'est pas la guerre', 'the sick man of Europe' and 'the thin red line'; in England even words for winter clothing – cardigan, balaclava and raglan sleeves – all derive from the war. The Anglo-Turkish alliance during the war gave the British the word 'bosh', and gave the Turks the naval expression 'fire up', meaning get cracking. In Paris the names of several stations on the Metro map provide ample testimony to the presence of the Crimean past. Even the former French colony Algeria has many Crimean place names on its map. In Russia, the Crimean War's siege of Sebastopol is known as that town's first defence, to distinguish it from its equally heroic second defence during the Second World War.

The image of Europe with a power vacuum at its centre is a curiously contemporary one as Russia unravels and a recently reunited Germany worries its European neighbours. Similarly, the war's ethnic and religious rivalries are all very much still alive: Chechen versus Russian and Muslim versus Christian. The hotspots that sparked the Crimean War – Jerusalem, the Balkans, Chechnya and the Crimea itself – are rarely out of the headlines 150 years later.

The day after Henry Clifford made his journal entry outside Sebastopol about *Hard Times*, Leo Tolstoy was sent into the besieged city. In his diary he wrote:

> **It's wonderful how beautiful Sebastopol is... I went to a hospital and spent time in a ward for the allied wounded. Most of the men had gone – dead or recovered – but the rest were convalescing. I found some five of them round an iron stove. French, English and Russians were laughing, chatting and playing cards, each one speaking his own language, with only the warders speaking some strange jargon in their attempt to make themselves understood by all...**

This book is an attempt to bring those voices, in all their different accents, and those faces, with all their expressions, back to life.

CHAPTER ONE

THE REASON WHY

OF EUROPE'S GREAT POWERS in the revolutionary year of 1848 only the Russian and British governments did not fall. The peace in Europe that had lasted since Waterloo was finally disintegrating. In France there was a republican revolution in February. In Italy, Austria, Hungary and Germany there were uprisings in March. Even in London, special constables had to be enlisted by the Prime Minister, the Duke of Wellington, to quell Chartist demonstrators in April.

THE MOSQUE OF TOPHANE, CONSTANTINOPLE (JAMES ROBERTSON).

CONSTANTINOPLE, BETWEEN THE BLACK SEA AND THE MEDITERRANEAN, WAS IN A KEY STRATEGIC POSITION.

This outburst of popular unrest could not be left unchecked for long. In August 1849 the revolution in Hungary was brutally put down by a joint force of Russians and Austrians. On 2 December 1851, President Louis Napoleon staged a *coup d'état* in France; exactly a year later he established the Second Empire and became Emperor Napoleon III. In 1852, in Britain, Napoleon Bonaparte's old enemy, the Duke of Wellington, died. A new world order appeared to be emerging. Writing in *The New York Tribune* on 7 April 1853 one journalist, Karl Marx, noted, 'Whenever the revolutionary hurricane has subsided for a moment, one ever-recurring question is sure to turn up: the eternal "Eastern Question".'

The Eastern Question concerned the uncertain

future of the floundering Ottoman Empire (commonly referred to as Turkey), particularly in relation to her neighbour, Russia. The frontiers of the Russian Empire in the nineteenth century extended in the north up to Finland and the Baltic Sea and in the south around both sides of the Black Sea, reaching the Danube delta in the west and penetrating the Caucasus mountains in the east. These Russian frontiers were met on both sides of the Black Sea by the northern frontiers of the Ottoman Empire, which included Bosnia, Serbia, Moldavia and Wallachia (present day Romania), and Bulgaria, in the west, and Anatolia (or Asia Minor), bordering the Caucasus, in the east. Throughout the century a series of disputes had erupted between these neighbouring empires. This one would be different.

The decline of the Ottoman Empire had started to arouse international concern. At the beginning of 1853 Tsar Nicholas I gave a diagnosis of Russia's imperial neighbour to the British Ambassador:

> **We have a sick man on our hands, a man gravely ill, it will be a great misfortune if one of these days he slips through our hands, especially before the necessary arrangements are made.**

Each of the major powers in Europe had their own idea of what these necessary arrangements might be. The tsar had his sights on Constantinople. He shared a long-held Russian ambition for access to the ice-free Mediterranean through the Bosphorus. Britain and France were described by the backbench MP Benjamin Disraeli as 'the policemen of Europe', but they were not without territorial concerns of their own. For Britain, Russian expansion in Asia or the Middle East was a potential threat not only to the Mediterranean but also to the northwest frontier of India. In France, Emperor Napoleon III was keen to reassociate his name with military prestige and imperial expansion. Prince Albert's remarks about Russia echoed public feeling: 'The Emperor of Russia is a tyrant and the enemy of all liberty on the Continent.'

Such sentiments rather concealed the fact that if Russian serfdom offended liberal sympathies so too must the Ottoman Empire's. But while Britain nursed hopes that careful diplomacy could sustain the *status quo* at least as far as the Ottoman Empire was concerned, Marx remained unconvinced:

> **Keep up the status quo in Turkey! Why you might as well try to keep up the precise degree of putridity into which the carcass of a dead horse has passed at a given time, before dissolution is complete. Turkey goes on decaying, and will go on decaying as long as the present system of 'balance of power' and maintenance of the status quo goes on.**

Marx's grim diagnosis was shared by both Russia and France. Both had their own imperial axes to grind, and both found what they were looking for in a long running quarrel over the right to worship in a remote part of the Ottoman Empire, Jerusalem. Since the early

Constantinople and the Bosphorus from the Seraskier Tower (James Robertson).

1850s Muslim policemen had been kept posted both inside and outside the Church of the Holy Sepulchre in Jerusalem, the Church of the Nativity in Bethlehem, and the Tomb of the Virgin at Gethsemane in an attempt to keep the peace between Catholics and Greek Orthodox Christians. In 1853, a British cleric, W.H. Bartlett, visiting the Church of the Holy Sepulchre, witnessed:

> **...different sets of warring monks, regarding one another with deadly hatred, exhausting every artifice of petty intrigue to supplant each other in the possession of these gainful shrines, and often coming to blows in the very holiest places. There is something so melancholy and degrading in the spectacle, that one almost wishes that the place were levelled to the ground, and its dust dispersed to the winds; that Christianity might no longer be degraded on the very spot where it first came into existence.**

According to James Finn, the British Consul in Jerusalem: '...the weapons used in such warfare were indeed carnal, even bodily fists, besides crucifixes and huge wax tapers taken from the very altars.'

Since Jerusalem was part of the Ottoman Empire, the Muslims were expected to settle this dispute and were blamed both for the casualties and the continuing controversy. But as Karl Marx perceived, the quarrels in the Holy Places were merely a pretext for a much wider struggle:

> **Imagine all these conflicting peoples beleaguering the Holy Sepulchre, the battle conducted by the monks, and the ostensible object of their rivalry being a star from the grotto of Bethlehem, a tapestry, a key of a sanctuary, an altar, a shrine, a chair, a cushion – any ridiculous precedence!...these sacred rows merely conceal a profane battle.**

France had historically seen itself as defender of Catholicism in the Holy Places, just as Russia saw itself as protector of Orthodox priests and places of worship. The Ottoman Empire's perceived weakness amplified what might otherwise have remained local power struggles. Both Napoleon III and Tsar Nicholas I were determined to win whatever victories they could over the issue. In the war of words that ensued, all of Europe's great powers were drawn into the negotiations, and increasingly frantic messages – dubbed the '1001 notes' by one diplomatic wit – were exchanged between Sultan Abdul Medjid, Emperor Napoleon III and Tsar Nicholas, with Britain acting as intermediary. The three autocrats failed to resolve the dispute and when, in May, Nicholas threw down the gauntlet by demanding the right to act as protector of the ten million Orthodox Christian subjects of the Ottoman Empire there was little room for manoeuvre. The tsar's ultimatum was rejected by the sultan and in

July 1853, to increase pressure on their ailing neighbour, Russia moved into the Principalities of Moldavia and Wallachia north of the Danube.

The Danubian Principalities were only nominally still part of the Ottoman Empire. Here, as in the Holy Places, the Russians could test the water, exercising their rights as protectors of the Orthodox Christian population. Perhaps they were assuming that not until they crossed the Danube into Bulgaria would their actions constitute an act of war. Neverthless they were drawing a fine line. On 5 October 1853 the Turks declared war.

The commander-in-chief of the Ottoman (Turkish) army was Omar Pasha. He was actually a Croat – his real name was Michael Lotis and he was a renegade from the Austrian army. Like all the European officers in the Ottoman forces he had been obliged to convert to Islam and take a Turkish name. On 8 October, with troops ready waiting in Bulgaria south of the Danube, Omar Pasha gave Russia's General Gorchakov two weeks to evacuate the Principalities. His ultimatum went unheeded and on 23 October, the Turks went on the offensive, crossing the Danube at Widdin in Western Bulgaria and advancing on the Russian positions. Ahmed Lutfi Efendi, the Ottoman court historian of the time, wrote:

> **The area seized could more properly be said to have been recovered, for this was not part of Russia. Our action was not an unlawful incursion, because the cannon burst on our soil.**

A cannon had burst nonetheless, and there followed a series of confrontations across the Danube. The Ottoman army won their first victory on 4 November at Oltenitsa, just south of Bucharest and opposite their base at Turtukai. Having forded the Danube to an island midway across and fortified their positions, they were ready to ambush the Russian attack when it came. Omar Pasha sent a letter to the sultan in Constantinople reporting the battle:

> **They could not stand the cannon shot from Turtukai and the island and the determined and lion-like onslaught of brave soldiers of the sublime Lord, who have the courage of Rustem. Many Russian soldiers were broken in the routs and after falling back, were repulsed in complete ignominy and defeat and destruction and devastating retreat.**
>
> **And in this pitched battle, many Russians were killed and wounded and more than two thousand rifles and helmets and other equipment were taken, while the Imperial Army sustained 30 martyrs and 150 wounded. With the grace and favour of God and the inspiration of the honoured Prophet and the sacred power of the most glorious and most just Sultan this commencement of war gave great honour to the Sublime State and to all people of Islam...**

The Russians counter-attacked but received many casualties and were forced to retreat. Over the next few weeks the Russians would be repulsed from other bases on the Danube, as the Turks, who had substantially larger forces, crossed the river and drove the invaders back. The sick man seemed to be reviving.

One problem for the Russians was that a worryingly high proportion of their troops was tied up in other campaigns. One of these involved fierce guerilla fighting in the Caucasus against a legendary Chechen tribesman, Shamil. He was a Muslim who had fomented a *jihad*, or holy war, against the Russian army of occupation and had for years been fighting for the independence of the hill tribes. His men were getting weaker, however, and when the Turks had finally declared war against Russia it seemed to Shamil and his mountaineer tribesmen that at last their hour had come. Earlier that year he had written to the Turkish Sultan:

> **Gracious and great Khalifa. We, your subjects, having for a long time fought the enemies of our Faith, have lost our strength. Furthermore, we, your subjects, have been hard pressed year after year [to such an extent that] now we have no force to furnish against our enemies. We are deprived of [all] means and are now in a disastrous position.**

Nevertheless Shamil was potentially a very useful ally for Sultan Abdul Medjid on the Caucasian border, especially as there was Russo-Turkish agitation in Asia Minor, quite near the Caucasus, at Kars. Although the Ottoman army had larger forces there than the Russians did, they had been forced into an undignified retreat.

While the conflict continued on various land fronts, the tension between Russia and Turkey finally came to a head on water. On 29 November the commander of the Ottoman Black Sea Fleet, Osman Pasha, saw Russian warships hovering menacingly near his base at Sinope Bay, 350 miles east of Constantinople but less than 200 miles south of the main port of Russia's Black Sea Fleet, Sebastopol, in the Crimea. He sent an urgent plea to the sultan in Constantinople:

> **The enemy naval base is near here. They could easily get reinforcements or open fire on us... This being the case, if you don't send us reinforcements and if your strategy stays the same, may Allah preserve us as the Imperial Fleet may well meet with losses.**

The following morning, 30 November, those on board the steamer *Taif*, anchored with the twelve other ships of the Ottoman Black Sea Squadron, heard gunfire:

> **Patrona Pasha signalled all the ships in the Turkish Squadron: 'The enemy's ships are all at sea and we cannot cope with them. If we put out to sea we will be lost. The best thing is to fight them, if they come, so long as we have a gun left. If there be any danger of their capturing your ship, slip your cables, run your ships on shore and set fire to them.'**

Not only did the Russians attack, but they used explosive shells for the first time in naval history. Captain Drummond, on board the British ship

Retribution, was one of the first on the scene:

> **One frigate blew up half an hour after the commencement of the action and almost all the crew perished, the other frigates were burnt, blown up and destroyed by the Russians...The Turkish town was completely destroyed having been set on fire by the shells or burning timber.**

Of the Turkish ships only the *Taif* had steamed to safety and arrived with the news in Constantinople two days later. Two British ships were sent back to treat the wounded and Captain Aldolphus Slade pieced together the story.

> **The shore of the bay was lined with wrecks and strewed with corpses. Havoc had done her worst. Not a mast was standing, not a timber was left whole. We found above a hundred wounded in various cafés, in every stage of suffering; some in agony, many of them frightfully disfigured by explosions.**

The Russian Admiral Nakhimov's complete destruction of the Ottoman squadron was exploited by the British media, and accounts like Slade's were eagerly recycled in London. Of a total of 4,490 men on

ABOVE: *THE BATTLE OF SINOPE* (ALEXANDER BOGOLYUBOV).
LEFT: *THE BATTLE OF OLTENITSA* (ANON).

board the Turkish ships it was claimed only 358 could be accounted for. According to Slade:

> **In an hour and a half the action was decided, and if Admiral Nakhimoff...had ceased fire there would have been no alloy to his credit...but he kept up a merciless fire of shot and shell which killed numbers of unresisting men...He did not cease firing till every ship save one was a stranded, bilged wreck.**

Admiral Nakhimov was quick to justify his action:

> **I sympathise with the sad fate of the town and its innocent inhabitants, but it was the obstinacy of the enemy ships in refusing to surrender and especially their firing which obliged us to use shells as the only way of quieting them. The greatest damage caused to the town certainly came from the burning wreckage of the Turkish ships which for the most part they had set fire to themselves.**

The use of explosive shells heralded a new era in naval warfare and spelt the end of the wooden warship. It was for this reason too that the battle of Sinope proved so controversial in London and was reported as a 'massacre'. Certainly it was a major victory for Russia, but it was also a tactical blunder. For it was a naval victory and Britain was not about to swallow a Russian naval victory – least of all one over a close commercial ally. As the Home Secretary Lord Palmerston put it, 'Something must be done to wipe away the stain.'

The Russian Black Sea Fleet had sailed from Sebastopol, and the Admiralty now started to consider the port as a good target for a revenge attack, if it came to war. The icy expanses of the Baltic were not navigable at this time of the year, but as the Russian Baltic Fleet, harboured at Krondstadt near St Petersburg, was only a few days' sail from Britain's east coast it was hardly surprising that by the time the thaw came in March 1854, before war had even been declared by the Allies, another fleet had sailed north to counter Russian aggression.

In Britain and France war fever was escalating. In France the conscript army was on stand-by. In Britain young men were signing up all over the country to take part in a brief campaign which would surely be over by Christmas. One of these young men was Private Timothy Gowing, a fusilier from Norwich:

> **The Turks were trying to defend themselves against their ancient foes the Russians, and thrilling accounts were appearing in our newspapers about the different fights at the seat of war on the Danube. I was now fast approaching my twentieth year...and the accounts that were constantly coming home from the East worked me up to try my luck...**

Just forty years after Wellington had defeated Napoleon at Waterloo, France and Britain signed a military alliance. Finally, on 28 March 1854, they entered the war.

CHAPTER TWO

TROUBLED WATERS

TO THE END OF his days Yanuari Kobylynsky had vivid memories of marching into the war that would eventually take him to the Crimea. On 10 March 1854, this young Russian infantry officer's regiment was among those facing the Ottomans across the Danube:

> **Our first night out on the march was cold and dark. The strong, piercing wind whistled and howled around the roofs of the old Galatsan town posts, as though playing a march to accompany the regiments. A large part of the town, set out up on the heights, opposite our positions, was sort of rejoicing and looking down at us; it was unusually bright and noisy there; but lower down, the Danube seethed, as though Neptune was about to appear, and rolled noisy waves on to the opposite shore.**

RECONNAISSANCE OF PRINCE GORCHAKOV ON THE DANUBE IN WALLACHIA (FILIPOV).

The Russians were about to advance under a newly appointed commander-in-chief, General Paskevich. He had persuaded the tsar to abandon the previous strategy of occupying Moldavia and Wallachia in favour of actually crossing the Danube and invading Bulgaria. The town of Silistria would be a serious obstacle to this southward march, but if it could be taken, the Russians' ultimate destination, Constantinople, would be well within reach.

At seven o'clock next morning, having loaded their guns and donned their packs, Kobylynsky and his comrades were in boats and ready to sail across the river:

> **On shore we moved forward cautiously but bravely, expecting at every step that a Turk would jump out of the reeds at us... We crossed and advanced along the**

Turkish shore without one shot and without even seeing a single Turk... At that time the cold and the biting north-east wind were a much more severe enemy for us than the Turks. By midday we arrived in the poor and bare settlement of Mervana...almost all the inhabitants came to see us at our positions and to look at our brave chaps, among whom there were some who could make themselves understood in Moldavian. We understood from them that before our arrival more than 600 Turks had been camped there with four cannon; upon our appearance, they quickly made tracks along the roads to Machin or Babadag, taking from the inhabitants everything they thought they might need for the journey.

ABOVE: OMAR PASHA, COMMANDER-IN-CHIEF OF THE OTTOMAN ARMY. (PHOTO BY ROGER FENTON.) LEFT: ARTILLERY OFFICER LEO TOLSTOY. (PORTRAIT BY VASILI TIMM.)

Russian troops crossed the river in several places. From Bucharest and Giurgevo to the west and the Dobrudsha in the east, they began to converge on Silistria, where General Paskevich took personal command of the assault. From his camp in the rose gardens of the region's displaced Turkish governor a young Russian artillery officer surveyed the scene below him:

...it was as if you could hold the town, the fortress and the little forts of Silistria in the palm of your hand. You could hear the cannon fire and rifle shots which went on night and day, and with a field-glass you could make out the Turkish soldiers. It's a strange sort of pleasure to see people killing each other, and yet every morning and evening I would spend hours at a time watching. I was not alone in doing this. The spectacle was truly beautiful, especially at night.

That officer was Leo Tolstoy, whose experiences in the front line during the war were to provide him with the raw material for what eventually became *War and Peace*.

Silistria had been fortified by a network of stone forts and earthwork ramparts. The most important fort, the Medjida, was defended by a huge earthwork, more than a 100 yards long, called the Arab Tabia.

Besides regular Turkish soldiers, the town's defenders included well-armed Egyptians, less well-armed Albanians and an irregular cavalry of Muslim volunteers called bashi-bazouks. Two young English officers, Captain Butler and Lieutenant Nasmyth, were also on the Danube at the time, as observers, watching the progress of hostilities. When Paskevich advanced to the siege of Silistria, they instantly went to render what assistance they could and ended up acting as military advisers to the Turkish commander of the garrison, Mustapha Pasha (nicknamed Moossa Pasha by the British). Captain Butler kept a daily journal of the siege, which starts by describing the state of the garrison:

With the exception of a small guard-room at the Stamboul gate, which Moossa Pacha has appropriated for his own quarters, there is not a bomb-proof building in the whole place: the inhabitants take refuge in caves (which they had constructed for the purpose under

ground) directly the siege commenced. The town appears quite deserted; nothing but soldiers and dogs to be seen.

From the opposite bank of the Danube, bridges had been constructed and troops sent across the river in boats. The Russians had busily dug trenches and now completely surrounded the town. Pyotr Alabin, a thirty-year-old officer in the Kamchatka Infantry regiment, also kept daily campaign notes:

Our work was carried out in this way: singers were selected from the whole regiment, they were placed at different points opposite one another, bonfires were lit here and there, there they were singing songs with drums, and here at this time, half of the regiment works at the earthworks until dawn. In the morning, Silistria looks and is amazed, when so much earth was dug up, the trench another several dozen feet longer, or the battery had sprung up higher.

At first trench duty was a shock to soldiers like Alabin:

The firing from our siege guns shakes my whole nervous system with its volume, but I am not saying that the shots are unexpected for me, no: I stand and wait for the shot - it fires and then I can barely stay upright on my legs, everything inside me is shaking so; that is what it means to be unused to it!

But as Leo Tolstoy described later in a letter to his aunt, one quickly got used to such scares:

At night our soldiers generally work on the trenches and the Turks throw themselves upon them to stop them; then you should have seen and heard the rifle-fire. The first night I spent at the camp this terrible noise woke me up and alarmed me – I thought an assault was taking place – and I very quickly saddled my horse; but those who had already spent some time at the camp told me just to keep calm; this cannon-fire and rifle-fire was quite normal and they jokingly called it 'Allah'.

By now the relative sizes of the opposing armies had been reversed and the Ottoman troops were severely outnumbered by the Russians. Mustapha Pasha wrote frequently to Omar Pasha urging reinforcements. But despite reassuring messages, none came and in the meantime the night attacks on the Arab Tabia intensified. At the end of May Captain Butler witnessed a particularly vicious assault:

No alarm was given till the enemy was actually in the redoubt. The first to enter was a Russian officer, who cut down a Turkish lieutenant of artillery, but was immediately knocked over with a handspike and killed by the men about. A fierce hand-to-hand conflict ensued with the enemy, who clambered up from the ditch and passed up through the embrasures and over the ramparts. They were driven back out into the ditch, where a terrific slaughter took place.

The next day he observed that the Turks seemed to be trying to terrify the enemy away:

Numbers of the townspeople went out and cut off the heads of the slain to bring in as trophies, for which they hoped to get a reward; but the savages were not

A BASHI-BAZOUK AND CAMP FOLLOWER. (PHOTO BY KAROL DE SZATHMARI.)

Karol de Szathmari

In 1839 the painter Paul Delaroche saw one of the first daguerreotypes and declared: 'From today, painting is dead!' Two years later a British artist, Roger Fenton (1819-1869), a pupil of Delaroche's, took up photography himself. Fenton is usually credited as being the first war photographer because of his work in the Crimea in 1855. But that title actually belongs to a little-known Rumanian, who was already in the field a year earlier documenting the conflict on camera. His name was Karol de Szathmari.

Karol de Szathmari (1812-1887) was a court painter and photographer in Bucharest. On the outbreak of war between Russia and Turkey, Szathmari compressed his photographic laboratory into a carriage and set off for the front line which lay along the banks of the Danube. There he became the first person to experience the danger of war photography: when he set up his camera to photograph a Russian quarantine station at Oltenitsa, a nearby Turkish battery opened fire on him.

Szathmari's connections gave him access to both sides. He photographed the Russian commander Prince Gorchakov, and officers including Generals Osten-Saken, Soimonov and Liprandi. From them, he obtained permission to photograph their camp. When the Turks occupied Bucharest, Szathmari also photographed their commander, Omar Pasha, as well as officers, musicians and groups of men in the field. Visible amongst these groups were British and French officers who had arrived in advance of the Allied armies as observers and may have included the two British heroes of the siege of Silistria, Captain Butler and Lieutenant Nasmyth.

Alongside such pictures he also photographed Turkish artillery in the field, Russian Cossacks and Ottoman bashi-bazouks, a Russian camp on the hillside by the banks of the river, a council of war, and the Russian retreat from Silistria with horses, wagons and infantry streaming away from the front.

Szathmari made at least four albums, each containing 200 photographs of the Danubian theatre of the war: one was presented to Queen Victoria, another to Napoleon III, and a third to Emperor Franz Joseph of Austria, while the composer Franz Liszt gave a fourth to his friend, the Duke of Saxe Weimar. The photographs were also exhibited at the Exposition Universelle in Paris in 1855. All these albums seem to have been lost; but the few pictures which survive, despite being faded or retouched, remain an extraordinary testimony to the achievements of the world's first war photographer. Some of them are shown here for the first time.

Above left: Szathmari.
Above: Omar Pasha and his aides.
Left: Turkish artillery in the field.

Russian Lancers

allowed to bring them within the gate. A heap of them, however, were left for a long time unburied just outside the gate. One ruffian, whilst we were sitting with Moossa Pacha, came and threw a pair of ears (which he had cut from a Russian soldier) at his feet: another boasted that a wounded Russian officer having begged for mercy in the name of the Prophet, he deliberately drew his knife and in cold blood cut his throat.

The Turks had kept the Russians at bay this time but they could not keep doing so and the Russians knew it. At the beginning of June, Mustapha Pasha was killed and the dwindling Turkish force became increasingly demoralized. The fall of Silistria was reckoned to be a matter of days away. In May, in response to Silistria's plight, the allied land forces finally arrived on the scene. Their destination was Varna, a port on the Black Sea only seventy miles south of the besieged Turkish garrison. It had been recommended by the Omar Pasha, whose own headquarters, at Shumla, was about sixty miles inland from Silistria. Between them, it was thought they could mount an effective relief operation.

The French arrived in Varna first and by the time British transports sailed into port, the best billets and campsites were taken and the main buildings and streets had French signs. William Howard Russell was a 34-year-old Irishman who had been sent out by *The Times* to cover the campaign and who was to become celebrated as the world's first-ever war correspondent. He was impressed to discover how carefully signposted the port had become – at least in the French quarter:

The names of the streets...were fixed to the walls so that one could find his way from place to place without going through the erratic wanderings which generally mark the stranger's progress through a Turkish town. One lane is named the Rue Ibrahim, another Rue de L'Hôpital, a third Rue Yussuf; the principal lane is termed the Corso, the next is Rue des Postes Françaises; and as all these names are very convenient, and have a meaning attached to them, no sneering ought to deter one from confessing that the French manage these things better than we do. Where is the English post office? No one knows. Where does the English General live? No one knows. Where is the hospital to carry a sick soldier to? No one knows. Does anyone want to find General Canrobert? Ask the first Frenchman you meet, and he will tell you to go up the Corso, turn to the right, by the end of the Rue de L'Hôpital, and then you will see the name of the General printed in large letters over the door of his quarters.

Right from the start, the superior organization of the French expeditionary forces was obvious.

On 1 June, Fanny Duberly, the dashing young wife of a cavalry paymaster, landed with her husband's regiment, the 8th Hussars:

...the landing place gave me a much greater realisation of the idea of 'war time' than any description could do. It was shadowing to twilight. The quay was crowded with Turks, Greeks, infantry, artillery and Hussars; piles of cannon balls and shells all around us; rattle of arms everywhere; horses kicking, screaming, plunging; and, 'Bob', whom I was to ride, was almost unmanageable from excitement and flies.

For Mrs Duberly and a handful of officers' wives like her, the expedition was a chance for sightseeing and adventure. By contrast many ordinary soldiers' wives accompanied their husbands 'on the strength' and prepared to work, most of them trying to avoid a life of grinding poverty if they stayed behind. As well as the women, the extraordinary variety of faces and costumes in the Allied camp made an impression. Colonel Cler, commander of the 2nd Zouaves, marvelled at the broad diversity of the Allied forces gathering at Varna:

It was a curious spectacle to look on, this assembly of troops, belonging to such various nations – so opposite in manners,costume and language – and yet drawn here from Europe, Asia and Africa, in defence of a common cause – and all on such good terms with one another! For, here, were the men of the North – English, Irish and Scottish - with their fair complexions, blue eyes and showy costume; the Frenchman, with his open and expressive countenance, smiling and intelligent look, and uniform made up of whatever he could find

War artists

Early one morning in October 1854 in London, the artist William Simpson (1823-1899) had a bad toothache. 'I had it pulled before going into the office,' he recalled:

> When I got there, I was queer about the mouth and I had had a bad night's rest; so I spread the morning paper I had been reading upon the floor, and laid myself upon it. I was in this position when the door opened and Mr Mackay of Colnaghi's came in. He put his glass up to his eye and looked at me suspiciously. I got up and he asked me if I would go to the Crimea.

Thus began the most detailed visual record of the Crimean War by a British artist. Simpson was despatched by the publisher, Colnaghi, to send back watercolours from *The Seat of War In The East* - as his paintings were called when published as a book. Initially, they were sold as coloured lithographs to a public eager for images of the war. Like Russell, Simpson referred to himself as a 'special' rather than 'war' correspondent. Unlike Russell, his work had almost official endorsement:

> I was in the habit of taking my sketches up to Headquarters on mail day. Calthorpe took me in to Lord Raglan, to show the sketches, and I was always invited to lunch. Lord Raglan kindly allowed me to send my sketches home in his letter bag, thus ensuring an extra security to them.

***The Interior of the Mamelon Vert* (William Simpson).**

Simpson stayed until after the fall of Sebastopol, joined the expedition to Kertch and even journeyed to Kars (and the Caucasus). His paintings have a meticulous topographical accuracy - he took great care with perspective and with geographical features - but he painted 'picture book battles' with troops in dress uniforms advancing in step, and the cavalry charging in neat, regular lines.

Significantly, Simpson was sent by a commercial publisher because, in Britain, there was no strong tradition of military art or of historical paintings commissioned by the state. In France, the situation was very different. At the outbreak of the Crimean War, Horace Vernet (1789-1863) travelled to Varna under the patronage of Prince Napoleon. After the battle of the Alma, the prince commissioned Vernet to paint a large-scale painting of this Allied victory, with himself in the centre of the canvas. He was emulating his uncle,

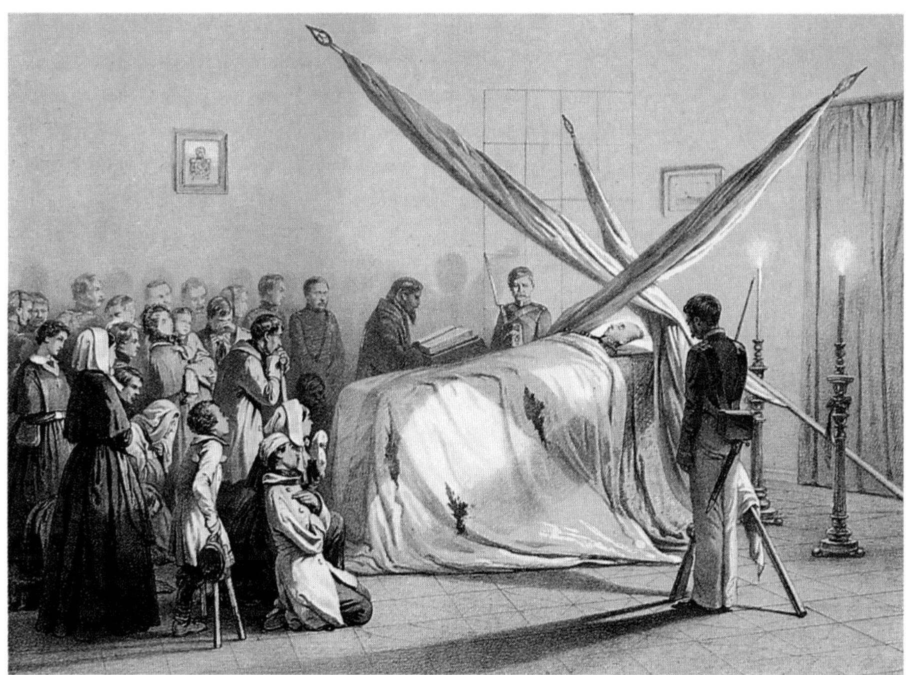

Above: *Nakhimov on his death bed* (Vasili Timm). Left: The war artist Constantin Guys on the battlefield.

Napoleon Bonaparte, who had been painted in heroic poses by artists such as Jacques-Louis David.

Vernet stayed in the Crimea until Sebastopol fell. At the beginning of 1856, Adolphe Yvon was commissioned to paint a major account of the capture of the Malakoff Tower. He spent six weeks in the Crimea making sketches, and his massive work, *La Prise de la Tour de Malakoff*, measuring six yards by nine, was destined to be hung in the Palace of Versailles.

Henri Durand-Brager (1814–1879) photographed the Crimea after the fall of Sebastopol, but he was also a prolific artist for the French illustrated weekly, *L'Illustration*. On returning to Paris, he embarked on a series of large panoramic paintings and at the Salon exhibition which opened in June 1857, he exhibited no fewer than twenty-one panoramic paintings featuring scenes from the Crimean War.

Another Frenchman, Constantin Guys (1805-1892), was one of six artists in the Crimea employed by *The Illustrated London News*. At the height of the Crimean War, the circulation of the *ILN* reached 100,000, and Guys had developed a style of working which suited the magazine. From the Crimea, he sent back copious sketches to London, where one or two would be selected and turned into wood engravings. Guys was part of an avant-garde group in Paris, which included Emile Zola and Edouard Manet; his greatest champion was Charles Baudelaire whose famous essay 'The Painter of Modern Life' celebrated Guys' achievement. Baudelaire was impressed by Guys' talent for capturing the ephemeral in his sketches. He was acclaimed as a new kind of artist whose work was at odds with the pretensions of state-sponsored military art. For Baudelaire, Guys was an artist who was in touch with the spirit of 'modernity', an artist more at home in the pages of a popular illustrated magazine than on the walls of an official Salon.

The Russian artist who created the most detailed visual record of his era was Vasili Timm. He began to publish his 'Russian Illustrated Pamphlet' in 1851, with this manifesto:

> All the illustrated works which fill our shops are brought, almost without exception, from foreign lands, and the public has before their eyes, views of foreign towns with their landmarks...In the meantime, our Russian traditions, people and places are almost entirely forgotten. Combining the past with the present and depicting all that is contemporary in its true aspect, the artist Timm proposes to include in the 'Russia Illustrated Pamphlet' all that is close to the heart of a Russian and everything precious to Russian life.

Timm published over 400 issues of his 'Pamphlet' between 1851 and 1863: a quarter of them are devoted to Sebastopol and the Crimean War - the key event during these years.

Nikolai Berg also published a detailed account of the war in his 'Notes On The Siege of Sebastopol' and his visual account of the siege, 'The Sebastopol Album' was published in 1858. He joined the Southern Army in the Crimea just as the war began, serving both as a pay-master and an interpreter to the main staff. He was present at the battle of Tchernaya and also visited the bastions during the siege.

TURKISH MUSICIANS IN THE ARMY. (PHOTO BY KAROL DE SZATHMARI.)

prettiest, most convenient and useful among those of other nations; the Turk with his grave air, and expression so full of dignity; the Algerian, with his swarthy and angular features; the Egyptian, with crisp hair, withered looks and gaudy dress; and finally, the inhabitant of Nubia, with his thick lips, and ebony skin; – and these, crossing and intermingling with one another, in the narrow streets of a Bulgarian town – a few leagues only from the great river of Europe, and in close proximity to the Russian outposts!

Henry Clifford, a captain in the Rifle Brigade, was less sanguine about Ottoman attitudes to the Allies:

The Turkish soldiers looked on in astonishment at the size and fine clothes of their English allies; but I do not observe any warmth of feeling between them and us. They look upon us I think with much suspicion and wonder how it will all end. The inhabitants look upon us almost with fear, and the old pashas and nobles with a sort of desponding, heart-broken civility, and think their empire will soon be at an end.

Captain Clifford was equally sceptical about Varna's suitability as the base for an Allied operation in defence of Silistria. On maps Varna may have looked like a good vantage point, but in practice the port was impracticable for overland manoeuvres:

It is out of the question our being able to go to the aid of the Turks at Silistria. The French are in just the same way as we are. There is the greatest difficulty in moving troops out of here, the country is very thinly inhabited, the transport very bad, and food hard to get.

In a richer and more densely populated countryside, the French might have been better able to relieve Silistria because, unlike the British, they were divided into relatively manageable and self-sufficient 100-men units that did not depend on cumbersome baggage-trains, but mid-nineteenth century Bulgaria did not have the population or the resources to sustain one invading army, let alone three or four.

When they set sail, the British expeditionary forces had a confidence in victory informed by little more than the illusion that backward, poorly trained Russian soldiers would drop their antique muskets and run back across the Danube at the very sight of Allied soldiers armed with their powerful and accurate new Minié rifles. At Varna it soon became obvious that no amount of new rifles or rousing songs could make up for an inefficient war machine. When she had settled into the Hussars' camp outside town, Mrs Duberly recorded the first of many instances of the administrative chaos that dogged daily life:

The headquarters and Captain Lockwood's troop have arrived in Varna, and were expected up today; but as they have no baggage ponies, nor any means of conveyance for the baggage, they were detained until we could send down our ponies to bring them up. This

does not strike me as being well arranged. Whose fault is it?

According to Edward Hodge, Lieutenant Colonel of the 4th Dragoons, the fault lay with the civil servants staffing the Commissariat, the Treasury department responsible for the organization and distribution of military personnel and supplies:

> **The Commissariat is infamous. The baggage arrangements are dreadful. They order us to carry certain things. They do not provide us with the means of transport, and they will not allow more than the regulated number of baggage animals to accompany the troops...**

Resourceful senior British commanders on the spot might have compensated for the shortcomings of the Commissariat, but alas, they too were in short supply.

Whereas Marshal Saint-Arnaud and his divisional commanders had seen recent active service in Algeria, few of their British counterparts had any comparable experience. In fact, much of the British army establishment was decidedly unsympathetic to those British officers who had served in India, the British equivalent of French colonial Algeria. As a living reminder of the great victory at Waterloo, where he had lost his right arm, the unflappable, unquestionably brave Lord Raglan had great prestige, but he had spent the best part of the previous forty years behind a desk at the Horse Guards. Faced with a difficult decision, he was inclined to ask himself what his mentor and former master, the Duke of Wellington, might have done in the same situation. The Iron Duke had died two years earlier, and Raglan himself was sixty-six years old when he arrived at Varna. As a military gentleman of the old school, Raglan might have made a good partner for Marshal Saint-Arnaud, but the previously tough and resourceful French commander-in-chief was already losing his battle against stomach cancer.

LORD RAGLAN, COMMANDER-IN-CHIEF OF THE BRITISH ARMY. (PHOTO BY ROGER FENTON.)

Lord Raglan had thrust greatness upon cavalry commander Lord Lucan, who was as fit as he was keen for action, and who had forgotten none of his previous skills as a drill-master. But Lucan had actually retired from the army sixteen years previously and by the time he rejoined and arrived at Varna, cavalry procedures had changed so much that the soldiers had no idea how to respond to his out-of-date orders, while officers did not know enough to teach them. Lord Lucan set great store by the most inconsequential regulations:

> **The Major General observes that officers do not wear their gold sword knots as prescribed by the regulations. It is to be observed that a gold sword knot has always been considered, in the English and foreign armies, as one of the distinctive marks of a commissioned officer. The officers comprising the cavalry division are to wear their regulation sword knots and no others.**

The cavalry division consisted of the Light Brigade and the Heavy. There was no love lost between Lord Lucan and his brother-in-law, Lord Cardigan, who, as commander of the Light Brigade, was his nominal subordinate. Cardigan's past was enlivened by quarrels and scandals, but he had had no direct experience of war and rather too much experience of the parade ground. Fanny Duberly regularly observed Lord Cardigan's penchant for showy hardship:

> **Captain Tomkinson, with a sergeant and nine men, has been away on patrol these three days, but is expected back tonight. Lord Cardigan forbids them to take their cloaks to wrap around them at night, as he considers it 'effeminate'.**

Later events forced attention on Cardigan's character, but there were others like him. Whereas French officers, promoted on merit rather than purchased commissions, had the confidence of their experience in the field, all too often their British counterparts compensated for their immaturity by continually giving orders. The letters of Harry Blishen, a young private in the Rifle Brigade who had run away from home to enlist, testify to the stoicism of the 'men' who served under such 'gentlemen':

> **We were drilled incessantly during the time we were there; in fact, almost harassed to death; and I am sorry to say we lost several men through the effect. We were drilled to give the young generals [sic. officers] an insight of what they would have to do on the field. Instead of their being drilled at home, or kept in an efficient state of discipline, which they ought to be, they are sent out here to reduce the strength of our army, and to render the men unfit for the fight when they are called upon. That is why the French have such an advantage over us; you will never see an inexperienced subaltern in their service... Omar Pasha, the**

ABOVE: THE SIEGE OF SILISTRIA (ANON).
LEFT: *THE LIGHT DIVISION CAMP AT VARNA.* ONE OF THE MANY WATERCOLOURS PAINTED WHEN NOT ON DUTY BY CAPTAIN HENRY CLIFFORD.

commander-in-chief of the Turkish army, came down from Silistria last Saturday and inspected us. He was delighted with the general appearance of the flower of the British army; and more especially the Rifles; for instead of marching past in quick time, we dashed past him in double time. He made us a present of one ration of rum.

Omar Pasha seemed to have forgotten his plan to send troops from Varna to the relief of the Ottoman army at Silistria, and by now they were on the verge of defeat. Captain Butler was all too aware of the collapsing morale of the Ottoman command:

Some of the officers said they were being sacrificed, and I actually saw one blubbering like a child, and rubbing his eyes in the presence of his men, who, poor devils, were behaving very well and ready to do anything they were ordered.

Captain Butler himself was shot in the forehead:

Thanks to a thick skull and the ball having just passed through part of the wall not yet cut through it did not penetrate the skull, although it left a tolerable hole and made me feel rather funny. This put a stop to the sortie at least for some days. I was assisted down to the town, where the surgeon did the needful.

The Russians were preparing for a final assault, and on 20 June, Pyotr Alabin could hardly contain his excitement as he wrote in his diary:

The fateful hour is striking for Silistria. Her time is running out. The storming of her advance fortifications

> **has been set for tonight... And now the night is here. The regiments have departed. At midnight they must be at their appointed places. The general ordered us to go there with him at 11 o'clock.**

But as soon as he had said his prayers and mounted his horse, Alabin saw the commander-in chief's adjutant approaching his general:

> **'What's this?'**
>
> **'Your excellency, order the troops to return – the storming has been cancelled.'**
>
> **My blood ran cold.**
>
> **'Do you have this order for me in writing?'**
>
> **'Allow me, your excellency...'**

Nobody could quite believe what was happening. On the ground the Russians were waiting for the flare that would signal their advance. One Russian soldier reported:

> **Quite a time had passed, we were bored with lying there, and the disappointed soldiers were whispering amongst themselves: 'The flare is a long time in coming. It's probably fallen asleep.'... Suddenly I hear somebody calling me in a whisper – this was our battalion adjutant who had crept up and said 'Retreat'. The soldiers were again whispering amongst themselves 'Isn't that treason?' Behind him crept up the regimental commander himself and said: 'Retreat!' Only then did we believe it and we all did an about turn, but from the enemy there was not a single shot fired; but when dawn came we saw that there were many people on the fortifications, singing and dancing national dances, probably as a sign that we had retreated.**

Not everyone inside Silistria was celebrating. Within a few days of Captain Butler's casual journal entry about his head injury he had contracted a fever. He died on 22 June, just a few hours after the Russian retreat was confirmed. Meanwhile Omar Pasha's reinforcements had never materialized. He wrote to Constantinople explaining the delay: 'I was preparing to march to the relief of Silistria. Then the Russians withdrew. During the forty days of investing Silistria, they lost 25,000 men killed'

Casualties had been high on both sides but Leo Tolstoy expressed the huge disappointment felt by the Russians at the anticlimax:

> **I can say without fear of contradiction that we all – soldiers, officers and generals – received this news as a real misfortune, all the more so since we knew through the spies who came to us very often from Silistria, and with whom I often spoke myself, that once this fort was taken – and there was no doubt that it would be – Silistria could not hold out for more than two or three days.**

Tolstoy was also at pains to point out that they were not alone in being disappointed. With the retreating Russians went...

> **...nearly 7,000 Bulgar families which we took with us to save them from the ferocity of the Turks – a ferocity which I've been obliged to believe in despite my incredulity. As soon as we left the various Bulgar villages that we were occupying, the Turks moved in and, except for the women young enough for a harem, massacred everyone they found there....**

After all the fighting, the siege had been brought to an end by diplomatic intimidation. For months the embarrassed Austrian government had been dithering over the dilemma posed by the latest Russo-Turkish conflict. The Austrians, who had an unwieldy empire of their own to contain, were always extremely sensitive to Russian activity around the Danube. If nationalist, anti-Turkish aspirations were encouraged in the Danubian Principalities, similar ideas might spread among the equally restive Balkan peoples within Austria's own borders. Despite their previous sympathies as part of the 'Holy Alliance', Austria finally made up her mind to present the tsar with an ultimatum: withdraw his troops from the Danube, or Austria would join the alliance that was backing Turkey. As the tsar saw it, retreat from Silistria was the only option.

If the conflict between Turkey and Russia in the Danubian Principalities had been the only reason behind the presence of British and French armies at Varna, the war should have ended with the Russian

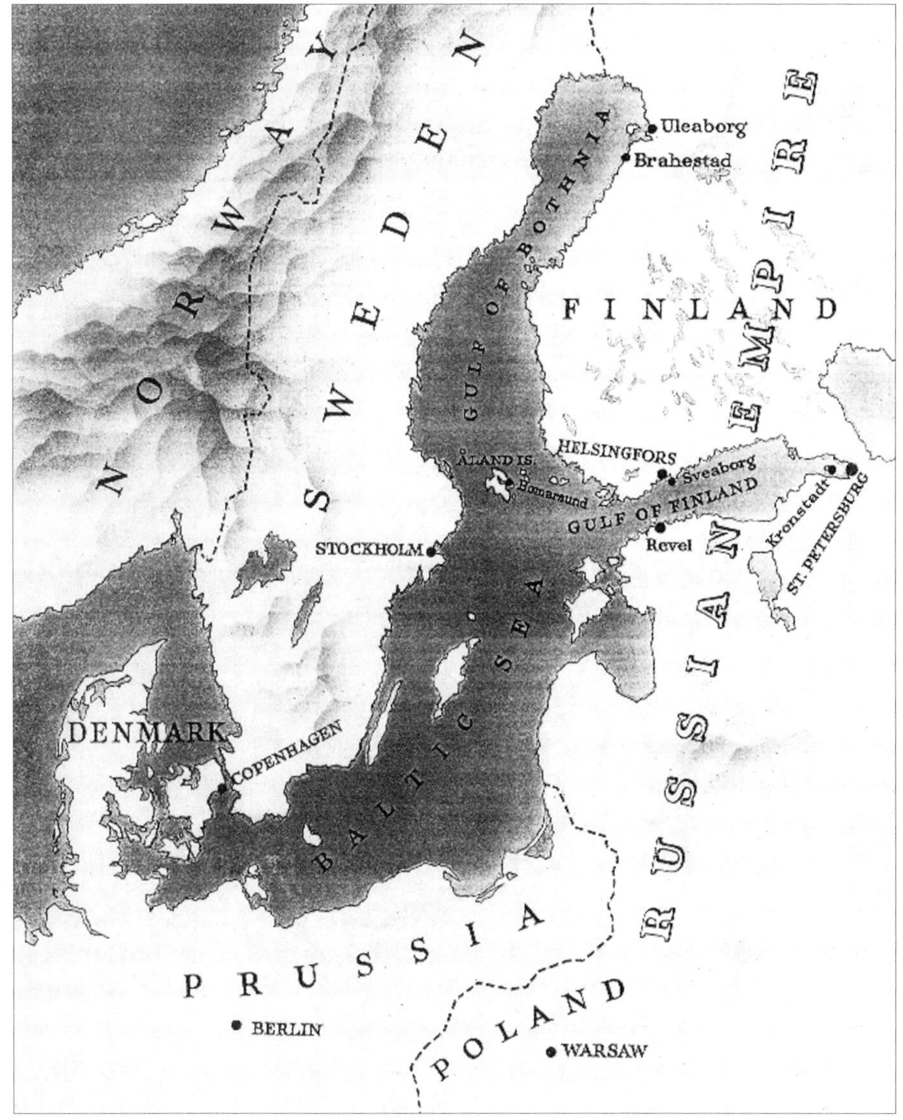

THE BALTIC SEA – NORTH-WEST FRONTIER OF THE RUSSIAN EMPIRE.

withdrawal. But Varna had also been selected as a likely launch base for an Allied invasion of the Crimea. Specifically, the Allied target was now Sebastopol, the base of the Russian Black Sea Fleet, which had annihilated the Ottoman naval squadron at Sinope. As *The Times* made clear: 'The grand political and military objects of the war cannot...be attained so long as Sebastopol and the Russian fleet are still in existence.'

On a warm evening in London on 28 June, a sleepy British cabinet at the end of a long and tedious agenda endorsed the Secretary of State for War's proposal that the Allies should assault Sebastopol. But destruction of the tsar's Black Sea Fleet was by no means the only aim in the British sights. The war was already unfolding on another front 1000 miles to the north.

Earlier, in March 1854, when war on Russia was declared, an Anglo-French naval squadron had been despatched to the Baltic where targets included the fortress at Sveaborg which protected the city of Helsingfors (present-day Helsinki) and the fortress of Bomarsund on the Åland Islands. One particular target however, aroused the excitement of the politicians, the press, and the public - the tsar's imperial capital, St Petersburg, and the heavily fortified island of Kronstadt which protected the approaches to the city.

Sir Charles Napier was appointed admiral in command of the Baltic Fleet, and he whetted the public's appetite for victory by boasting that he 'would treat the Russians to the old Nelson trick in the Baltic'.

The Allied fleet made their presence felt when they anchored off Kronstadt on 26 June. For a week their sails were clearly visible to the Russian imperial family, as they looked out from the balcony of their summer palace at Peterhof. But no onslaught followed. After his reconnaissance, Napier decided that Kronstadt could not be taken without a much larger force.

Instead of delivering a knock-out blow to the Russian capital, much of the naval campaign, which could only be waged in the summer months when the Baltic was ice-free, consisted of harassing 'enemy' shipping. The Grand Duchy of Finland was part of the Russian Empire, and some British naval commanders interpreted this as a license to 'take, burn, or destroy' Finnish boats and cargo. Captain George Giffard described his progress in June 1854, when they anchored off the town of Uleaborg:

> **A flag of truce came off, begging us to spare the town. Informed the deputation that the town and private property would be spared, as long as the people kept quiet and did not fire on the boats; we would only destroy the shipping and naval stores. 9 pm: Sent the armed boats of the squadron under Lieutenants Priest and Graham, to take, burn, or destroy. 2 June, 8 am: Boats returned having found the Russians had scuttled all the shipping afloat, but our men burnt them as well as a number of buildings with large stores of timber, tar, and pitch, estimated as worth half a million. The fire from the immense quantities of pitch, tar and timber could be seen for many miles around.**

One Finnish eye-witness described just such a visit from the British navy:

> **One of the officers asked, 'Are there any troops there?' When the reply was negative, he said, 'What a pity. We are going to set fire to the shipyard and that fine vessel will have to be burnt'. He was referring to a newly-built vessel which had just been copper-sheathed. When all the workers had been driven out of the shipyard, the British set fire to it. One by one, 13 vessels, the timber store, 5 buildings and many barrels of tar, salt and pitch...fell prey to the flames.**

In July, *The Times* denounced the raids, pointing out that the fleet was not destroying military supplies but goods intended for export – much of it to Britain and already paid for. It had been hoped that British naval operations in the Baltic might encourage the King of Sweden to join the alliance against Russia, but the raids were having the opposite effect. The Swedish and Finnish press compared the British raids to the plunder and arson of the Vikings. Finally Napier prepared for his big offensive on a military target, and the Allied fleet set off to attack Bomarsund in the Åland Islands.

The novelty of war had inspired a number of wealthy gentlemen to attach themselves to the Allied forces as a kind of military tourist. They were known to the forces as Travelling Gentlemen – or 'TGs' – and when the Bomarsund expedition landed on 8 August, it was accompanied by no fewer than five private yachts. The smallest of these was *The Pet* from the Royal Thames Yacht Club which belonged to the Reverend Mr Hughes, a fellow of Magdalene College, Cambridge. Hughes described his vessel as a 'very small cutter-yacht, about as long as a moderate-sized drawing room and scarcely so wide as a four-poster bed'.

Accompanied by his brother, Hughes went ashore with the landing party:

> **All morning, the shore...was crowded with boats and barges landing the French troops. It was a bustling scene and everyone spoke in admiration of the orderly manner in which the French managed the landing. No sooner did a boat touch the beach, than the men were ashore and away on their respective duties, some chopping fuel, others clearing a road; a party of carpenters were soon busy running out a pier. In an hour...water had been found, tents pitched, cooking under way, cows pillaged and most artistically butchered, a canteen with a smart vivandière in full swing; and a little thriving military village was already extemporized, and in full vitality.**

The Russian fortress at Bomarsund consisted of three round towers, each heavily armed, and a 'Great Fort' built in a semi-circle. After successfully establishing both an English and French base camp, the next task was to bring ashore the heavy artillery that would pulverize these forts into submission. Hughes observed:

> **The business of the next day was dragging the heavy**

THE LANDING OF THE FRENCH TROOPS AT BOMARSUND (E.A.DOLBY).

guns up to the camp. It was a strange sight to see the long trail of 150 seamen to a gun come winding up the rough and narrow road. First in the procession came the band, dusty way-worn, and red-hot with puffing; next came the seamen tugging away at the hawser, while officers rushed about to guide their course; lastly came the gun mounted on a sledge, which rolled, pitched, and slewed about the rough ground, while half-a-dozen smart fellows did their best to steady it.

On 13 August 1854, the batteries opened fire on Fort Branklint:

My brother was off soon after dawn and secured an excellent position among the French sharpshooters, where he got a capital view of everything. I followed soon after, and quickly came into view of the fort, which was blazing away pretty briskly.

In this war, Allied and Russian officers could still show courtesy while fighting each other. During the bombardment of Branklint, there was a lull in the battle and one British officer described how he approached the tower to get a better view of the main fort, accompanied by a French captain and a British lord. The Russian commander of Fort Branklint suddenly appeared and advised them in French that they should withdraw as the fighting was about to begin again:

We were obliged for our honour to thank him and to proceed leisurely until we were hidden by a ledge of

rocks from the fortress, when we finally took to our heels and got to our battery just as the firing re-opened! We should have been in an embarrassing position between the two fires, for our people did not know we were gone to the front; we were also much indebted to the Russian officer, who might have begged us to walk into the fort as prisoners, for our only arms were spy glasses and cigars!

Fort Branklint surrendered and on Tuesday 15 August, the bombardment of the next target, the main fort, was interrupted by birthday celebrations. Reverend Hughes reported:

Suddenly, at noon, the whole fleet roared out a royal salute in honour of the Emperor's birthday [Napoleon III]. The ships saluted with shotted guns, and the brightest colours flew out in the merry breeze, which was blowing stinking smoke and burnt gunpowder into the eyes of the over-matched and unhappy foe.

Finally, on 16 August, the main fort at Bomarsund surrendered. Hughes was one of the first to enter and he gloated over the defeated Russian force:

We passed into the fort, and there we saw a strange sordid crowd of convict-looking wretches in long workhouse drab coats, scrambling and huddling together in all the attitudes of drunken, senseless merriment. They tore off their uniform, they stamped on it and threw it in heaps, they sang, they laughed and danced... Little squeezy bald-headed old men, or raw loose-spun boys, they looked more like a herd of half-starved emigrants than the imperial troops of a great military power.

On their way to the Crimea, the British troops stopped off at Scutari, a suburb of Constantinople, later to become famous as the site of Florence Nightingale's hopsital. (Photo by James Robertson.)

At the end of their excursiön, the Reverend Hughes and his brother wandered back to the round tower, Fort Notvik, which had surrendered to the British:

We passed into a room which had a cold feeling about

it; I was walking hastily on, when my brother called aloud; I looked round and saw...the cold, clean silent forms of the dead. The shock of the surprise was fearful; the light linen cloths that shrouded the stiffened figures wavered and flickered in the draught, as if stirred by the breaths of those who could breathe no more. What did these poor fellows know about the Turkish question? And yet they had fought and trembled, they had writhed in agony, and now father and brother, maid and mother were weeping and breaking their hearts for them, and all about the Danubian principalities. 'Those', said my brother, as we hastened into the air, 'are the first Russians I have seen clean and sober yet'.

Bomarsund was the first Anglo-French victory of the Crimean War. Until October, Napier's fleet maintained an effective blockade of the Baltic and the Gulf of Finland. They destroyed merchant vessels, and kept a quarter of a million Russian troops tied down in the defence of the Baltic region and St Petersburg, without losing a single ship. But to the press and the public, eagerly anticipating an attack on Kronstadt, Napier's campaign was an anticlimax. After Bomarsund, the Admiralty pointedly asked him 'what further operations' he was planning. No major action followed, and by October *The Illustrated London News* wrote sarcastically of how:

The Baltic fleet, with fifty thousand men
Sailed up the seas – and then sailed home again

The destruction of Bomarsund encouraged naval strategists to focus upon the more important target of Sveaborg, and ultimately on Krondstadt – the gateway to the tsar's capital. In the short term, however, Napier's failure to deliver a decisive blow in the Baltic increased the political pressure for a quick victory in the Crimea. The Allied armies, however, were still on the wrong side of the Black Sea.

In Varna Frederick Robinson, an assistant surgeon with the Scots Fusilier Guards, was struggling to cope with casualties – though the Allied armies had yet to fire a single bullet in anger:

The hospital tents present a ghastly spectacle of suffering, beyond all relief by human aid. The detachment here have already begun what is likely to be their chief occupation – burying the dead... My great fear is that the disease will affect the company now here, to an extent incapacitating them from affording them adequate assistance to the sick.

In the blazing heat the Allies had been struck by a devastating bacteriological offensive: cholera. It had only been a matter of time before the disease, which had been following the French troops from Marseilles, ravaged the men who were crowded into the hot and insanitary camps and warships around Varna. First hit

THE BALTIC FLEET LEAVING PORTSMOUTH, MARCH 1855. (PHOTO BY ROGER FENTON.)

were the French forces, which had been sent into the Dobrudsha on a reconnaissance. One zouave told how:

> **Towards evening the bugle sounded, but many of the men found they couldn't get up. By seven o'clock that evening four hundred soldiers were dead or on the verge of death.**

Within days the same scene was repeating itself in British camps. Private Harry Blishen was already regretting running away from home:

> **We have harder work against the cholera, dysentery and lake fever, than we should have had against five times our number of the enemy in Russia. The number of deaths with us and the French has been fearful...dear mother, if you can, give me a better example of the 'frailty of life' than many of my comrades have offered me of late; that of being in robust health one hour, and the next hour groaning in the agonies of death; one poor fellow invoking the Almighty to forgive him his sins, and another raging with fever...**

Captain Henry Clifford was equally pessimistic:

> **So bad has it been with the French, the medical men say it is no use trying to fight it. Fine young men in perfect health are taken with it and die in four and five hours. I grieve very much for a young officer of the 77th who came out here with a Draft from England. He came up here on the Tuesday, was taken ill on the Wednesday morning and buried that evening.**

TOURISTS LOOK AT A CANNONBALL ABOARD HMS *HECLA* (E.A.DOLBY).

Besides taking so many lives, cholera took a huge toll on the spirits of the living. Albert Mitchell of the 13th Light Dragoons watched both fellow privates and officers succumb to it:

> **At first we had regular funeral parties, with trumpets sounding in front of the procession, but as it soon became an every day occurrence, and the number of men in hospital increased daily, the 'Dead March' was ordered to be discontinued; for to say the least of it, it was a most doleful noise, and must have had a depressing effect on the sick, some of whom were hourly expecting to go the same road.**

Depressed by her own powerlessness, Fanny Duberly found herself:

> **...encamped on the cholera-stricken ground just vacated by the Heavies. We had appalling evidence of their deaths! Here and there a heap of loose earth, with a protruding hand or foot, showed where the inhabitants had desecrated the dead, and dug them up to possess themselves of the blankets in which they were buried.**

In just three months, before they even got to the Crimea, disease was to take the lives of 10,000 men. To add to the misery, on 10 August a fire broke out in Varna. The French claimed that it was sabotage, the work of Greeks in sympathy with their advancing Russian co-religionists, and five luckless Greeks were bayonetted to death. Cornet Fisher, of the 4th Dragoon Guards, bored by the long sojourn at Varna, was quite amused by what ensued:

> **There is not a shop left open that I can see since the fire, for the very reason that there is nothing left to sell; although not half the town is destroyed by fire, the whole is sacked. Our gallant generals adhered to their usual policy and did nothing, although there are troops enough to have kept order and prevented plunder in a town 50 times the size... The English, according to all accounts, behaved very well, confining themselves strictly to getting as drunk as possible on the liquor**

Interior of the chamber at Fort Notvik, Bomarsund (E.A.Dolby).

which was washing all over town. The fire is hardly put out yet, although the fire commenced three nights ago. The ration biscuits burn beautifully, and will not be put out... There is not a Turk to be seen anywhere. I hear that any of them who have been lucky enough to save a towel have encamped under it, where they sit smoking their pipes, which they did not lose, as I believe they sleep smoking... We know nothing as to where we are going, but there will most likely be a move on Sebastopol before this season is finished...

Two weeks later, when the day of embarkation was set as 5 September, Fisher was thrilled: 'Hurrah for the Crimea, we are off tomorrow; fine country, people very friendly; take Sebastopol in a week or so, and then into winter quarters for the winter.' But his commanding officer, Lieutenant-Colonel Hodge, was not so cheery: 'I hear that the spot that was selected for the army to land on now has a large Russian force encamped upon it. For this we may thank *The Times* newspaper...'

William Howard Russell's response to this charge of treachery by journalism was robust:

Even if the Czar believed that plan to be correct – and he might well entertain suspicions on that point – is it likely that he would take the trouble as soon as he has read his morning paper to send off a courier to the Crimea to prepare his Generals for an attack on a certain point, which they must (if the article in the paper is of any service to the enemy at all) have hitherto left undefended? Surely the Russian engineers are not so utterly ignorant that they do not know their weak points, and do not see where a disembarkation of troops is probable or practicable.

In fact, it was the Allied commanders on board the ships that sailed from Varna who had little or no idea about what sort of landing might be probable or practicable.

The armies

The British Army
Britain was primarily a sea-power, which was one reason why its army was less efficient and more old-fashioned than its navy. Another reason was the purchase system, dating back to 1683 and still in force during the Crimean War, by which 'gentlemen' became officers if they could afford the substantial price of a commission. In contrast with his French equivalent, the ordinary British soldier who had proved his ability in action had little or no hope of earning promotion beyond the rank of sergeant. Often, these men were more fervently attached to their regimental 'Colours' (the squares of silk that functioned as standards and rallying points in battle) than they were to any general religious or patriotic ethos.

At the outset of the Crimean expedition Britain was proud of its amateur army, which had, after all, contributed to the defeat of Napoleon's professional forces, but soon after the war the most conspicuous obstacles to the army's modernization - the purchase system and punishment by flogging - were abolished.

Above: Lieutenant-Colonel Hallewell and his servant. (Photo by Roger Fenton.)

Left: *Russian peasant family say goodbye to their son* (Vasili Timm).

The French Army
Napoleon III's army was run along the lines that had been established, and vindicated, by his uncle, Napoleon Bonaparte. The French army was organized into relatively small, mobile units, which were backed up by the technical services of dedicated cooks, surgeons, nurses and engineers. The status of officers in the French army depended on a combination of experience and ability, and though it was clear that the French Crimean commanders were also prominent supporters of Napoleon III's regime, it was their experience as hard-nosed colonial generals that had recommended them for that coup d'état. Ordinary French soldiers were better fed and better supported than their British counterparts, and morale was correspondingly higher.

Some of the most colourful French regiments had been created in the colonies. The zouaves, for example, were originally Berber soldiers commanded by French officers in Algeria. By 1854 they retained their exotic uniforms and legendary audacity, although many of the zouaves who fought in the Crimea were Frenchmen. The French forces also included a cavalry brigade from Algeria, the Chasseurs d'Afrique. Besides its fighting men, each French regiment included a contingent of non-combatant female auxiliaries, the vivandières. These women – the majority of whom were married to junior officers or regimental musicians – saw to the material needs of soldiers: supplying drink, tobacco and extra rations, organizing the laundry, and caring for the sick and wounded.

The Ottoman Army

The ethnically diverse Ottoman army was made up of soldiers drawn from all the countries of the empire's traditional influence, including Egypt, Tunisia and Albania, although they are commonly referred to as Turks. For all the Ottoman Empire's political image as the 'sick man of Europe', its army was comparatively young and healthy, although the different nations had different levels of miltary experience. The Ottoman army was open to talent, and military schools were set up and staffed by foreign instructors, including several Prussian and British officers. Even at the highest level, after conversion to Islam, there was no impediment to the rise of Michael Lotis (or Omar Pasha), the versatile, ex-Christian Croatian who was commander-in-chief of the Ottoman forces on the Danube and in the Crimea.

The Ottoman army comprised both regular and irregular troops. The most famous irregulars were Muslim volunteers called bashi-bazouks. About 14,000 bashi-bazouks volunteered for action against the Russian 'infidels', and the French General Yussuf tried, and failed, to organize them like a regular cavalry division. These Muslim volunteers refused regular pay on the basis that this would compromise their heavenly reward if they were martyred during the Crimean holy war or *jihad*. Since they supported and equipped themselves through plunder and flouted all conventional military discipline (routinely stripping and mutilating dead Russian soldiers) the bashi-bazouks were something of a mixed blessing. Although they were among the defenders of Silistria, they were not involved in the Crimean theatre of war.

Turkish infantry. (Photo by Szathmari.)

French zouaves. (Photo by Fenton.)

The Russian Army

Traditionally, the strength of Russia's army was its size and its capacity to survive harsh conditions. The rank and file of the Russian army were drawn from the lowest class of society: the serfs. Every Russian landowner was obliged to equip and dispatch a number of serfs from his estate – the number depended on the size of the estate – for the imperial army, and the regiments were named after the districts in which their members had been recruited. These men were expected to serve for twenty-five years, but distances were so great, and life so cheap within the Russian army, that few families would expect to see their sons alive again. With such huge numbers at his disposal – the million-strong Russian army of 1853 was twice as big a year later – the tsar did not have to worry too much about modernizing recruitment procedures.

The tsar was, however, an enthusiastic patron of the latest military technologies, such as the detonation of explosives by electrical currents during the defence of Sebastopol. Artillery was another of Tsar Nicholas's special interests, and Russian artillerymen were regarded as an élite force. They were inclined to withdraw prematurely from a position, rather than staying to defend it at the risk of an unbearable disgrace: that of losing a gun to the enemy. Although the Russian military machine was extremely corrupt – riddled with the rackets by which middlemen and colonels took their cuts from army supplies and equipment – the soldiers' morale was high. 'With all my strength and with the aid of a cannon I shall assist in destroying the predatory and turbulent Asiatics,' was the resolve of Leo Tolstoy, and from the top to the bottom of the enormous Russian army this attitude was typical.

The Sardinian Army

Victor Emmanuel, king of Sardinia had no particular quarrel with Russia, but like the other Allied leaders he recognized that the changing pattern of Europe and its empires would be decided after the war by its winners, and he wanted to rule over a united Italy. Cavour, Sardinia's wily Foreign Minister, realized that by participating in the fighting, Sardinia would have a place at the peace conference tables, whereas Austria, the oppressors of Italy, would not. Therefore, in May 1855, a contingent of Sardinian troops under General della Marmora arrived in the Crimea. In fact, two Sardinian officers had ridden in the charge of the Light Brigade the previous year. The Sardinians were admired for their practical uniforms and fine music, and would play a vital role at the battle of the Tchernaya.

CHAPTER THREE

THE DOOMED CITY

FROM THE MIDDLE OF the Black Sea, Captain Fred Dallas of the 46th Foot wrote daily updates in a letter to his sister:

We cast anchor in the middle of the sea entirely out of sight of land the day before yesterday and here we still are just as near as when we started. I can only write our different opinions about our destination as we know nothing.

We have been hanging about some time ever since the 11th waiting for each other and I think wasting time. We are now on the Coast of the Crimea, we fancy Eupatoria, and are skirting along in the direction of Sebastopol. Where we are to land we don't know...

THE ALLIES LANDING AT EUPATORIA, IN THE CRIMEA (ANON).

It was not only the men who were ignorant of their destination. When the Allied armies set sail for the Crimea on 5 September 1854, even the commanders had only a vague idea where they were going to land. A larger amphibious operation than any that had previously been mounted, it was equipped with rudimentary maps, and the Allies' information about Russian military strength was almost non-existent. In search of a beach-head for landing, HMS *Caradoc* carried the Allied commanders past Sebastopol, the naval base they intended to destroy. A mere 3000 yards offshore, the British commander Lord Raglan, and the second in command of the French forces, General Canrobert, heard the bells of the cathedral tolling, and they solemnly tipped their hats to the enemy. Finally, Raglan decided on Kalamita Bay as a landing place and the waiting fleet sailed north up the coast to disembark.

In Sebastopol there were rumours of the Allied landing. A troop of Russian cavalry was sent north to assess the enemy armada of 600 vessels, which stretched for nine miles along the coast, and they were astonished. Captain Hodasiewicz of the Taroutine cavalry regiment reported:

> **On reaching the position on the heights, one of the most beautiful sights it was ever my lot to behold lay before us. The whole of the Allied fleet was lying off the salt lakes to the south of Eupatoria, and at night their forest of masts was illuminated with various coloured lanterns. Both men and officers were lost in amazement at the sight of such large number of ships... The soldiers said, 'Behold, the infidel has built another holy Moscow on the waves!' comparing the masts of the ships to the church spires of that city. The officers...were not quite so sure of victory as they were two days before.**

The Russian cavalry returned to Sebastopol to inform their commander, Prince Menshikov, who had been sceptical about an Allied attack so late in the year. Many of the officers from the Sebastopol garrison were at the theatre watching Gogol's satire on bureaucracy, *The Government Inspector*, when the play was interrupted by news of the invasion.

Early on the morning of 14 September, the Allied force of 27,000 British, 30,000 French and 7,000 Turks began to disembark. William Howard Russell described the scene for the readers of *The Times*:

> **We are an 'army of occupation' at last. The English and French armies have laid hold of a material guarantee in the shape of some score square miles of the soil of the Crimea and they are preparing to extend the area of their rule in their progress towards Sebastopol...**
>
> **By twelve o clock in the day, that barren and desolate beach inhabited but a short time before only by the seagull and wildfowl was swarming with life. From one extremity to the other, bayonets glistened and red coats and brass-mounted shakos [hats] glinted in solid masses. The air was filled with our English speech and the hum of voices mingled with loud notes of command, cries of comrades to each other, the familiar address of 'Bill' to 'Tom' or 'Pat' to 'Sandy' and an occasional shout of laughter.**

Unlike the French, the British left bulky items including tents and ambulances on board ship, to ensure swift progress. Their absence was soon noticed by Private Donald Cameron of the 93rd Highlanders:

> **My comrade and I got grass or anything we could gather for a bed and lay down, having a stone for a pillow, and then the rain came pouring on us. So we lay on our backs holding up our blankets with our hands, so as the rain would run down both sides, and so keep our firelocks and ammunition dry, but there is worse on before.**

Relations between the French and the British were still a little awkward. French infantry captain, Jean-Jules Herbé, writing home to his parents, described this first brush with his allies:

> **The day after we landed, the English officers still had not been able to get cooking equipment ashore due to the rough sea. Deprived of food, they were quite at a loss and we saw three or four of them go past carrying a cow's head without a scrap of meat on it... We were about to sit down to eat – bread, soup, boiled beef, salad, and dried beans – when I suggested to my comrades we share our meal with these English officers. As graciously as possible I invited them and was accepted on the spot with undisguised satisfaction. Imagine how surprised we were when they tucked in without further ado, taking more than half a dish in one go. They probably hadn't eaten for 36 hours and we would have forgiven them such manners borne of an empty stomach if on leaving they had thanked us. But no, they withdrew haughtily and the next day they passed our tent twice without even saying hello.**

The medical situation was as dire as the catering. On the beach, Russell met some senior medical officers who complained:

> **Do make a note of this! By—! They have landed this**

> **army without any kind of hospital transport, litters, or carts, or anything! Everything was ready at Varna! Now with all this cholera and diarrhoea about, there are no means of taking the sick down to the boats.**

The Allies had landed on territory that had become part of Russia only seventy years earlier. In 1783, Catherine the Great had annexed the Crimean peninsular, as Russia extended her territory south into the Ukraine, winning land from the Ottoman Empire. The massive naval dockyards at Sebastopol, home of the Russian Black Sea Fleet and now the Allies' main target, had been built by British civil engineers as recently as the 1840s and 1850s, at the command of the present tsar, Nicholas I. But they stood in a Crimea that was still overwhelmingly Tartar and Turkish in its population. William Howard Russell described the inhabitants and their reaction to the invasion:

> **The men are apparently of pure Tartar race, with small eyes very wide apart, the nose very much sunk, and a square substantial figure. They wear turbans of lamb's wool and jackets of sheepskin with the wool inwards. They speak indifferent Turkish, and are most ready with information respecting their Russian masters, by whom they have been most carefully disarmed. A deputation of them waited on Lord Raglan to-day to beg for muskets and gunpowder.**

Some Allied officers moved into the nearby town of Eupatoria, taking over the houses of the wealthy Russians who had fled. Fanny Duberly was entertained by the newly appointed governor of Eupatoria, Captain Brock, who accompanied her as they explored on horseback:

> **After we had finished our ride, we went to one of the deserted houses, where we found a grand piano – the first I had played on for so long! It was like meeting a dear and long absent friend. The house and garden were soon...echoing to the magnificent chords of 'Rule Britannia'; whilst Tennyson's sweet words, 'Break, Break, Break' and the 'Northern Star' fitted both the occasion and the place.**

Meanwhile the army on shore slowly assembled itself into marching order. The idea was to descend on Sebastopol, destroy the naval base and withdraw as quickly as possible. There was no desire for long-term occupation of the Crimea – the commanders hoped they were embarked upon a swift strategic 'raid'. From now on they would never be more than twenty four hours march from the sea.

As the army tramped south towards Sebastopol, shadowed by their warships sailing with them down the coast, one song rose above the brackish lakes and the flocks of wildfowl:

Cheer Boys Cheer
No more of idle sorrow
Courage, true hearts, shall bear us on our way
Hope points before and shows the bright tomorrow
Let us forget the darkness of to-day.

'Cheer Boys Cheer' became the 'hit' of the Crimean War, sung by British soldiers on their way to war in the same way that 'It's a Long Way to Tipperary' became the marching song of 1914. Finally on the morning of 20 September, the two sides came face to face. The first battle between major European powers since Waterloo, forty years earlier, was about to begin.

Menshikov had planned a warm reception for the Allies. As soon as the fleet had been observed from Eupatoria a force of 36,000 Russian infantry, 3,400 cavalry and 2,500 artillerymen with 122 guns had been sent north from Sebastopol to take up a commanding position on a stretch of heights overlooking the River Alma. They had time to build earthwork batteries, so their big guns dominated the ground sloping down to the river. They also transformed the small village of Burliuk, next to the bridge carrying the main road, into a fire bomb, stuffing the houses with hay and explosives. Menshikov was confident of holding this position for weeks while Sebastopol fortified itself and he invited an audience to witness what was planned as a spectacular repulse. Many of Sebastopol's fashionable citizens arrived armed with rugs, picnic baskets, cold chicken, bottles of champagne and opera glasses.

The previous night, the Allied commanders Lord Raglan and Marshal Saint-Arnaud had devised their

battle plan, and had given their respective troops quite distinct roles. The French were to advance along the seashore towards the mouth of the Alma and then scale the cliffs to capture the heights overlooking the Russian positions. These heights were almost entirely undefended. Either Menshikov thought the cliffs were impossible to climb, or he believed any of his troops stationed there would be easy targets for the guns of the Allied ships anchored just offshore. Meanwhile, the British would proceed in a line two men deep and two miles long up the steep slope and straight towards the Russian artillery battery of the so-called 'Great Redoubt'. Russell described the British infantry lining up as 'a sight of inexpressible grandeur':

FIRST NIGHT BIVOUAC IN THE CRIMEA (CAPTAIN HENRY CLIFFORD).

Red is the colour, after all, and the white slashings of the breast of the coat and the cross belts, though rendering a man conspicuous enough, give him an appearance in size which other uniforms don't create.

At six in the morning on the day of battle General Bosquet's division got under way, and they were full of excitement at the thought of their first clash with the enemy. Although they were now on the same side, there were still slight hitches in Anglo-French co-operation. In a letter to his parents, André, a zouave private (only his first name is known), wrote:

> **The humidity of the night had slightly numbed us, but we were full of spirit. Besides we were being drawn towards the unknown, and we were proud to be leading the way for once... But all of a sudden a messenger arrived riding flat out to invite General Bosquet to call a halt. 'Messieurs les Anglais' weren't ready to leave, so we would have to await their pleasure. We weren't particularly polite about them, I can tell you. A battle, after all is like a surgical operation – nobody knows if they will come out of it alive, but once the necessity for it has been recognized, and the hour has come, it is best to get it over with.**

Although the zouaves were accustomed to battle from their colonial duties, many British men, like Private Timothy Gowing of the 7th Fusiliers, were going into battle for the first time in their lives. The opening shots were fired at about noon:

> **As soon as the enemy's round shot came hopping along, we simply did the polite – opened out and allowed them to pass on; there is nothing lost by politeness even on a battlefield. As we kept advancing, we had to move our pins to get out of their way. Presently they began to pitch their shot and shell right amongst us, and our men began to fall. I know that I felt horribly sick – a cold shiver running through my veins – and I must acknowledge that I felt very uncomfortable.**

As soon as they saw the Allies advancing, the Russians ignited Burliuk. Smoke engulfed Private Harry Blishen in the Rifle Brigade:

> **They managed to set fire to the town before we could get near it, and under cover of the smoke, they opened their fire. We crossed a river and faced a strong entrenchment camp. We shot and made dreadful havoc**

Photography

When Britain declared war on Russia in March 1854, the War Office decided to send a photographer with the army. They contacted a Bond Street photography firm, which recommended Mr Richard Nicklin for the job. Nicklin set sail for the East with two assistants and a lot of equipment; they photographed the Allied army in Varna and in the Crimea. At the battle of Balaklava, in October 1854, there were two photographers attached to the British army. One was Nicklin, the War Office photographer. The second was Major Halkett of the 4th Light Dragoons, for whom a small portable camera had been made in London by Marcus Sparling (who later visited the Crimea as an assistant to Roger Fenton).

Sadly, not a single one of these images has survived. Major Halkett rode into the Russian cannons at the charge of the Light Brigade, but he did not ride back. Richard Nicklin and his two assistants also met an untimely death: they drowned when their transport ship sank outside Balaklava harbour during the hurricane of 14 November 1854. All of their pictures went down with their ship, the *Rip Van Winkle*.

After these early mishaps, the best known photographer of the Crimean War, Roger Fenton, was sent out by a commercial gallery, Thomas Agnew & Sons. Not only was Fenton's passage supplied by the Secretary of State for War, he also carried a letter of introduction from Prince Albert to Lord Raglan. This gave him unusual access and privileges. Fenton came from a prosperous mill-owning and banking family in Lancashire. He studied painting and photography in Paris, and then studied law in London. He was the central figure in a group which established the Photographic Society in London in January 1853 – the present-day Royal Photographic Society. Queen Victoria and Prince Albert visited its first exhibition, so he was well connected.

When Fenton arrived at Balaklava on 8 March 1855, he brought with him his 'Photographic Van' (originally a wine-merchant's vehicle from Canterbury) and two assistants: William, as handyman and cook, and Marcus Sparling, as photographic assistant and groom for the horses. Fenton stayed in the Crimea until June 1855, when, infected by cholera, he returned to England in a very weak state. He brought back with him a total of 360 photographs, taken under very difficult conditions. To make a successful photograph, Fenton and his assistants had to coat a glass plate with an emulsion of wet collodion in their van, transport the plate to the camera, expose it, and return to the van for processing. They probably had about five minutes to do this, because the plate had to be developed while still moist. Exposure times varied between three and twenty seconds, so all Fenton's portraits and informal photos had to be carefully posed.

Fort Constantine, Sebastopol (James Robertson).

Fenton produced many memorable images of the Crimean War, but he also operated under conditions of considerable self-censorship. He arrived in the Crimea after reports in *The Times* had caused an outcry and helped to bring down the government. He was very conscious of his friendship with the royal family; when his work was published as an album, it was 'Dedicated by Special Permission to Her Most Gracious Majesty the Queen and under the Patronage of His Imperial Majesty the Emperor of the French and His Royal Highness Prince Albert'. Neither publisher nor photographer wished to destroy their patronage. Although he witnessed the bloody assaults on the Mamelon Vert, the Redan, and the Malakoff Tower in June 1855, which resulted in huge losses, there are no dead bodies in Fenton's photos.

On his return to England, Queen Victoria and the Prince Consort summoned Fenton to an audience to question him about his adventures. Because he was still weak from cholera, he was permit-

Top: Panorama of the Tchernaya (Leon Méhédin). Above: Roger Fenton and his photographic van.

ted to lie down and address his royal audience in a horizontal position. In Paris, he was asked to present his images to Napoleon III. During this audience, which lasted an hour and a half, the emperor smoked cigarettes incessantly and asked Fenton to return the next day as he 'was not able to satiate his curiosity in one long seance', as *The Times* reported. When his photographs were exhibited in London in October 1855, the magazine *Notes & Queries* wrote:

> An exhibition of deeper interest was never opened to the public... The stern reality stands revealed to the spectator. Camp life with all its hardships, mixed occasionally with some rough-and-ready enjoyments, is realized as if one stood face to face with it.

Fenton left the Crimea before the fall of Sebastopol, but the captured town was recorded in detail by James Robertson. He had trained as an engraver at the Royal Mint in London, and became chief engraver of the Imperial Mint in Constantinople. He was also an enthusiastic photographer and made impressive images of Constantinople, Jerusalem, and Sebastopol. Robertson photographed the ruins of the Redan and the Malakoff Tower, and dramatic 'before' and 'after' pictures of the destruction of the Sebastopol dockyards. His photographs capture the violence and chaos of the ruined naval base.

French photographers and artists were also at work in the Crimea after the fall of Sebastopol. Colonel Charles Langlois had already created a celebrated panoramic painting in Paris, and in Sebastopol he decided to use photography as the basis of his next work. Working with the photographer Leon Méhédin, they made a series of photographs from the top of the ruined Malakoff. Back in Paris, these became the basis for the panoramic painting *The Taking of Sebastopol*, which opened to the public in 1860. As well as working with Langlois, the young Méhédin became ambitious to make a more 'picturesque' series of panoramas of Sebastopol and its surrounding countryside. His images convey a Romantic view of the desolation of the ruined city.

The French artist, Henri Durand-Brager, worked as a reporter and artist for several French journals. In the winter of 1855, he began to take photographs with the assistance of a professional photographer, Lassimonne. They travelled to Kinburn to photograph the fort at the mouth of the Dniepr, and took atmospheric pictures of ships frozen in the ice. It seems likely that Durand-Brager (like Fenton and Robertson) was responding to a commission from a publisher who wished to capitalize on public interest in the war. Thus photographers began to displace artists and illustrators as the principal providers of war images.

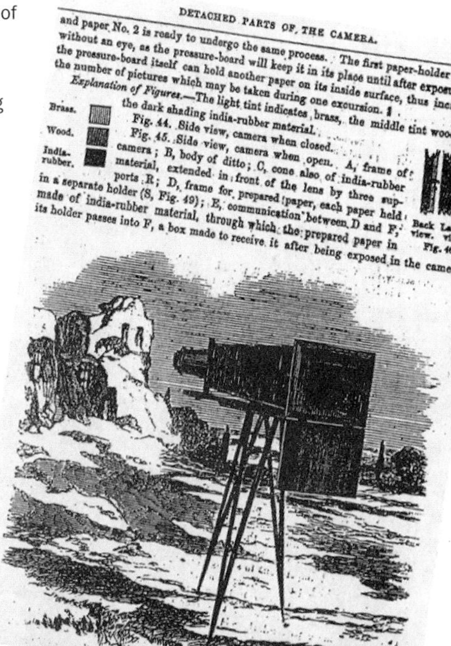

DETACHED PARTS OF THE CAMERA.

and paper No. 2 is ready to undergo the same process. The first paper-holder
without an eye, as the pressure-board will keep it in its place until after exposur
the pressure-board itself can hold another paper on its inside surface, thus incre
the number of pictures which may be taken during one excursion.

Explanation of Figures.—The light tint indicates brass, the middle tint wood, the dark shading india-rubber material.

Fig. 44. Side view, camera when closed.

Fig. 45. Side view, camera when open. A, frame of camera; B, body of ditto; C, cone also of india-rubber material, extended in front of the lens by three supports R; D, frame for prepared paper, each paper held in a separate holder (S, Fig. 49); E, communication between D and F, made of india-rubber material, through which the prepared paper in its holder passes into F, a box made to receive it after being exposed in the camera

Brass.
Wood.
India-rubber.

Back view. Late[ral] view.
Fig. 46.

The battle of the Alma (Captain Henry Clifford).

Clifford wrote that: 'It was sad to see the poor fellows, Russian and English, lying on the ground groaning and suffering so much at the first.'

amongst them, for as we advanced we stumbled over their dead and wounded, knapsacks and horses, and I am sorry to say that our poor fellows fell like grass before a scythe.

Just as the French attack had been delayed by the British in the morning, now Raglan ordered his troops to lie down until the French were in command of the heights. The 2nd Zouaves were standing by in the river itself, being rained on by enemy artillery. Their commander Colonel Cler gave the order to advance:

The branches of the great trees which line the bank, torn away by round shot, came crashing down in every direction... I had the charge sounded and putting my horse into a gallop was followed by the whole of my battalion. The soldiers crossed the river under a hurricane of iron and lead and swinging themselves up the bank reformed at the foot of the hill where they were protected by the very steepness of the overhanging ridge. Making but a brief pause here, the battalion quickly scaled the face of the cliff and hurled themselves on the Russians...and after a short, sharp struggle, the enemy was compelled to abandon their formidable position.

Meanwhile, Private Gowing and the 7th Fusiliers, climbing straight up towards the 'Great Redoubt', were equally successful :

We were only about 600 yards from the mouth of the guns; the thunderbolts of war were not far apart – and Death loves a crowd. The havoc among the Fusiliers, both 7th and 23rd, was awful. Still, nothing but Death could stop that renowned infantry.

The weapon that enabled the British to get up the slope and force the Russians to retreat was their powerful, modern Minié rifle, which was accurate over 500 yards. Russian soldiers had been expecting to engage the enemy with their bayonets. Like his fellow soldiers, Naum Gorbunov, an aide-de-camp of the Vladimir Regiment, could not understand what was hitting his men:

Artillery fire had not yet opened from our battery, so we dismounted our horses and watched with curiosity these strange things...even the artillery men could not name them, suggesting that these bullets, which fell burning from within an explosive device, were aimed at our artillery's cartridge boxes but were in no way meant for us. Expecting to grapple with the approaching enemy, with characteristic Russian courage...we looked death right in the eyes. But after a few seconds we learnt from experience the significance of these 'thimbles'.

Meanwhile Gunner Cox and the Royal Artillery were dragging their heavy guns up to the Great Redoubt:

We limbered up, and advanced again into the din and confusion of the fight; and when the order was again 'Action front,' we found one of our gunners seated on the trail plate without his head, and holding on to the guard-iron with a death grip. A shell had taken his head off without our noticing it, and we had to loosen his hands, and lift his body down, before we could unlimber the gun.

Menshikov, realising that the British would take the 'Great Redoubt', ordered the Russian guns to be withdrawn. Captain Hodasiewicz was shocked by the size and speed of the defeat:

Our army was utterly routed and beaten out of an almost unassailable position. The retreat then began in earnest; a few minutes afterwards we became exposed to a crossfire from the English and French batteries, and on all sides the men cried out 'To the right!' 'To the left!' to avoid the shot, and in one place they broke into a run.

I asked the commander of the battalion where we were going – and I was ashamed to ask where we were retreating, or rather running, for such it was. But the Major did not know; he had no orders where to go...

By four o'clock in the afternoon the Allied victory was complete. The Russians, who had thought they would hold out for three weeks, had been dislodged in only a few hours. Russell observed the plight of the spectators:

Thirty Russian ladies went out of Sebastopol to see the Battle of the Alma as though they were going to a play or a picnic. They were quite assured of the success of the Russian troops, and great was their alarm and dismay when they found themselves obliged to leave the telegraph house on the hill, and to fly for their lives in their carriages.

Throughout the battle, the British cavalry waited to one side, protecting the flank but otherwise inactive. Frustrated, they now wanted to pursue the fleeing Russians. Raglan, as usual, advised caution, fearful of over-extending his forces. Cavalry Captain Lewis Nolan complained bitterly to Russell about this wasted opportunity:

There were one thousand British Cavalry looking at a beaten army retreating – guns, standards, colours and all – with a wretched horde of Cossacks and cowards who had never struck a blow, ready to turn tail at the first trumpet... It is too disgraceful! Too infamous!

One month later, at the charge of the Light Brigade, Nolan would vent his frustration about the role of the cavalry. That evening William Howard Russell walked over the battlefield:

One who has not seen, cannot conceive the relics of a great fight, especially on such a field as that of the Alma on which there had been an army bivouacking for several days. There was an immense accumulation of camp-litter on the hill-sides. There was a sickening, sour, foetid smell everywhere, and the grass was sloppy with blood.

The same night, Marshal Saint-Arnaud wrote a report to Emperor Napoleon:

> **My tent is on the very site which Prince Menshikov occupied this morning, so sure of beating us that he left his carriage. I have taken it, along with his pocketbook and his correspondence, and I will use the precious information that I find in it profitably.**

The Russians had suffered heavy losses and now fled back to Sebastopol. On the way Captain Hodasiewicz witnessed the brutal reality of the aftermath of battle:

> **We passed numbers of unfortunate men who cried out to us for help we could not give them. Some asked for water to quench their intolerable thirst, while others begged hard to be put out of their agony by a speedy death. These sights and sounds had a very visible effect on the morale of the men, as they saw how little care was taken of them when they most required it. They exclaimed among themselves while passing through these horrors, 'Happy is he who a merciful Providence permits to die on the field of battle.'**

Things were no better for the British. Private Albert Mitchell of the 13th Light Dragoons passed an uneasy night after the battle:

> **By this time, the greater part of the army was asleep, and then it was that we heard around us the groans of the wounded and the dying; some calling for the love of God for a drop of water. Others were praying most devoutly, well knowing this to be their last night in this life. We had already seen sufficient to harden our feelings, and make us callous to human suffering, but I lay some time thinking very seriously and praying to God for protection from all dangers.**

For two days the Allied army tended their wounded and buried their dead while the British and French commanders tried to agree on a strategy. On 23 September, the army set off once more towards Sebastopol.

On the morning the battle had taken place, Fanny Duberly had been sleeping on board ship at Eupatoria, but had been woken by the sound of guns and asked herself what they could mean: 'Oh this suspense! How could I be so weak as to allow myself to be separated from my husband? A lifetime of anxiety has been crowded into these...days.' Three days later she got a confused report of what had happened:

> **Was awoke from a restless sleep by the entrance of my maid - with her apron over her eyes. I naturally asked what was the matter. 'Oh, ma'am!... There has been a dreadful battle - 500 English killed, and 5,000 Russians; and all our poor cavalry fellows are all killed; and, the Lord be good to us, we're all widows.'**

Fanny was not in fact a widow, the information had become garbled on the way. But it made up her mind always to be at the scene of the battle, just in case. News of the victory travelled 1,500 miles back to London. Along the way it, too, became garbled. In Paris, Emperor Napoleon III told the crowds 'I have little doubt the flags of the Allied army are waving on the walls of Sebastopol.' In London, *The Times* reported his speech and their headline on 2 October was 'The Fall of Sebastopol'.

The Russians themselves were also convinced that the fall of Sebastopol was imminent. Prince Menshikov had been confident that his troops at the Alma would hold out for at least three weeks. Now he was equally sure that the Allies were coming to take Sebastopol from the north. Naum Gorbunov had survived the battle and returned to the Russian base:

> **In Sebastopol itself there was an inordinate fuss going on, the inhabitants were expecting to be given weapons; the boats standing in the bay and other vessels were still waiting to be given instructions, so unclear yet was the overall state of affairs.**

However the fall of Sebastopol would not be so straightforward. The leading strategist of the British army, Sir John Burgoyne, had been sent out to advise Raglan. He brought with him the conviction that a raid would not succeed and that Sebastopol could only be taken by a formal siege. Events were now playing into his hands.

Saint-Arnaud, the commander-in-chief of the French forces, was dying of cancer of the stomach. As the Allies approached the north of Sebastopol, only one fortification stood in their way – the 'Star Fort'. Saint-Arnaud refused to commit the French to an assault on this fort. Raglan, reluctant to press his views on his dying co-commander, sent Sir John Burgoyne to hammer out a strategy. Not surprisingly, Burgoyne advocated his own plan – for a flank march around the city, so that the Allies could benefit from the natural harbours at Balaklava and Kamiesch and besiege Sebastopol from the south. His argument was that Sebastopol's defences must first be reduced by heavy artillery and that only then could the town be taken. Burgoyne's strategy was accepted by the French and almost by default became the basis of the war in the Crimea.

For thirty hours, the Allied army marched towards Sebastopol, Lord Raglan leading the way. All of a sudden he found himself surrounded by a Russian army. It was nothing less than the baggage train of their commander, Prince Menshikov, being hastily evacuated from Sebastopol towards Simferopol in the interior of the Crimea. The Allies took a few prisoners, including one drunk artillery captain, and captured some ladies underwear and a few risqué French novels into the bargain! William Howard Russell described this strange encounter in *The Times*:

> **A Russian artillery officer, who was found in one of the carriages, was in a very jovial mood, and had evidently been making rather free with the bottle. Plenty of Champagne was discovered among the baggage, and served to cheer the captors during their cold bivouac that night... This plunder put the soldiers in great good humour, and they marched on the whole day, leaving Sebastopol on their right.**

Beneath this champagne-fuelled jollity, the crucial decision was made. The raiding party had turned away from Sebastopol, and had begun the 'flank march' around the city, committing themselves to a siege. This decision would transform the Crimean campaign from a swift raid into an offensive that would drag on for a year of trench warfare and mounting casualty figures. Looking back on the war later, Russell summed up the almost farcical situation:

> **The French General was dying. The English General...in order to take Sebastopol was marching round it! The Russian General, anxious to save Sebastopol, was marching away from it! Neither of them had the least notion what the other was doing.**

Pyotr Alabin was part of a large contingent of reinforcements marching back around the Black Sea from the Danube and down to Sebastopol. When he arrived in the town he heard the astonishing news:

> **Those who were in Sebastopol when the Allies moved from the northern to the southern side could not believe their eyes. The defenders of the town, which was weak from the land side, had decided to fight to the very last but no-one held out any hope of staving off the enemy hordes; the sailors, fired with the resolve of...their commanders...vowed that they would blow themselves up with their ships so as not to see the enemy's triumph... When the Allies moved from a position beneath the northern fortifications, which was defended by two cargo battalions, and a few naval squadrons, to the Tchernaya River, nobody could understand what they were thinking of.**

Harry Blishen's Rifle Brigade was among the first of the regiments to reach Balaklava and wrest control of the harbour from a handful of local militia:

> **On the 26th we marched to Balaklava and in two hours stormed a fort and took every living Russian in the place prisoner. There is a nice little Harbour which admitted of our landing our Siege train which consists of 90 pieces of heavy cannon. We are now lazing in the rear of Sebastopol within range of their guns and expect to go to work at it in every hour. I imagine it will be a rather tough job. I have been sleeping in the open air with my clothes on now for 19 days.**

By now the French commander-in-chief was unable even to climb into his saddle. Paul de Molènes, a captain of the Spahi cavalry regiment, which acted as Marshal Saint-Arnaud's personal guard, reported:

> **The Arabs say the day a warrior leaves his horse, he lies down by his grave. The Marshall lay down in a waggon and we Spahis escorted him for the last time. The**

The harbour at Balakava. (Photo by Roger Fenton.)

journey had a cruelly sad appearance. The dilapidated wagon resembled a hearse, the men holding it together looked as if they were carrying a coffin.

At Balaklava, the marshal was carried on board a boat bound for Constantinople, but he died at sea on 29 September.

The British had made Balaklava their base, but the men were camped on the plateau in front of Sebastopol. Most of their army was positioned on the right, directly opposite the Karabalnaya suburb and the all-important Russian dockyard. The French made their base at Kamiesch, and took up camp and artillery positions on the left hand side of the plateau facing the besieged city. Henry Clifford was on the staff of the Light Division. From two Polish deserters he learnt about the Russian plans:

They say Prince Menshikov has spoken to the troops in Sebastopol, and told them that our arms...are superior to theirs, but that at the Battle of Alma, one of the Regiments with big caps (the Fusilier Guards) wavered when the bayonet was used against them, and that is the weapon to use against the English. I only hope they

will try it on, how they will catch it! This no doubt gave rise to the ludicrous sight we saw from our picket house last evening. The Russians brought out some planks about six feet long and fixed them to the ground, and then charged them with fixed bayonets, shouting - such shouting!!

But the Allies were thinking on a bigger scale than the fixing of bayonets and were already bringing their artillery ashore, as Harry Blishen had witnessed. Cornet Fisher, of the 4th Dragoon Guards noted:

The ships have furnished more than a thousand sailors to work their own guns. They are most wonderful fellows, they come along, singing, and shouting, harnessed to an araba [cart] in which their kits are conveyed; as they come opposite they are received with loud cheers, which they return with a power of lungs extraordinary.

Despite the enthusiasm of the 'Jack Tars', the Allies now frittered away their advantage gained at Alma with lengthy preparations. It took the artillery and naval units three weeks to drag their big guns into position. Meanwhile, entrenchments had to be dug and batteries made for the siege trains. Officers such as Captain Dallas welcomed the activity as a way of relieving their frustration:

These last few days we have been having really desperate hard work and though one is utterly exhausted, it is infinitely better than the stupid inaction we have been suffering from for nearly a fortnight. We are still hard at work preparing the trenches and the position for our guns. The ground is hard as iron & full of stones so that the work is most laborious.

Some of the commanders argued that a serious mistake had been made. Dallas's own general, Sir George Cathcart, looked down on Sebastopol appalled by this wasted opportunity, and wrote to Raglan:

I am sure I could walk into it, with scarcely the loss of a man – at night or an hour before day. We could leave our packs and run into it even in open daylight, only risking a few shots while we passed the redoubts. We see people walking about the streets in great consternation.

All too soon, however, the moment had passed. As the British and French struggled to commence their siege, the Russians wasted no time organizing their defence. After the defeat at the Alma, Menshikov made a difficult decision for the naval garrison – to scuttle part of the Black Sea Fleet and to use the ships' guns to defend the town. Some ships resisted their fate, as Captain Hodasiewicz observed:

The 'Three Prelates' would not sink after being scuttled, so about 8 a.m. on September 22nd the steamer 'Vladimir' fired three shots into her from a very short range but still she floated on the waters. At this moment, a man belonging to the 'Vladimir' went to his captain and asked if he might go to the doomed ship and take out of her a holy icon that had been given by the Bishop of Odessa when the ship was launched. That is the cause of her not sinking, said the man. The captain granted his request with a smile and he returned triumphantly with the prize which he showed to the captain exclaiming, 'How could you expect something so holy to sink!' Two more shots sent the vessel to the bottom.

Seven Russian warships were sunk across the entrance to Sebastopol harbour, forming an effective barricade. The naval commander, Admiral Kornilov, who took charge of the operations, was helped by an extraordinary man. Lieutenant-Colonel Eduard

RUSSIAN FORTIFICATIONS AT SEBASTOPOL AND, IN THE FOREGROUND, THE BRITISH BASE IN BALAKLAVA.

Wives and Warriors

One woman who caused a stir in Constantinople was Kara Fatima, a sixty-year old Albanian woman, who arrived at the head of a bunch of picturesque looking Kurdistan warriors. Captain Adolphus Slade remarked:

> Constantinople swarms with spectators curious to see the amazon. [The people are], somewhat scandalised by sight of Moslem woman unveiled..., dressed in Damascene riding attire & armed with sabre & pistols.

The Allies themselves had created a bit of excitement, as Captain Henry Clifford observed:

> I am afraid that the old Pashas with their 100 young wives are not over-pleased with the appearance of so many young officers, and I think one or two more promenades at the 'Sweet Waters' will make an even greater change in the ladies of these dear old gentlemen. The fact is, the Turkish ladies are quite as fond of admiration as English or any other women, and like to be looked at better by a dashing handsome young officer with a fine uniform, than by an old gentleman with one foot in the grave. In vain the guardians of these fair dames walk after them, with frowns and hints that the old gentleman shall hear all about it when they get home. The veil will drop, and the head will turn over the shoulder to exchange a smile and a glance with some young admirer. However sorry others may be, I have no doubt the old Turks are delighted the troops are leaving Constantinople.

Above: Mrs Fanny Duberly, eager to experience the thrills of war (Fenton). Right: Kara Fatima rides through Constantinople.

Some of the British soldiers had brought their wives with them. According to 'Queen's Regulations', a fixed number of women, about 6 to every 100 men, was permitted to travel 'on the strength' of each regiment. Since a good many left-at-home soldiers' wives faced destitution, these expeditionary positions were highly desirable, and had to be filled by a ballot. Despite that ballot, it was late in May 1854 before they were allocated full rations and their own tents. Wherever the army landed the women were left to make their own way to shore, and follow on as best they could. As Florence Nightingale knew, at least 250 of the women who left England with their husbands' regiments ended up in the verminous cellars under Scutari hospital:

> In the Barrack are now located some two hundred poor women in the most abject misery. They are the wives of soldiers who were allowed to accompany their

husbands; a great number have been sent down from Varna; they are in rags and covered with vermin. My heart bleeds for them, and they are at our doors daily, clamouring for everything; but it is impossible for me to attend to them, my work is with the soldiers, not with their wives.

They were eventually rescued by Lady Alicia Blackwood, one of several philanthropic 'ladies' who rushed to the Crimea in response to news of the terrible conditions.

If I entered into any description of these dens, it would be to say they must have been fitly likened to a Pandemonium full of cursing and swearing and drunkenness. The arrangements of a barrack room for married soldiers in those days were such, that other than this result could hardly be expected. They were certainly as much sinned against as sinning!

Independently of the bodily suffering, insepera-ble from such a state of things, it is difficult to realise the terrible demor-alisation produced by the fact that there was no actual division between the portions of the floor appro-priated by the married couples; only here and there some of them had attempted to make a sort of screen by hanging a rug or two on a piece of cord.

Lady Alicia established a laundry where the women could earn money. She then set up a store and a shop, selling gifts sent by the charitable to the employed women at low rates, and using the resulting funds to buy tea, soap and other necessaries.

A wife 'on the strength' of the 4th Dragoon Guards (Fenton).

In France women known as *vivandières* were an integrated part of the army both at home and on campaigns. Each regiment had at least one *vivandière* and their role was to provide food and drink for the men, to wash their clothes and to tend the wounded. British officers, like Lieutenant William Young of the 49th Foot, visited their allies whenever they could:

Have been over to the French Camp all day listening to the band and having a jolly good feed at the canteen where Mademoiselle Marie Henri (and I don't know how many other names she has) has a stuning (sic) place for officers.

Vivandières had the same status as normal soldiers regarding their treatment and decorations. They had their place in the order of battle, between the musicians and the staff, and they participated in all military parades, reviews and campaigns. They even dressed in a feminized version of their regimental uniform.

As the war progressed and the siege of Sebastopol became a reality, Pyotr Alabin observed how Russian women also became war wives:

The whole of the northern side and west of the Malakoff Tower are covered with the sailors' little houses, filled with their families. The women wash the officers' linen, giving this task a special importance; they trade their wares not only at two bazaars on the Karabelnaya side but even at the Malakoff Tower itself, sitting behind their stalls at the dug-out gates, offering the crowd of soldiers who've come in their free time to have a little treat, blini, pies, pieces of chopped herring, apples, buns of different types, wonderful bread, kvass, nuts, jellied meats and all kinds of edible delights which the soldiers would consume there and then with a hot honey drink, spending any spare money they had.

The sailor's wife brings her husband's food to him at the bastion and sits with him by the gun while he eats so as to take the dish away again, she spends two, three hours with her husband, in spite of the relentless flight of enemy shells. During the general bombardment, the women brought water to the bastion, never stopping, so as to refresh the soldiers, tormented by their labours and the intense heat.

ABOVE: *THE TRENCHES AT NIGHT* (CAPTAIN HENRY CLIFFORD).
RIGHT: SHIPS SUNK ACROSS THE HARBOUR AT SEBASTOPOL (JAMES ROBERTSON).

Totleben, a brilliant young engineer in the Russian army, had been despatched from Silistria by his commanding officer to assist with the defence of Sebastopol. Totleben reported to Menshikov in August, and was treated as an unwelcome intruder. Now Menshikov changed his mind. Together with Kornilov, Totleben set to work to build an ambitious series of earthwork defences, armed with cannons from the boats.

Totleben ordered six major bastions to be built around Sebastopol. As with the Allies, it was Russian sailors who manned the guns taken from the ships, while the men, women and children from the town were also drafted into the defence. Unlike their enemy, however, in only thirty-six hours they had 100 naval guns in position. Captain Hodasiewicz noted:

> **In the town the people were as busy as ants, working day and night at their defences. The greater number of the wives and families of the naval officers were at this time in the town. As it was not known where the enemy might be expected, they were afraid to retire to Simferopol. In fact, all seemed to be seized with a kind of panic. Korniloff appeared to have a power of multiplying himself, for he was everywhere, promising large rewards to all if they could only keep the town.**

Admiral Kornilov was already becoming a local legend. Troops returning to Russia from the Danube, including Leo Tolstoy, heard stories of his defence of the town:

> **The army's spirit defies description. There wasn't so much heroism in the days of ancient Greece. When Kornilov does his round of the troops, instead of saying, 'Hello, lads!', he says, 'If you have to die, lads, will you die?' and the troops shout, 'We'll die, Your Excellency! Hurrah!'**

While Kornilov was organizing his naval defences inside Sebastopol, Menshikov led his army into the interior of the Crimea. From there they could keep the supply lines to Sebastopol open and harass the Allies. By keeping the northern flank open, Menshikov prevented the city from ever being completely encircled by the British and French.

By now Fanny Duberly had sailed to Balaklava to join her husband. She took one look at the tent that Henry was sharing with three other men, and decided she would sleep on board ship. Nevertheless, she visited the British camp at night and was thrilled by the preparations for the siege:

> **From the forts of Sebastopol, the shot and shell came hissing every two minutes. I could not but feel a high degree of excitement, and I think it was not unnatural. We were standing on the brow of a hill, backed by our magnificent troops and fronting the enemy; the doomed city beneath our feet and the pale moon above; it was indeed a moment worth a hundred years of every-day existence.**

The etiquette of the alliance demanded that British and French guns should open fire simultaneously. While being bombarded by the Russians, and waiting

LOOKING AT SEBASTOPOL (CAPTAIN HENRY CLIFFORD).

COULD THEY HAVE MARCHED STRAIGHT IN? SOME OFFICERS CONSIDERED THEY HAD WASTED AN OPPORTUNITY.

for their own guns to open up, officers and men alike discussed which house they would take over in Sebastopol and what it would be like to celebrate mass in a Sebastopol church that Sunday. For Captain Dallas, as for most of the troops the city really did seem 'doomed':

> **How ominous it must seem to them, seeing us quietly sitting around their city. Our batteries when up (and they say it will be in a day or two) will all open up at once, and then Heaven help the poor city. I am told we have three times as large a battery as has ever been brought against any city or fortress, and the most commanding position to place them in... I expect that in a few days the whole town will be a heap of ruins, and that we shall be sent to wherever we are intended to winter.**

Dallas's forecast was wildly over-optimistic. By the

Lieutenant Colonel Totleben (portrait by Vasili Timm).

The intelligence behind the earthworks that would 'checkmate the Allies in engineering'.

time the Allied guns finally opened fire on 17 October, the Russians had made very good use of the delay. But for ordinary Russian soldiers and civilians the bombardment was still a terrifying ordeal. Inside Sebastopol, Lieutenant-Captain Reimers had been sent to take charge of the men defending the Flagstaff (fourth) bastion:

> **Finally, the awful day of the beginning of the bombardment came... What a frightening picture! Everywhere you could hear the moans and cries of the wounded, in a second everything was covered in smoke, and we, thinking that the enemy is about to assault, opened fire from all our guns, firing, of course, heaven knows where!**
>
> **I will never forget the moment when, on the first day of the bombardment, Kornilov, Nakhimov, Totleben and a venerable priest with the cross blessed everyone and went all around the bastion. With what feeling did each of us go up to the cross and how the calm spirit of all these worthy people animated us.**

Timothy Gowing, who had been made a sergeant at the battle of the Alma, reported on the first day's progress:

> **...from 6 until 9 a.m. they were hard at it; as fast as our men could load and fire it was ding-dong hard fighting. At 9 a.m. one of the French magazines went up with a crash. Still our people kept at it – it was, as far as we could see, all fair give and take. The White Tower was knocked all to pieces very quickly, but huge works were erected all around it, and called the Malakoff.**

The first day of the siege was hardly a triumph: the French guns had been silenced by an explosion in their magazine, and the British guns had not performed well. However, the Allied bombardment had scored one extraordinary hit. Captain Hodasiewicz first heard the news at six in the evening:

> **The rumour began to spread that Admiral Kornilov had been wounded on his favourite spot – the Malakov Hill. His right leg had been carried off and there was little hope of saving his life. This was all passed from one to another in whispers, as it was forbidden to speak openly of this event, as Kornilov was much respected and**

Soldiers learnt to adapt to new methods of transport. (Photo by Roger Fenton.)

beloved by all belonging to the town, of which he was regarded as the chief defence, and his death would have a most discouraging effect, especially upon the sailors.

Allied morale may have been boosted by the death of the commander of Sebastopol's garrison, but as the bombardment went on they had little to cheer about. Every time they destroyed part of the Russian defence, it was immediately rebuilt. On 19 October Colonel Charles Windham wrote in his diary:

The pounding match went on as usual, without our gaining the slightest advantage, and I am more convinced than ever that we shall lose double the number of men in taking the place (if we do succeed) than we should have done had we attacked it twenty-four days ago. This long range firing is all nonsense; moreover the Russians are better at it than we are, and, from all I can see, our present attack is an absurdity.

Weeks of delay by the Allies had enabled Totleben to construct a formidable defence. The principal Russian army under Prince Menshikov remained outside the city. In a few days they would return and attack the British camp at Balaklava.

CHAPTER FOUR

VALLEYS OF DEATH

THE RESERVE ARMY THAT Prince Menshikov had led out of Sebastopol was gradually getting stronger and, with the arrival of new troops, the Russians were determined to try and force the invading army back into the sea. Kamiesch, the French base, was secure, but with most of the Allied troops caught up in the siege, only a small defence corps had been appointed to protect Balaklava, the more vulnerable of the two. This became the Russians' target.

THE CAVALRY CAMP AT KADIKOI, JUST OUTSIDE BALAKLAVA. (PHOTO BY ROGER FENTON.)

Balaklava was defended by British and Ottoman troops under the command of Sir Colin Campbell, one of the few generals from a humble background. There were two lines of defence. In front of the town itself were some heights occupied by the Royal Marine Artillery and a small hill occupied by a battery of artillery and the 93rd Highlanders. Beyond this lay the Causeway Heights, a low ridge that carried the Woronzoff Road, and which separated the ground between the British and the Russians into two valleys. The Causeway Heights had been fortified with six redoubts containing British twelve-pounder guns, and was manned by Ottoman infantry troops. After the brave defence of Silistria such confidence was placed in these troops that it was assumed they could hold the redoubts by themselves. But these men were not the Egyptian heroes of Silistria, but untrained Tunisian militia, and, according to Captain Adolphus Slade, the positions they were responsible for defending were unenviable at best:

[They were] above 2000 yards away from any support, requiring the staunchest troops of any army to hold...[and had been]...entrusted to men under depressing influences; men not long enrolled, and never in action. Ignorant and suspicious, in a strange army, they may have fancied themselves placed there by the 'infidel' to be sacrificed.

Among the other troops stationed near Balaklava was the pride of the British army – the cavalry. Its contribution, now that the war strategy was to besiege Sebastopol, had been reduced to patrolling the roads between base and camp. A large Russian force was a constant presence on the Fediukhin Heights above Balaklava from which raiding parties would occasionally appear out of the bushes. No serious notice was taken of reported attacks, but turning out every morning at four or five o'clock and standing to arms for an hour took its toll. Private Farquharson of the 4th Light Dragoons wrote:

Every day now the Russians loitering or moving in great masses about the Chernaya [river separating the two forces]...began to keep us on the alert morning, noon and night. If we came in from picket fagged, cold and hungry, we might hear the trumpet sound 'boot and saddle' at any moment.

There were numerous false alarms. Once an unfortunate cow was mistaken for a Cossack and killed. Lord George Paget, the son of Wellington's cavalry commander at Waterloo, wrote to his new wife:

Every fool at the outposts, who fancies he hears something, has only to make a row, and there we all are, Generals and all... Well I suppose 500 false alarms are better than one surprise.

They were to be surprised nevertheless. On 24 October 1854 a spy came to Sir Colin Campbell with the news that General Liprandi intended to attack Balaklava the following day, but the same tale had been told several times already that week and Raglan ignored the warning.

Early the next morning two flags were spotted flying from one of the Turkish redoubts, the agreed sign for a Russian attack. Captain Temple Godman was watching through binoculars:

Up the hill came the Russian infantry, meeting a warm fire from the Johnny [Turk] who at that moment turned and rushed up again under their fort. On came the Russians, shouting and running up in fine order and giving a heavy fire.

In the first redoubt the 500 or so Turks resisted bravely. Outnumbered by around fifteen to one they held the Russians back for two hours, losing over a third of their men in the process, but winning the British precious time. At eight o'clock in the morning Troop Sergeant-Major Smith arrived to see them being 'sacrificed':

As they gained the plain, a number of Cossacks swept round the foot of the hill, killing and wounding many of them. Some of them being unarmed raised their hands imploringly, but it was only to have them severed from their bodies... Had a dozen or two of us been sent out numbers of these poor fellows might have been saved.

Raglan also did not arrive on the scene until two hours after the attack had begun, just in time to see the Turks retreating from the other redoubts. Seeing the Russians advancing on Balaklava Lord Raglan sent an urgent request for infantry to support the Turks. The messenger to the 1st Division needed only to say that there was 'a row going on down in Balaklava plain and you fellows are wanted' and the Duke of Cambridge ordered his men to march. Sir George Cathcart, in charge of the 4th Division, was not so ready to jump to order. He was already said to be angry with Raglan, particularly over the latter's failure to assault Sebastopol, and on hearing of the Turks' plight said to the messenger:

I can't help that, sir. It is impossible for my division to move, as the greater proportion of the men have only just come from the trenches. The best thing you can do, sir, is to sit down and have some breakfast.

If Cathcart could not do without his breakfast, Fanny Duberly's appetite was for action. This time she was not going to miss the chance to see a battle:

TURKISH ARTILLERY.

A note was put into my hands from Henry... It ran thus 'The battle of Balaklava has begun, and promises to be a hot one. I send you the horse. Lose no time, but come up as quickly as you can: do not wait for breakfast.'

I was hardly clear of the town, before I met a commissariat officer, who told me that the Turks had abandoned all their batteries, and were running towards the town. He begged me to keep as much to the left as possible, and, of all things, to lose no time in getting amongst our own men, as the Russian force was pouring on us; adding, 'For God's sake, ride fast, or you may not reach the camp alive.'

With no immediate support forthcoming from their Allies, some Turks did run toward the port screaming 'Ship! Ship! dok (too many) Rus!', but the rest rallied and joined forces with the 93rd Highlanders. A single battery of artillery and these men were now all that stood between a large body of advancing Russian cavalry and Balaklava itself. On the small ridge where they were based, Sir Colin Campbell told these men, 'Remember there is no retreat from here. You must die where you stand.' Private Donald Cameron, of the Highlanders, was one of those standing:

Now is the time to try our courage and steadiness with a mass of cavalry coming on us, but there we stood like a rock, determined to stand or fall together.

A crowd had now gathered on the heights overlooking the Highlanders' position, where they had a good view of both valleys. William Howard Russell and Fanny Duberly had joined Lord Raglan and the other officers, who Russell described as:

...spectators of the scene as though they were looking

down on the stage from the boxes of the theatre. Nearly everyone dismounted and sat down, and not a word was said...

The silence is oppressive; between the cannon bursts one can hear the champing of bits and the clink of sabres in the valley below.

Fanny Duberly held her breath:

Presently came the Russian Cavalry charging, over the hillside and across the valley, right against the little line of Highlanders. Ah, what a moment! Charging and surging onward, what could that little wall of men do against such numbers and such speed? There they stood. Sir Colin did not even form them into square. They waited until the horsemen were within range, and then poured a volley which for a moment hid everything in smoke.

As the smoke cleared, Private Donald Cameron and the obstinate line of Highlanders did not give an inch:

ABOVE: THE VARIOUS STAGES OF THE BATTLE OF BALAKLAVA (A. MACLURE).
ABOVE RIGHT: *THE CHARGE OF THE HEAVY BRIGADE* (WILLIAM SIMPSON).

The Russians coming again towards us, we opened fire on them the second time and turned them. They seemed to be going away. We ceased firing and cheered. They wheeled about and made a dash at us again. We opened fire on them the third time. They came to a stand, wheeled about and off at a canter. We ceased firing and cheered. Our heavy guns fired after them. They were soon back over the hill the way they came.

At the retreat of the Russians, the valley echoed to British cheers of 'Bravo, Highlanders! Well done!'. Russell turned this clash into journalistic legend:

The Russians on their left drew breath for a moment, and then in one grand line dashed at the Highlanders. The ground flies beneath their horses' feet; gathering

> **speed at every stride, they dash on towards that thin red streak tipped with a line of steel.**

He had coined a phrase – his 'thin red streak' became the thin red line.

Meanwhile the main body of Russian cavalry, a mass of 2,000 troops, had started to descend the south valley towards a Heavy Brigade that was a mere 600 strong. In command of this brigade was General Scarlett, whose first ever battle this was to be. The Russians had caught him unprepared and at a disadvantage, on lower ground. But in spite of this he decided to charge the enemy – and to charge uphill.

Scarlett's troop officers started to form up unhurriedly as if on a parade ground. Without concern, they turned their backs on the enemy until they were ready. The incredulous Russians halted. On the heights no one spoke. Captain Henry Clifford, who was not involved that day, was a spectator:

> **The Scots Greys and the Enniskillen Dragoons advanced in a slow, steady trot towards them, the Russians looked at them as if fascinated, unable to move. The distance between the two Cavalries at last decreased to about 50 yards, and the shrill sound of the trumpet, ordering the charge, first broke the awful silence.**

When the charge sounded, Scarlett calmly led his cavalry forward into the centre of the enemy. There was no time to think. One dragoon wrote:

> **Oh God! I cannot describe it. They were so superior in numbers, they outflanked us, and we were in the middle of them... I hope God will forgive me, for I felt more like a devil than a man.**

From the heights, the charge made thrilling spectator sport. William Howard Russell was now in full swing:

> **The Greys rush on with a cheer that thrills to every heart – the wild shout of the Enniskilliners rises through the air at the same instant. As lightning flashes through a cloud, the Greys and Enniskilliners pierced through the dark masses of Russians. The shock was but for a**

moment. There was a clash of steel and a light play of sword blades in the air, and then the Greys and the redcoats disappear in the midst of the shaken and quivering columns... It was a terrible moment. 'God help them! they are lost!' was the exclamation of more than one man, and the thought of many. With unabated fire the noble hearts dashed at their enemy. It was a fight of heroes.

It looked as if the brigade had been completely enveloped and was about to be destroyed. Luckily, at that moment reinforcements arrived, including Major Forrest of the 4th Dragoon Guards:

We had very bad ground to advance over, first thro' a vineyard, and over two fences, bank & ditch, then thro' the Camp of the 17th [Lancers], & we were scarcely formed when we attacked , & had but very little ground to charge over. Still we did not go in at so good a pace as we might have done. Once in, we did better, but the confusion was more than I had expected. The men of all regiments were mixed & we were a long time reforming... When once in amongst them I scarcely saw anybody – that is to recognise them. One could not look about much until the Russians began to run.

There was terrible confusion. One Enniskillen officer carried a dead Russian across his saddle into the close-packed ranks, unable to throw the corpse off for lack of room. In fact, because of the lack of space to manouevre there were relatively few casualties. The British swung their swords with great energy but did not inflict severe wounds on the Russians who were also protected to some extent by their heavy coats. The swords on both sides were blunt and rusty from the wet weather, and Lieutenant-Colonel Griffiths reported: 'When our men made a thrust with the sword, they all bent and would not go into a man's body.'

Nonetheless, in only eight minutes the Heavy Brigade, according to William Howard Russell, had 'put them to utter rout' and:

A cheer burst from every lip – in the enthusiasm, officers and men took off their caps and shouted with delight, and thus keeping up the scenic character of their position, they clapped their hands again and again.

Certainly Scarlett's charge had unsettled the Russian cavalry. Equally certainly it had not defeated them. For, having re-formed at the top of the hill – and only forty or fifty having been knocked from their horses, the Russians were ready to attack again. That they did not was due to the artillery which then opened fire on the Russians, the 24-pounder howitzers doing far more damage than the blunt swords of the British cavalry, however heroic the horsemen had been. But the urge to print the legend, to make the romantic cavalry rather than the prosaic artillery the heroes of the war, was supreme.

By 9.30am both sides thought they were winning the battle of Balaklava.

Against the expectations and conventions of cavalry combat, the Light Brigade had remained motionless. Private Mitchell, of the 13th Lancers, was confused:

All this time we sat expecting an order to pursue, but no order came, and soon the opportunity was lost. We all felt certain that if we had been sent in pursuit we should have cut up many of them, besides capturing many prisoners.

But the private's lot was not to reason why. A misunderstanding between Lord Lucan, commander of the Cavalry, and his brother-in-law Lord Cardigan, commander of the Light Brigade, exacerbated by their personal hostility for each other had been enough to keep the Light Brigade out of action.

As Raglan watched the battle, his staff told him that the Russians were removing the British guns that had been abandoned in the redoubts. For the next hour he tried, with increasing impatience, to get either his cavalry or his infantry to respond to orders to prevent this intolerable humiliation. Finally, he dictated a fourth order to Lord Lucan. It was delivered by Captain Lewis Nolan, an expert horseman, but someone already riled by Lucan's caution. The note read:

Lord Raglan wishes the cavalry to advance rapidly to the front follow the enemy and try to prevent the enemy carrying away the guns. Troop Horse Attily may

accompany. French cavalry is on y left. Immediate.

From the Light Brigade's position the guns in the Turkish redoubts were not visible. All that Lucan and Cardigan could see was the Russian cavalry, turned back by the Heavy Brigade, re-forming at the far end of the valley behind the guns of the Don battery, the artillery which had earlier routed the Turks. Private Mitchell was waiting to act:

> **Things were in this state when Captain Nolan, of the 15th Hussars, and who belonged to the headquarters staff, came galloping down and handed a paper to Lord Lucan. We now felt certain there was something cut out for us, but Lords Lucan and Cardigan both appeared to demur at the order, when Captain Nolan, pointing to the guns, said something, which caused us to get the order to mount and move off at a trot.**

Which guns Nolan pointed at have been the subject of controversy ever since. Lucan was understandably reluctant to launch into such a suicidal attack. But orders had to be obeyed. At 11.10am, the Russian cavalry commander, General Ryzhov, got a surprise:

> **The sharp eyes of the Don gunners noted the far distant cloud of dust raised by enemy cavalry coming down the slopes into the valley. Two minutes later it was clear that the enemy was coming along the valley in to the attack.**

To the Russians it must have seemed that Cardigan and his 632 cavalrymen coming the one and a quarter miles down the valley to the guns, were riding to certain death. The charge of the Light Brigade had begun.

One of the men charging was William Pennington:

> **The word was given to 'charge guns to the front'. We advanced at a gallop to these guns, amid a fearful fire from the front, with ditto on the left and right flanks, of grape, shell and canister, and infantry also pouring in a tremendous fire. The effect was that horses and men fell thick and fast, but even this did not check our onward rush.**

Only after they had covered some 200 yards did it become evident to William Howard Russell and the other spectators that Lord Cardigan was leading his men not to the right, towards the redoubts, but straight down the valley toward the Russian Don battery.

> **We could scarcely believe the evidence of our senses! Surely that handful of men are not going to charge an enemy in position? Alas! it was but too true – their desperate valour knew no bounds, and far indeed was it removed from its so-called better part – discretion.**

Someone had blundered. Suddenly Nolan rode out in front of Cardigan gesticulating wildly. Whether he was trying to redirect the Brigade will never be known as he became the first casualty of the charge when a shell splinter pierced his chest. But by now it was too late to divert the charge even if that had been Nolan's intention.

The Heavy Brigade, following them up the valley was also under fire. Lucan himself was hit and he made the decision not to sacrifice the Heavy Brigade as well as the Light. The halt was sounded, and he retreated a little way back up the valley. The Light Brigade, unsupported by either Heavies or infantry, was left to go it alone. But nothing could restrain the troopers now: 'It was something more than kill or be killed. It was kill whether or no and in any way, don't mind it and I didn't.'

On the field that day was the regimental butcher of the 17th Lancers, John Fahey known as 'Butcher Jack', who had been under guard for being drunk on duty the previous night and had awoken to find the Light Brigade camp empty. Hastening to the battlefield he grabbed a riderless Russian pony and, still wearing his butcher's apron and wielding his axe, galloped down the valley to join his regiment:

> **Nearer and nearer we came to the dreadful battery, which kept vomiting death on us like a volcano, till I seemed to feel on my cheek the hot air from the cannon's mouth. At last we were on it. Half a dozen of us leaped in among the guns at once, and I with one blow of my axe brained a Russian gunner just as he was clapping the linstock to the touch-hole of his piece. With another I split open the head of an officer who was trying to rally the artillery detachment in the rear.**

The Russian guns made instant gaps in the ranks, horses were flying wounded and riderless across the plain. Lord George Paget, who had placed a cheroot between his teeth which was to stay there throughout the charge, worked his way through them:

> **Bewildered horses from the first line, riderless, rushed in upon our ranks in every state of mutilation...one was guiding one's own...so as to avoid trampling on the bleeding objects in one's path – sometimes a man, sometimes a horse...the poor dumb brutes, who by this time were galloping about in numbers, like mad wild beasts.**

Private Mitchell's horse was one such casualty, struck by a shell as he approached:

> **I found my horse was lying on his near side; my left leg**

was beneath him...I tried to move...at that moment I heard the second line come galloping towards where I lay, and fully expecting to be trampled on, I looked up and saw the 4th Light Dragoons quite close. I called out, 'For God's sake don't ride over me.'

But with cannons thundering on all sides of them, the troopers had to keep riding. Private Wightman, of the

ABOVE: *AFTER THE BALAKLAVA CHARGE* (CAPTAIN HENRY CLIFFORD).
LEFT: A CAREFUL DEPICTION OF THE CHARGE OF THE LIGHT BRIGADE (WILLIAM SIMPSON, SEE P. 71).

17th Lancers, made it as far as the Russian guns:

> **My horse made a tremendous leap into the air, though I know not what at. The smoke was so dense that I could not even see my arm in before me. Then suddenly I was in the battery, and in the darkness there were sounds of fighting and slaughter...In this gloom we cut and thrust and hacked like demons.**

On the heights, Russell's disbelief turned into awed admiration at such extraordinary heroism:

> **With diminished ranks, thinned by those thirty [sic] guns, which the Russians had laid with the most deadly accuracy, with a halo of flashing steel above their heads, and with a cheer which was many a noble fellow's death-cry, they flew into the smoke of the batteries, but ere they were lost from view the plain was strewed with their bodies and with the carcasses of horses.**

Some of the British cavalry had ridden straight through the Russian gunners and found themselves face to face with the Russian cavalry. The latter were so astonished at the sight of these madmen that many of them wheeled about and galloped away. Captain Kubitovitch described how they rode towards them sabring a number of gunners as they passed through:

> **The majority of the gun crews made off, mounted on horse teams and limbers. The enemy spiked some of the guns hoping to drag them off...but most of the cavalry continued the headlong chase after the hussars, slashing at them without mercy.**

Recovering from their surprise, however, the Russians realized that the advantage of numbers was on their side, and they soon regrouped and turned once more on the Light Brigade. Russell watched as the the remains of the British cavalry cut their way back through the enemy lines:

> **With courage too great almost for credence, they were breaking their way through the columns which enveloped them, when there took place an act of atrocity without parallel in the modern warfare of civilized nations. The Russian gunners, when the storm of cavalry passed, returned to their guns. They saw their own cavalry mingled with the troopers who had just ridden over them, and, to the eternal disgrace of the Russian name, the miscreants poured a murderous volley of grape and canister on the mass of struggling men and horses, mingling friend and foe in one common ruin.**

'Butcher Jack' was part of the mêlée riding back down the valley:

> **I was sober as a bishop by this time, take my word for it, and I joined [the retreat] right cheerfully; but the chances of getting back again to our own side of the valley looked very blue. The Russian cavalry were hard on our heels, and we suffered sorely from the devilish battery in our rear, which kept pelting into the thick of us, without much discrimination between friend and foe. The guns on those forts on the left...which had been pounced on by the Russians were not doing us much good neither, I assure you, and it was for all the world like being between the devil and the deep sea. Soon**

FRENCH CHASSEURS D'AFRIQUE. (PHOTO BY ROGER FENTON.)

what little formation we had got was knocked to pieces, and then the word was, 'Every man for himself, and God help the hindmost' ...

Earlier that morning word had been sent to General Bosquet and he had dispatched a regiment of Chasseurs d'Afrique – tough Algerian cavalrymen. They arrived as the Light Brigade was retreating to see them being attacked by gunners on the Fediukhin Heights to their right. Vicomte de Noé, a French cavalry officer, was watching:

A cloud of dust, from which came a chorus of British 'hurrahs' advanced towards us; it was the unfortunate cavalry who were returning mutilated and decimated. The Russian artillery, who were on the heights to our left, began to open fire on this noble debris. General Morris didn't hesitate and the Chasseurs d'Afrique raced towards the Russians. They attacked bravely sabring two lines of riflemen...then retreated in good order. The Russian artillery, recoupled their guns and hurriedly withdrew.

Thanks to the French intervention, more of the 'noble debris' rode back down the valley than might have done. Russell now brought his account to a climax:

Wounded men and dismounted troopers flying towards us told the sad tale – demi-gods could not have done what we had failed to do... It was as much as our Heavy Cavalry brigade could do to cover the retreat of the miserable remnants of that band of heroes as they returned to the place they had so lately quitted in all the pride of life. At thirty five minutes past eleven not a British soldier, except the dead and dying, was left in front of these bloody Muscovite guns.

It was hard to tell whether it had been twenty-five minutes of tragedy or farce. Henry Clifford was overcome: 'The tears ran down my face, and the din of musketry pouring in their murderous fire on the brave gallant fellows rang in my ears.' General Bosquet was also on the heights watching, but his reaction was more ambivalent: 'C'est magnifique, mais ce n'est pas la guerre. C'est de la folie.'

Fanny passed a 'lurid night'. Her husband Henry had not charged, but this time her maid's husband really had been killed. Private Wightman had been taken prisoner as he 'hacked away like a demon' at the Russian gunners. He learned later that night that the Russians were convinced the Light Brigade must have all been drunk to have charged at all:

'Come now men,' said General Liprandi genially, and in excellent English. 'What did they give you to drink? Did they not prime you with spirits to come down and attack us in such a mad manner?' 'You think we were drunk?' replied one of the other wounded privates. 'By God, I tell you that if we had so much as smelt the barrel we would have taken half Russia by this time...' 'On my honour, sir, there is not a man who has tasted food or drink this day.' Liprandi was moved. 'You are noble fellows' he said, 'and I am sincerely sorry for you. I will order you some Vodka.'

Certainly the Russians had been impressed by their enemy's mad bravery that day, and they did not risk another encounter with British cavalry for the rest of the war. But they nevertheless saw Balaklava as a Russian triumph. In practical terms they were left in possession of the Woronzoff Road. More importantly perhaps, as a 'chasseur' of the Taroutine Regiment put it:

The brilliant victory of 25th October had an important influence on our morale: it lifted the spirits of our troops after the unsuccessful Alma affair, proving our ability to triumph over the enemy.

The triumph was not that clear-cut, however. Russell's account and everything that followed would soon turn the charge into a glorious act of tragic daring, creating mythic heroes of the chargers.

The battle of Balaklava appeared in *The Times* on 14 November. Alfred Lord Tennyson, sparked by the reference to a military 'blunder', and the use of the phrase 'valley of death', began writing a poem about it almost at once. 'The Charge of the Light Brigade' was published in *The Examiner* in early December.

The poem soon proved so popular that it was printed and sold as a single sheet, and by the new year

War reporting

During the Crimean War, the novelist William MakepeaceThackeray, who had turned down an offer from *The Illustrated London News* to cover the campaign for them, gave a speech on the condition of literature. The speech has been lost but Thackeray's notes survive. He made two key points. The first noted 'book trade frozen up' – taking the image of 'frozen up' from the situation of the British army outside Sebastopol. The second explained why this situation had come about: 'reality more interesting than novels... Heroines and heroes – what are they compared to the Crimea.'

Novelists felt readers only wanted to read about the war – an appetite satisfied by newly proliferating weeklies like *The Illustrated London News* and *The Graphic* and by the daily reports in *The Times*. How could fiction compete with the extraordinary facts reported in the press?

The Crimean War was the first war to have so-called 'Special Correspondents', such as the Irish-born war correspondent William Howard Russell, who was dispatched to the front to document the campaign. It took over a fortnight for Russell's reports to reach London by sea. The battle of Balaklava on 25 October 1854, for instance, was not reported in *The Times* until 14 November. The telegraph between Balaklava and London via Varna – completed in April 1855 – reduced this to forty-eight hours. In spite of the delays however, the press was peculiarly important since Parliament was in recess from 14 August to 12 December. The fourth estate stepped into the political vacuum. *The Times'* readers, after all, were also influential voters.

In Paris, St Petersburg and Constantinople press censorship – and, in the latter two, mass illiteracy – meant that coverage of the war was limited and unreliable. In Constantinople there were only two newspapers, *Takvim-i Vekayi* and *Ceride-i Havadis,* founded by an Englishman, William Churchill. All the dispatches of the French correspondents in the Crimea went first to a government office in Paris to be checked and censored before being passed on to the newspapers. In St. Petersburg the tsar's censors were swift to blue pencil anything that seemed critical of the war effort, although Vasili Timm's *Russian Illustrated Pamphlet*, which was suitably pro-Russian, was published three times a month, and produced more than a hundred issues devoted to the war.

Tolstoy's writing ambitions, on the other hand, were more controversial. His military life had begun in the Caucasus, where he took part in the campaign against Shamil and the Chechens. It was in this period that he wrote the first draft of *Letter From The Caucasus*, which was published as *The Raid* in 1853. While he was there he also formed the idea of setting up a military gazette to bolster the army's morale. Its purpose would be:

> ...to publish less cut-and-dried and more accurate accounts of the battles than the other papers; reports of heroic deeds, biographies and obituaries of the bravest men, chosen chiefly from among the humble and unknown; war stories, soldiers' songs, simplified articles on artillery and military engineering.

Tolstoy began writing articles for the new journal – 'How Russian Soldiers Die' was one of the first. A sample issue was sent to the Minister of War. When the tsar himself refused permission for such a publication Tolstoy wrote to the editor of *The Contemporary* offering to send articles and stories on a monthly basis from the front line – in this sense he could be called Russia's first war correspondent. His first suggestions were 'A Letter About the Sisters of Mercy', 'Memories of the Siege of Silistria' and 'Letter From a Soldier in Sebastopol'. There are what may be early drafts of the first two of these ideas in Tolstoy's letters; the third finally emerged as the fictionalized *Sebastopol Sketches*.

Above: William Howard Russell.

Right: Back home battles were not only sung about, but were even reenacted in London theatres.

copies were available in the Crimea, where the poem was read to revive the spirits of wounded soldiers who had ridden in the charge. By then, the myth was gaining momentum in the Crimea itself. Arriving just after the battle, the artist William Simpson tried to produce definitive images of the charge by interviewing the participants:

> **The Battle of Balaklava...had taken place before I arrived in the Crimea, but it was necessary for me to give pictures. I could easily make sketches on the ground, but I had to trust to those on the spot for a description of the events. Here I may mention, I had my first experience as to how men who have been actors in an event will differ in their descriptions... I then did a sketch and took it to Lord Cardigan. He gazed at it with a vacant stare, and pointing to something, asked, 'What is that?' On being told, he said, 'It is all wrong' and gave expression to one or two remarks of a critical kind, objecting to the picture. I...made another sketch, in which I tried to avoid the points objected to. On my taking this to the yacht next day, sketch and artist were treated in much the same way as on the first occasion. I felt rather nettled at the cold, haughty style of his Lordship, but I was anxious to be able to send home the sketch bearing with it the approval of the principal hero... I went on board a third time, and...was rewarded with the warmest praise, and was able to send it home with the expression of Lord Cardigan's highest admiration. The real truth was that in the last sketch I had taken greater care than in the first two to make his Lordship conspicuous in the front of the brigade.**

In spite of the doctoring, it was clear that someone had blundered. As the need for a scapegoat became paramount, both Cardigan and Lucan were forced to defend their actions. But whoever was responsible, the extent of the disaster is another of the many myths of Balaklava. As Colin Frederick Campbell, an officer of the 46th Foot, later commented:

> **The actual loss to the army of the Light Cavalry was not so important as has been imagined, as many horses would have died of starvation if they had not been killed then; and as for the men, we bury three times the number every week and think nothing of it.**

THE CHARGE OF THE LIGHT BRIGADE

Half a league, half a league,
Half a league onward,
All in the valley of Death
Rode the six hundred.
'Forward the Light Brigade!
Charge for the guns!' He said.
Into the valley of Death
Rode the six hundred.

'Forward, the Light Brigade!'
Was there a man dismay'd?
Not tho' the soldier knew
Someone had blunder'd.
Theirs not to make reply,
Theirs not to reason why,
Theirs but to do and die.
Into the valley of Death
Rode the six hundred

Cannon to right of them,
Cannon to left of them,
Cannon in front of them
Volley'd and thunder'd;
Storm'd at with shot and shell,
Boldly they rode and well,
Into the jaws of Death,
Into the mouth of hell
Rode the six hundred.

Flash'd all their sabres bare,
Flash'd as they turn'd in air
Sabring the gunners there,
Charging an army, while
All the world wonder'd.
Plunged in the battery-smoke
Right thro' the line they broke;
Cossack and Russian
Reel'd from the sabre-stroke
Shatter'd and sunder'd.
Then they rode back, but not,
Not the six hundred.

Cannon to right of them,
Cannon to left of them,
Cannon behind them
Volley'd and thunder'd;
Storm'd at with shot and shell,
While horse and hero fell,
They that had fought so well
Came thro' the jaws of Death,
Back from the mouth of hell,
All that was left of them,
Left of six hundred.

When can their glory fade?
O the wild charge they made!
All the world wonder'd.
Honour the charge they made!
Honour the Light Brigade,
Noble six hundred!

Of a total of 632 men who charged, 110 were killed in action (including seven who died of their wounds), 196 were wounded, 57 taken prisoner, and 362 horses died or had to be put down. Astonishingly 276 men rode back down the valley with barely a scratch. A year later, after the prisoners had been released, over 500 cavalrymen could claim to have ridden in the charge.

Ten days later another battle was fought in which the casualties on both sides would put Balaklava in the shade.

The attack on the British base had ended in a stalemate and activity on both sides was now heightened. In front of Sebastopol, the French were coming increasingly close to storming the town's defences. Outside the besieged town, the Russian reserve army was growing, with reinforcements arriving from the Danube and Moscow.

Prince Menshikov's headquarters were at the ruined town of Inkerman, on the heights opposite the British camp. The latter believed that the ravines and gullies separating them from the enemy were uncrossable. But the Russians were determined to take the offensive once more before the winter struck. At the beginning of November the tsar sent two of his sons, the grand dukes, to spur Menshikov into action.

This time their aim was to attack the British observation camp (comprising the 2nd Division and the Guards, with the Light Division in reserve) at a place called Home Ridge, to occupy these heights, and to force the Allies back into the sea once and for all. General Soimonov was to lead troops out of Sebastopol and General Paulov was to bring his down from Inkerman. When they converged, the two armies were to to be commanded by General Dannenberg. Meanwhile the French were to be kept back, and from within Sebastopol a continuous barrage was to bombard the Allied ranks.

At four o'clock on the morning of 5 November, Pyotr Alabin, who had joined the reserve army at Inkerman after marching down from the Danube, jotted a quick note in his diary:

> **The night is dark. The rain, though it has completely abated, has made thick mud, which must inevitably make our ascent up the slope more difficult... But time does not wait. The regiments are beginning to move. Our horses are being saddled... We put the samovar on the embers of the fire and drank our fill of tea, perhaps for the last time? The regiments are standing at attention. Our horses are impatiently dancing. It's time to close my diary. Close it!...and will it be my fate once again to open these pages which are so close to my heart?**

The Russians wanted the benefit of surprise. They would advance quietly on ground that was completely covered by scrub very early in the morning. On 5 November they received unexpected extra help in the shape of a fog so thick that the combatants could hardly see more than a few feet in front of them. Although the Russian officers knew what was going on, the young chasseurs of the Taroutine Regiment were almost as ill-informed as their British counterparts:

> **Slowly and sleepily, the soldiers moved their feet; there was no talking, not a sound... No one knew where we were being taken so early, or why, although the night-time meal and extra cup of vodka and our route towards the enemy positions forced us to make a guess.**

During the night one British sergeant thought he heard the sound of wheels in the valley below, as though the enemy were approaching up the hill. His superior decided it was just local produce being taken to market, and the noise was ignored. Unsuspecting, Sergeant Richard Barnham in the 2nd Division camp was going about normal routine the next morning, when he got a surprise from the Russian artillery:

> **The morning was thick and hazey and as heavy rain had visited the camps a day or two previous in and out it was a complete trough. The men of the division had just returned off trench duty and some were preparing breakfast... others enjoying a short sleep, but were soon aroused by a rough salute from the enemies guns ploughing up the ground and tearing the tents down about their ears and the poor fellows half of them naked under the blankets.**

One man had his legs blown off in his own tent. The Russians had devastated the British camp before the Allies were aware quite what was happening.

General De Lacy Evans, commander of the 2nd Division, had fallen off his horse and was stuck on board a transport ship in Balaklava harbour. So British command fell to General Pennefather, whose rule of thumb was 'whenever you see a head, hit it.' This was to prove apt advice during this battle of scattered pickets where the fog made it impossible to gauge either the size of the enemy or their position.

Captain Henry Clifford was part of the first reinforcements to reach the destroyed camp at Home Ridge, where he saw a large group of Russians emerging out of the fog only fifteen yards away:

> **It was a moment or two before I could make General Buller believe they were Russians. 'In God's name,' I said 'fix bayonets and charge.' He gave the order and in another moment we were hand to hand with them. 'Come on,' I said 'my lads' and the brave fellows dashed in amongst the astonished Russians bayonetting them in every direction. I drew my sword and cut off one man's arm who was in the act of bayonetting me and a second seeing it, turned round and was in the act of running out of my way, when I hit him over the back of the neck and laid him dead at my feet... I saw one poor fellow's head carried away by a shot and some 10 or a dozen blown into the air by a shell.**

Meanwhile, on the extreme right flank, the Taroutines were still struggling up the slippery slopes:

> **Getting up the hill was very difficult. The silty loam had come loose from the rain so that, sliding in it, we grabbed hold of the bushes, steadied ourselves with the butts of our firearms, and sometimes even pulled one another down.**

The ground was as unfamiliar to most of the Russians as it was to the Allies. They too were nearly all new to the Crimea. By the time the two Russian corps met their plan had already gone wrong. Pyotr Alabin was in the division under General Paulov, advancing towards a position called the 'Barrier', behind Home Ridge:

> **Soimonov attacked with his detachment at the point meant for our attack, and both detachments were forced into the space for one, having destroyed the English whom we met in our path there. Then, not seeing, not knowing and not receiving any orders from anyone as to what we were to do next, we stood and perished in our masses, until the battle turned into practically individual fist-fights.**

On this confusing terrain and in this terrible weather the battle became a dispersed and disorganized affair. Pickets and outposts were fighting isolated battles with Russian units, seeing only their own fights and knowing nothing of what was going on elsewhere. Being forced to fight at close quarters because of the fog, both sides made much use of the bayonet. Sergeant Timothy Gowing could scarcely see beyond the end of his nose:

> **The drunken yells of their massive columns were answered by volley after volley at point-blank range and then, with a clear and distinct cheer for Old England, we closed upon them with the bayonet and stuck to them like wax until they were hurled from the field.**

While desperate fighting continued at the main defensive position on Home Ridge, a number of troops got caught up on the extreme right of the British position. The Sandbag Battery was really nothing more than a hastily constructed earth wall, but the Russians, assuming it to be part of the British defences, seized and occupied it. Captain Hodasiewicz, of the Taroutine Regiment, was among them:

> **Close to me stood a young ensign Protopopoff, and, seeing that he looked dull, I asked what was the matter. 'Ah!' said he 'tell my uncle to write home, and say that I was killed at the battle of Inkerman!' His uncle was in our regiment. I told him that he ought not to joke like that, 'for don't you see the day is ours?' I had hardly had time to pronouce these words before he was struck in the left side by a rifle ball and died almost immediately.**

This marginal, but psychologically important, battery changed hands several times during the next few hours. The struggles that went on there epitomized the chaos of the entire battle. Sergeant Timothy Gowing wrote home later with what he had heard from his surviving friends:

> **The 41st and 49th regiments held the Sandbag Battery and were fairly mobbed out of it by the overwhelming numbers of the enemy, who were exulting in their victory with yells of triumph when up came the Guards, and in they went with a cheer and a rush that told heavily upon the foe.**

The Guards, all must admit, set a glorious example; for if they had to die, they acted upon the old 57th motto, 'Let us die hard!'

Men were also dying hard in the ravines and gullies beneath the heights. Captain Fred Dallas formed part of one such advance:

We were so close to the enemy that they threw stones & clods of earth in our faces. Poor Sir George Cathcart fell there, shot I believe through the brain. As I was coming up the hill he was just in front of me. As I passed him he recognised me & said 'There is nothing for us but the bayonet, Dallas!' Noble hearted old hero! I shall never forget him sitting quite calmly on his horse, certainly not 12 yards from the front rank of the enemy. He was wounded in the head when he spoke to me. If ever a man lived who knew not what fear was, he was the one.

As soon as General Bosquet had heard the firing that morning he had offered his assistance to Cathcart and Sir George Brown, commander of the Light Division. This had been politely refused. With Cathcart dead and Sir George Brown badly wounded, Bosquet took the initiative. He arrived at a gallop with a group of Chasseurs à Pied, zouaves and 'Turcos' (or Algerian riflemen). His aide-de-camp, Captain Charles Fay, heard him shout to them in Arabic, 'Show what you're made of, children of fire!' Fay wrote:

Nothing can describe the effect that was caused by the arrival of these African veterans with their bronzed skins and their strange outfits, dashing forward with their bayonets.

Bosquet's arrival secured the right flank, which had absorbed so many troops in fighting for the 'abattoir', as he called the strategically unimportant Sandbag Battery. Meanwhile the main body of Russians, who had got as far as Home Ridge, had then been forced back by a handful of troops and were desperately trying to hold the Barrier. But to Pyotr Alabin it was clear that Russian command structure had broken down:

ABOVE: *BATTLE OF INKERMAN* (WILLIAM SIMPSON).
LEFT: THE SAME BATTLE DEPICTED BY CAPTAIN HENRY CLIFFORD, WHO WAS LATER AWARDED A VC FOR HIS BRAVERY.

> **There are no general instructions...these advances are far from being the development of some unified thought process; far from being the carrying out of the ideas of one man, who with his bloody staff is draughting on the field of death signs incomprehensible to the majority, but the secret meaning of which is, all nevertheless one and the same – victory; no, all these disjointed actions are the children of chance – nobody knows what all this is leading to!**

At about 9.30am two British 18-pounder guns arrived and proved the turning-point of the battle, but the disjointed actions and desperate slaughter continued for another three hours. Finally, supported by his artillery, Pennefather ordered his few remaining men to attack and this gallant attempt convinced Dannenberg to abandon the field. Captain Hodasiewicz described the chaos of the Russian retreat:

> **During the retreat, or rather flight...we lost a great many men from our ignorance of the ground; everyone ran according to his own judgement, and many found themselves at the top of high precipitous rocks or the quarries and such was the panic that had taken possession of the men that many of them, making the sign of the cross, threw themselves over and were dashed to pieces...numbers, especially wounded men, crept into the caves that abound here and were never heard of more.**

If the fate of the Allies at Balaklava had hung on largely inept commanders but extremely courageous officers and men, at Inkerman the command structure was to prove simply irrelevant. Indeed, if Inkerman meant anything at all it was every man for himself. One captain told how, 'Colonels of regiments led on small parties and fought like subalterns, captains like privates. Once engaged every man was his own General.'

Fred Dallas had escaped unhurt, the shoulder-belt plate over his heart having deflected a near-fatal shot. But he had lost many friends and was angry at the fruitless waste of life:

> **It was a great victory for our men & a great disgrace to our Leaders, that such a slaughter should have been necessary. A few hours work would have rendered our position unassailable, but they allowed us to be surprised & nothing but our noble men saved our Camp and our Generals' reputation.**

Hodasiewicz was equally scathing about the lack of interest shown at the right time by his Russian leaders:

> **Suddenly, as if he fell from heaven, appeared amongst us the General of our division, Kiriakoff, whom we had not seen for some days. 'Halt, halt!' shouted he, frantically waving his Cossack whip; but the soldiers paid little attention to him, so, in order to gain proper respect from the men, he began to beat them with his whip, shouting that the officers did not attend to their duty, or the men would never have run. Some of the men who could not bear to see this, shouted, 'Go up there yourself. He was not to be seen in the fight, but he makes himself felt now it's over.'**

General Bosquet. (Photo by Roger Fenton.)

The battle, which consisted largely of separate, heroically fought infantry and artillery combats, had lasted eight hours. The following day Henry Clifford reflected on what he had done in the heat of battle:

> **The excitement certainly was tremendous while it lasted, and it is well perhaps it is so, for I am sure in cold blood I never could strike at a man as I did then, and if I had not, in all probability, those with me would not have charged and we should have lost our lives. This morning as I passed the Russians, prisoners and wounded, a man amongst them ran up and called out to me and pointed to his shoulder bound up. It was the poor fellow whose arm I had cut off yesterday; he laughed and said 'Bono Johnny'. I took his hand and shook it heartily and the tears came in my eyes. I had not a shilling in my pocket; had I had a bag of gold he should have had it. I enquired if he had been cared for and the Doctor told me he had and he was doing well.**

Leo Tolstoy had returned to Russia in September. Like many he was strongly affected on hearing reports of the battle. In his diary he called Inkerman 'Dannenberg's terrible action in which we attacked again and were beaten again' and continued:

> **It was a treacherous, revolting business...we had to retreat, because half our troops had no artillery owing to the roads being impassable, and – God knows why – there were no rifle battalions. Terrible slaughter! It will weigh heavy on the souls of many people! Lord, forgive them.**
>
> **The news of this action has produced a sensation. I've seen old men who wept aloud and young men who swore to kill Dannenberg... Among the useless sacrifices of that unfortunate action were Soymonov and Komstadius, who were killed. It is said of the first that he was one of the few honest and intelligent generals in the Russian army. The second I knew well: he was a**

Some of the horses killed at Inkerman (Captain Henry Clifford).

member of our society and a would-be editor of our journal. His death more than anything has impelled me to ask to go to Sebastopol. He made me feel somehow ashamed.

It was the death of Komstadius that finally persuaded Tolstoy to start work on some literary sketches of the war. A few days later he was transferred to Sebastopol, which would provide him with the framework for the first of these *Sebastopol Sketches*. Because of censorship, Tolstoy's fiction was as close as any Russian came to war reporting.

William Howard Russell described Inkerman as 'the bloodiest struggle ever witnessed since war cursed the earth'. His tone was very different from the heroics of Balaklava:

We have nothing to rejoice over, and almost everything to deplore, in the battle of Inkermann. We have defeated the enemy indeed, but have not advanced one step nearer toward the citadel of Sebastopol. We have abashed, humiliated, and utterly routed an enemy strong in numbers, in fanatacism, and in dogged resolute courage...but we have suffered a fearful loss, and we are not in a position to part with one man.

The Allies' assault on Sebastopol had been postponed, but this time the cost in casualties on both sides had been far too high and far too horrific.

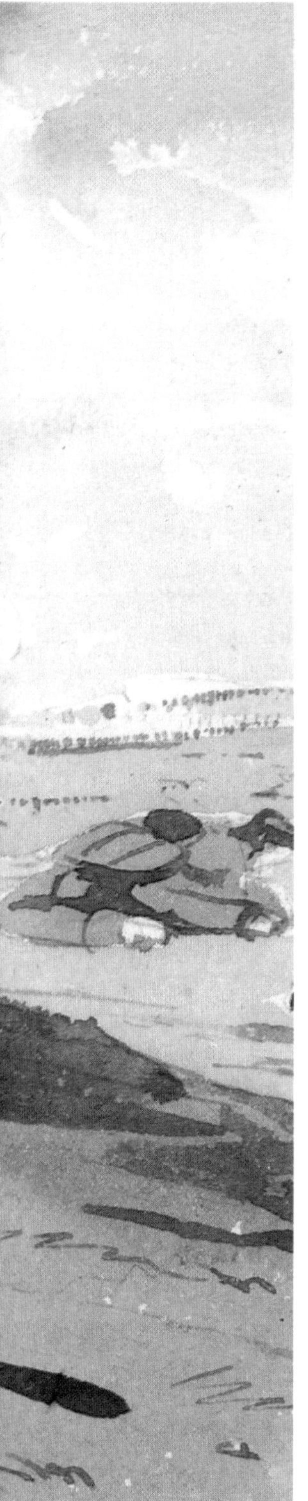

CHAPTER FIVE

SISTERS OF MERCY

FOR PYOTR ALABIN THE aftermath of the battle of Inkerman on 5 November 1854 brought home the horrific reality of war:

> **Your heart was torn in two looking at these wretches and at the circumstances of their hospital life. The sick and wounded were packed tight like herrings in a barrel. They were in their dirty clothes and linen, covered in blood, stained beyond measure; the men were unshaved, unwashed, many had not had their dressings changed more than once since the battle of Inkerman; lying on plank-beds with their uniform for a pillow and cloth trousers for bedding – for those who still had them – many had no bedding at all; the only coverlet for many of the wounded and sick was their immutable great-coat. Together with the lightly wounded, lie many badly wounded, hopelessly ill and dying people. Oh, for the sake of God do not think that I am exaggerating!**

AGONY! (CAPTAIN HENRY CLIFFORD).

CLIFFORD WAS ONE OF THE FEW TO RECORD THE HORROR OF WAR IN ALL ITS GRUESOME DETAIL.

For Russia's top surgeon Nikolai Pirogov back in St Petersburg, it also showed up the terrible lack of organization of treatment for the wounded:

> **During that unforgettable time every heart in St. Petersburg beat harder and with more alarm, awaiting the results of the battle of Inkerman. Several weeks before this I had already made known my readiness to make available all my strength and knowledge to the army in the field of battle. I had long since submitted my request but it was still doing the rounds of the various medical administrators. I was beginning to despair of ever getting a decision when I received an invitation from the Grand Duchess.**

As news of the state of the wounded got back home to both sides, high-ranking and influential philanthropists mobilized themselves. In Russia, Grand Duchess Elena Pavlovna founded the Community of the Cross, an organization intended to send female assistance to the sick and wounded on the battlefield. She proposed that Pirogov select the medical personnel and take charge of its direction. Tsar Nicholas was sceptical, but he gave in to her request and consented to this unprecedented experiment.

In England, news of the conditions in the East was also creating a scandal. Medical officers had accompanied their regiments to the front without a single hospital bed or marquee, the transport ships were overcrowded, and the base hospital was a mess. *The Times* denounced the authorities angrily. Sidney Herbert, the Secretary at War and a passionate reformer, wrote to his long-standing friend, the manager of the 'Establishment for Gentlewomen During Illness' in Harley Street, asking her too to superintend a new enterprise – the introduction of female nurses into the military hospitals in Turkey:

> **There is but one person in England that I know of, who would be capable of organising and superintending such a scheme and I have been several times on the point of asking you hypothetically if, supposing the attempt were made, you would undertake to direct it. The difficulty of finding women equal to a task after all full of horror, and requiring besides knowledge and goodwill, great energy and great courage will be great. The task of ruling them and introducing system among them, is great; and not the least, will be the difficulty of making the whole work smoothly with the medical and military authorities out there. This it is, which makes it so important, that the experiment should be carried out by one with administrative capacity and experience...**

Florence Nightingale accepted immediately. Nightingale and Pirogov would not only influence the fate of sick and wounded soldiers during the war, but would also change the course of military medicine for ever.

On 10 November 1854, Pirogov set out for the Crimea with two doctors and a medical assistant. He arrived in Sebastopol shortly after Florence Nightingale had disembarked, with thirty-eight nurses, on the other side of the Black Sea at Scutari, a suburb of Constantinople. They found themselves confronted by similar situations – hospitals full of the wounded from Alma and Balaklava, and many more about to arrive after the terrible recent battle at Inkerman. Pirogov wrote to his wife with his first impressions:

> **I spend from eight in the morning until six at night in the hospital where the blood flows in rivers... We reproached the English for doing nothing to help**

ABOVE: FLORENCE NIGHTINGALE
RIGHT: SURGEON NIKOLAI PIROGOV

THE HOSPITAL AT SCUTARI RECORDED BY TWO OF THE WOMEN IN THE CRIMEA
ABOVE: PANORAMA BY LADY ALICIA BLACKWOOD
LEFT: LINEN ROOM SKETCHED BY NURSE ANN MORTON

the wounded enemy after Alma; and we ourselves did nothing for them after Inkerman either. Arriving in Sebastopol eighteen days after the event, I found over 2000 wounded, all lumped together, lying on dirty mattresses, soaked with blood, all mixed together; and, once I'd sorted them into groups, I spent a whole ten days practically from morning to nightfall operating on those who should have been operated immediately after the battle... Who did they take the soldiers for? Who will fight well when he is convinced that the wounded will be thrown down like dogs?

Florence Nightingale's first letter back to England also talked of the overwhelming numbers of wounded, and of blood, filth and inconsiderate treatment. At Scutari the wounded were lying right up to the door of the hospital:

In all our Corridors I think we have not an average of three limbs per man – and there are two ships more 'loading' at the Crimea with wounded, this is our phraseology... We have four miles of beds – and not eighteen inches apart. All this fresh influx has been laid down between us and the Main Guard in two corridors with a line of beds down each side, just room for one man to step between, and four wards... Yet in the midst of this appalling horror (we are steeped up to our necks in blood) – there is good. As I went my night rounds among the newly wounded that first night, there was not one murmur, not one groan, the strictest discipline, the most absolute silence and quiet prevailed, only the step of the sentry. The poor fellows bear pain and mutilation with unshrinking heroism, and die or are cut up without a complaint.

Back in October Dr John Hall, the principal medical officer of the army, had inspected the Hospital at Scutari and had reported to London that it was in a highly satisfactory state. Florence Nightingale found, on the contrary, that despite the heroism of the men, almost everything about Scutari was unsatisfactory. Not only were the buildings unsuitable, the staff ill-disciplined and the supplies insufficient, but there was not even an effective system of hygiene. On 25 November she wrote to Sidney Herbert:

> **It appears that in these hospitals the Purveyors consider washing both of linen and of the men as a 'detail' and during the three weeks we have been here, though our remonstrances have been treated with perfect civility, yet no washing whatever has been performed for the men either of body-linen or of bed-linen except by ourselves and a few wives of the wounded, – and a story of a contractor, with which we have been amused, turned out to be a myth. The dirty shirts were collected yesterday for the first time, and on Monday *it is said* that they are to be washed...**
>
> **When we came here there was neither basin, towel nor soap in the wards, nor any means of personal cleanliness for the wounded except the following – Thirty were bathed every night by Dr McGrigor's orderly in slipper baths, but this does not do more than include a washing once in eighty days for 2300 men.**

Florence Nightingale's immediate priority was clearly going to be less in the sphere of nursing, and more in that of domestic management. The problem was that the hospital organization itself was weak and there were no models to follow. She therefore set to work to apply her own principles of 'sanitary science' to improve the hygiene of the hospital building, and used her skill as a manager to reorganize the laundry and kitchens and to improve the supply of bedding, linen and other hospital necessities. She was soon to run into problems over supplies, however. One of her nurses, Margaret Goodman, made this laconic observation:

> **Generally speaking, the chief medical officers resolutely closed their eyes to the great want in the hospitals of every comfort for the patients: they would have said, from time immemorial a prescribed course has been resorted to in order to meet certain exigencies, and if it did not meet them, it was supposed to; which was, they persisted, as far as they were concerned, the same thing. For instance, shirts were needed: a requisition would be written, calling upon the official belonging to the commissariat to provide them; if they did not appear, and the chief was again applied to, he would treat the matter precisely as if the patients were enjoying their comfortable garments: he had written the order, and so far as he was concerned the men were clothed**

Florence Nightingale would bombard Sidney Herbert throughout the campaign with complaints about the deficiencies of the Purveyors in the Commissariat and the stupidity of those in charge.

> **December 21**
>
> **This morning I foraged in the Purveyor's store – a cruise I make almost daily, as the only way of getting things. No mops – no plates, no wooden trays – no slippers, no shoe brushes, no blacking, no knives & forks, no spoons, no scissors (for cutting the men's hair which is literally alive) – no basins, no towelling – no Chloride of Lime.**
>
> **January 8**
>
> **...the fact is I am now clothing the British Army. The sick were reembarked at Balaklava for these hospitals, without recovering their kits, also half-naked besides. And when discharged from here they carry off, small blame to them, even my knives and forks. – Shirts, of course – and hospital clothing also.**

Florence Nightingale was extremely attentive. She would often be up in the night compiling statistics, making notes and writing to Sidney Herbert. She also spent every evening walking the miles of hospital corridors checking on patients. In February 1855, *The Illustrated London News* christened her 'the Lady with

Jan 23rd – The Transport that never fails –

Burying The Dead: The transport that never fails (Captain Henry Clifford).

the Lamp', but this underplayed the fact that in the three months since she arrived she had also seen major structural improvements effected. At Scutari Hospital work had begun on a new drainage system, on repaving the corridors and reflooring the wards. And she was aiming for overhaul at an even higher level:

> **There is a far greater question to be agitated before the country...this is of whether the system or no-system which is found adequate in time of peace but wholly inadequate to meet the exigencies of a time of war is to be left as it is – , or patched up temporarily, as you give a beggar halfpence, – or made equal to the wants, not diminishing but increasing, of a time of awful pressure... Each one of these points would require a pamphlet. Will you let me write my notes & experiences to you, never mind whether I am superseded or not? You need not take the suggestions of poor me, but consult somebody (not an official hoping for promotion) who understands the question.**

Between November 1854 and April 1855, as many as four parliamentary commissions were sent out to investigate the state of the British army in the East. The most significant of these (and the one which may have been subtly initiated by Florence Nightingale herself) was the Sanitary Commission, which consisted of Dr John Sutherland, a progressive official of the Board of Health and Mr Robert Rawlinson, a distinguished civil engineer. Arriving in Scutari on 4 March 1855 they got going with great energy. Florence Nightingale was impressed:

> **The Sanitary Commission is really doing something, and has set to work burying dead dogs and white washing infected walls, two prolific causes of fever. Lord William Paulet looks out of his window and sends word to us to remove four pieces of white paper at the corner of our store, while five dead dogs lay all of a row in the principle thorough fare from the Hospital to the wharf. A Liverpool Inspector of Nuisances has been left us to do what we should have done long ago.**

Their recommendations were acted upon quickly, the necessary labour force was at last forthcoming, and the work was now directed by skilled engineers and sanitary inspectors. Florence Nightingale soon developed a close and lasting friendship with Sutherland, who stayed in the Crimea for the rest of the campaign to supervise the work he had initiated, and she believed that 'the arrival of this Commission saved the British Army'.

While Nightingale's Scutari Hospital was an appropriated Turkish army barracks, Pirogov's main hospital building in Sebastopol was the House of the Nobles' Assembly, a ballroom with pink marble floors and gold wallpaper. Nikolai Berg, a translator with the staff of the Russian High Command, visited him there:

> **Pirogov sat here without a break, in a corner of the room, by a green table, silent and pensive. He wore as always one and the same soldier's greatcoat, undone, under which poked out a long red jersey. On his head he wore a cap. Clumps of grey hair stuck out at the temples. It seemed as though he was sitting apart, like a stranger, but he heard and saw everything. From time to time he would stand and go towards the table, take a surgical knife and his inspired, unequalled incisions astonished the surrounding medical attendants, but only the medical personnel – to others, unenlightened, the poetry of his brilliant operations was inaccessible.**

RUSSIAN NURSES. (PORTRAIT BY VASILI TIMM.)

Pirogov, like Nightingale, was impressive for his sheer energy. Unlike Florence Nightingale, he was literally up to his elbows in blood. He worked at the Nobles' Assembly for about ten months and personally undertook or supervised 5,000 operations – only about 400 operations were done without his presence. On the days of major attacks surgical operations were performed simultaneously on three operating tables. Pirogov himself would amputate a leg in seven or eight minutes. Berg observed a typical day:

> **The soldiers swore continuously during their operations, in spite of the action of the chloroform which apparently put them into a deep sleep. On a special little table, purpose-built for operations, there was always someone lying. A few medical orderlies bustled around, knives and files flashed bright, blood flowed in streams, and its rich smell assaulted the nose of every passerby off the street. The attendants – soldiers and nurses – mopped up the puddles of blood. In one corner there stood a vat from which amputated arms and legs peeped out. Stretcher after stretcher appeared at the doors...**

This was the first war in which chloroform was used – although neither Prince Menshikov nor Dr John Hall approved of anaesthetics:

> **Dr. Hall takes this opportunity of cautioning medical officers against the use of chloroform in the severe shock of gunshot wounds, as he thinks few will survive if it is used. But as public opinion, founded perhaps on mistaken philanthropy, he knows is against him, he can only caution medical officers and expect they will narrowly watch its effects. However barbarous it may appear, the smart of the knife is a powerful stimulant,**

Turkey's sick men

As soon as the Allies arrived in Constantinople, General Canrobert astonished the Pasha by declaring that if they could not find wood for fires they would use Turkish houses. When it came to establishing hospitals they were equally single-minded, as Captain Adolphus Slade observed:

> The Allies had demanded and obtained nearly all the public edifices at Constantinople, including the naval, military and medical schools, for barracks and hospitals; leaving, in their liberality, two barracks for the native garrison and hospital room for about 800 men. The French thus obtained accomodation for 12,000, the English for 5,000 patients.

In Slade's view the Allies had left their hosts in appalling straits:

> We have debated in our mind if the Allies, in their laudable anxiety about their own sick, ever asked themselves what became of the Turkish sick, who were more numerous and more intensely diseased. They had deprived them of their hospitals and barracks, and knew that no others would be extemporised. Devoid of resources, with no public to stimulate their rulers, the Turkish sick, all more or less influenced by the dogma of fate, in general died where they had sickened.

There were huge cultural differences in the attitudes of the Allies and their Turkish hosts in the East towards sanitation and medicine. The Allies' perception of the Turks from the beginning was that they were filthy and unhealthy. Henry Clifford's first impression of Constantinople was that:

> ...you step in all sorts of filth. In trying to get out of the way of a dead dog the other day, I found my foot on a dead rat. The streets are never cleaned in any way, so the stench beats anything I have ever smelt.

By comparison with Western standards of hygiene, the way they buried their dead, the proximity of their cemeteries to water supplies, the pestilential stench and the conditions of the streets, littered with animal carcasses, made it unsurprising to the Allies when the Turks were seen to die in vast numbers. This shocking mortality was viewed quite unsympathetically by people like Fanny Duberly:

> I hear Balaklava is to be given up to the sick. The place stinks already with the number of sick Turks, who have turned it into a half-putrid hospital. I never saw people die with such dreary perseverance as these Turks. Two hundred of them were buried in one day a short time since.

The Turks, partly for religious reasons, also had a different attitude towards death. Being conveyed to hospitals on mules or packhorses, patients often fell off. In these cases the Turk leading the animal would 'sit and smoke philosophically until the patient was ready to carry on'. From Scutari hospital, Margaret Goodman could see men arriving:

> A long file of stretchers, each with a gaunt soldier clothed in his tattered grey coat, lying helpless (and very often senseless) upon it, being borne by noisy, careless Turks, who really appeared to resort to little expedients in order to increase the sufferings of the soldier...on one occasion the Turkish bearers, while jesting among themselves, threw a sick man off the stretcher, cutting his face and giving him a severe shock. When able to speak, his first words were, 'Those frightful men have murdered me.' He did not live long; though the fall would not have killed a man in health.

and it is much better to hear a man bawl lustily, than to see him sink silently into his grave.

VIVANDIÈRE TENDING A WOUNDED ZOUAVE. (PHOTO BY ROGER FENTON.)

Like Nightingale, Pirogov was convinced that 'not medicine but administration plays the major role in the task of helping the wounded and sick at the battlefield'. Pirogov's major administrative achievement in military hospital care was to devise a system of sorting patients into four categories: the hopelessly sick and mortally wounded who were entrusted to the Sisters of Mercy and the priests, the seriously wounded who needed immediate surgical attention, the less seriously wounded whose operations could wait until the following day, and those with minor injuries who were treated swiftly and returned to their regiments.

From the Nobles' Assembly the patients were sent to what were called 'dressing stations', according to their category. Ekaterina Bakunina, one of the Russian nurses who served with Pirogov, described the system in action:

> **...everything in the grand hall was ready: glasses, vodka, the samovar was boiling. In the operating-room, the doctors were sitting around Nikolai Ivanovich**

(Pirogov). At 11 o'clock there began to be heard the sounds of firing, and immediately our main, ceremonial doors were thrown open wide: two stretchers, and then three came running in; then two men came in holding a wounded man by the arms. The doctors would inspect them, when the cases were complicated they would call one another and confer, and then the words would ring out: 'This one to Nikolaevsky battery!' (that meant he was lightly wounded) 'This one to the Gushchin House!' (that meant there was no hope for him) 'This one to remain here!' (that meant that there would be an amputation).

Sometimes, however, like Nightingale, Pirogov still had to fight against what he called 'the insatiable rapacity of the hospital administration' and 'the stupidity of the official medical personnel'. On one occasion, due to an administrative fault, about 2,000 wounded men had to spend the whole night outdoors after an artillery bombardment because there was no transport. In the end, the sisters had to carry them to the dressing station.

Since the fighting was taking place around Sebastopol, transporting the wounded was slightly easier for the Russians than for the Allies. The major British and French hospitals were at Scutari and Pera, suburbs of Constantinople on the other side of the Black Sea, and at least four days away by boat. Even getting to the boats was a problem, as Fanny Duberly described:

We have no ambulance waggons; they are nearly all broken down, or the mules are dead, or the drivers are dead or dead drunk: as well one as the other, as far as usefulness goes. Our poor Cavalry horses, as we know full well, are all unequal to the task of carrying down the sick; and the French have provided transports for us for some time... Why can we not tend our own sick? Why are we so helpless and so broken down?

The French had a well-functioning medical system. At the outbreak of war everything had been in place, each duty was defined and provided for. As ambulances, for example, they had introduced *cacolets* – mules furnished with couches slung on either side, previously used by tourists to get up mountains in the Pyrenees - which proved very efficient in the Crimea. In the British army plans had been confined to sending out a bunch of army veterans. Thomas Chenery was scathing in *The Times*:

At the commencement of this war a plan was invented, and carried out, by which a number of Chelsea pensioners were sent out as an ambulance corps to attend on the sick. Whether it was a scheme for saving money by utilizing the poor old men or shortening the duration of their lives and pensions, it is difficult to say, but they have been found in practice rather to require nurses themselves than to be able to nurse others... The man who conceived the idea that the hard work of a military hospital could be performed by worn-out and aged cripples must have had slight knowledge of warfare or have profited little by experience. To attend the sick who lie by hundreds in the wards of a vast hospital, and require unceasing care by night and day, is no easy task, and certainly cannot be performed by such old men as may be seen at Scutari — the remains of the body who were sent out six months ago.

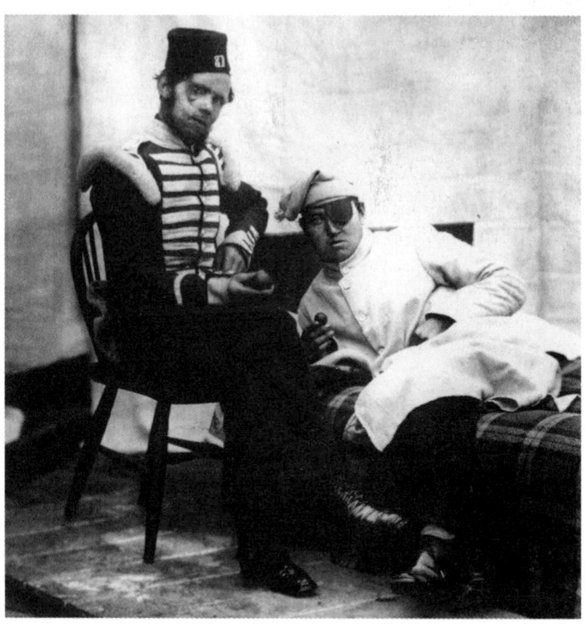

WOUNDED PRIVATES JESSE LOCKHURST (31ST) AND THOMAS O'BRIEN (1ST ROYALS).
(PHOTO BY CUNDALL AND HOWLETT.)

Florence Nightingale was constantly making comparisons with the French:

> **The French have a permanent system of orderlies, trained for the purpose, who do not reenter the ranks. It is too late for us to organise this. But if the convalescents, being good orderlies, were not sent away to the Crimea as soon as they had learnt their work – if the Commander-in-Chief would call upon the Commanding Officer of each Regiment to select ten men from each as Hospital Orderlies to form a depot here (not young soldiers but men of good character) this would give some hope of organizing an efficient corps.**

There were many complaints about the British orderlies, who were basically men unfit for active service. They were often drunk or just not very good, and some were caught stealing money and belongings from dying soldiers. Nevertheless, Florence Nightingale thought that male orderlies and not nurses should be tending the sick, and when she found men who could do the job, she was even accused of holding on to them and not letting them go back to the front. Meanwhile, the female nurses performed domestic chores and gave the patients 'womanly attentions'.

THE CASTLE HOSPITAL AT BALAKLAVA.
(PHOTO BY JAMES ROBERTSON.)

Margaret Goodman wrote that she was moistening lint over inflamed wounds, helping patients to turn in bed, and placing cologne-filled handkerchiefs next to the stinking stumps left after their limbs had been amputated .

Florence Nightingale did not think it proper for female nurses to come into close contact with male patients. She may have been 'the Lady with the Lamp', but she did not allow her nurses in the wards after 8.30pm, and she thought it was only acceptable for certain parts of the men's bodies to be washed or cooled by the nurses. Bromide was given to the patients to curb their sexual urges, but flirtation still bothered her. After all, as Fanny Duberly pointed out, certain nurses did have the nickname 'The New Matrimony-At-Any-Price Association'. During the course of the campaign a few nurses announced their intentions to marry soldiers whom they had nursed back to health. They were immediately sent home.

Other nurses annoyed her by their silliness, so much that she transcribed their ignorance for Sidney Herbert. A certain Mrs Lawfield, for instance, had complained:

> **I came out Ma'am, prepared to submit to every thing - to be put upon in every way – but there are some things, Ma'am, one can't submit to – There is caps, Ma'am, that suits one face, and some that suits anothers, and if I'd known, Ma'am, about the caps, great as was my desire to come out to nurse at Scutari, I wouldn't have come, Ma'am.**

However, the majority of Florence's nurses were very competent, sturdy older women. For some of them the fact that real nursing duties were simply not being fulfilled was frustrating. Elizabeth Davis felt she could be used better in a more practical role. The only possibility of doing this was to leave Scutari against Florence Nightingale's wishes, and go nearer to the front, where other hospitals were now being set up. Davis joined the General Hospital at Balaklava:

> **One soldier there had been wounded at Alma by a shot which passed through his left breast, above the heart, and came out below the shoulder blade. His wound had not been dressed for five weeks, and I took at least a**

Mary Seacole, who was nicknamed 'Mother' by the troops.

quart of maggots from it. From many of the other patients I removed them in handfuls. When the wounds were regularly attended to, these men soon got well. I do not believe that maggots ever occur in cases where the wounds are properly cleansed and dressed. I always consider their presence as proof of neglect.

Another woman was determined to make her way as close to the front as possible. Mary Seacole was a widowed West Indian 'doctress' who had got to know, and earn the respect of, some of the British regiments, including high-ranking officers like Sir John Campbell, from treating many of their ailments in Jamaica. When she read of the outbreak of war in the Crimea she paid her way to London only to be turned down by the Nightingale mission.

Her experience was similar to that of other black women who applied for posts as nurses in the Crimean War. A certain Miss Belgrave was rejected because a 'West Indian constitution is not the one best able to bear the fatigue of nursing...though Mrs B. looks robust – and some English patients would object to a nurse being so nearly a person of color [sic]'. Similarly Elizabeth Purcell, who was first described as an 'exemplary character', was then rejected at fifty-two, some ten years younger than many of the nurses who went out to the Crimea, for being 'too old and almost black'.

Undaunted Mary Seacole made the three week journey to the Crimea at her own expense. She stopped at Scutari on the way to the front:

One thought never left my mind as I walked through the fearful miles of suffering in that great hospital. If it is so here, what must it not be at the scene of war – on the spot where the poor fellows are stricken down by pestilence or Russian bullets, and days and nights of agony must be passed before a woman's hand can dress their wounds. And I felt happy in the conviction that I must be useful three or four days nearer to their pressing wants than this.

Mary Seacole was keen to put her practical experience into use as much as possible. As soon as she arrived in Balaklava she threw herself into the work of relieving the suffering among the troops:

The very first day that I approached the wharf, a party of sick and wounded had just arrived. Here was work for me, I felt sure. With so many patients, the doctors must be glad of all the hands they could get. Indeed, so strong was the old impulse within me, that I waited for no permission, but seeing a poor artilleryman stretched upon a pallet, groaning heavily, I ran up to him at once, and eased the stiff dressings. Lightly my practised fingers ran over the familiar work, and well was I rewarded when the poor fellow's groans subsided into a restless, uneasy mutter. God help him! He had been hit in the forehead, and I think his sight was gone. I stooped down, and raised some tea to his baked lips.

> **Then his hand touched mine and rested there...**

She was also a succesful practitioner of herbal remedies, and William Howard Russell observed:

> **Her hut was surrounded every morning by the rough navvies and Land Transport men, who had a faith in her proficiency in the healing art, which she justified by many cures and by removing obstinate cases of diarrhoea, dysentery, and similar camp maladies.**

Once she had settled in to the Crimea, she was often seen riding out to the front with baskets of medicines of her own preparation, and as the siege progressed, she was the the most active of the few women who helped the British wounded on the battlefield.

The Russian initiative, on the contrary, had from the start anticipated the possibility of the nurses serving nearer to the action. The women were, after all, going into Sebastopol, a city under siege. When Pirogov arrived in the Crimea he had already found local women caring for the wounded in dangerous situations:

> **Everyday when the wounds are being dressed, you can see three or four women, one of these is the famous Darya, one is the daughter of some civil servant, a girl of about 17, and one is the wife of a soldier... At the Battle of Alma, she (Darya) brought linen which had been given to her to launder, and it was here that her noble inclination to help the wounded was first revealed.**

Darya, the orphaned daughter of a Black Sea Fleet sailor, was one of the first Russian women to care for the injured on the battlefield itself. Her father was one of the very few Russians killed at the battle of Sinope. She followed the Russian troops under fire at the Alma, creating the first battlefield 'dressing station' in the process and then went on to care for the sick at the hospitals and dressing stations of besieged Sebastopol.

The work of these local women paved the way for the Sisters of Mercy, but it was the Allies who had

SISTERS OF CHARITY DURING THE BATTLE.
(R. DE MORAINE)

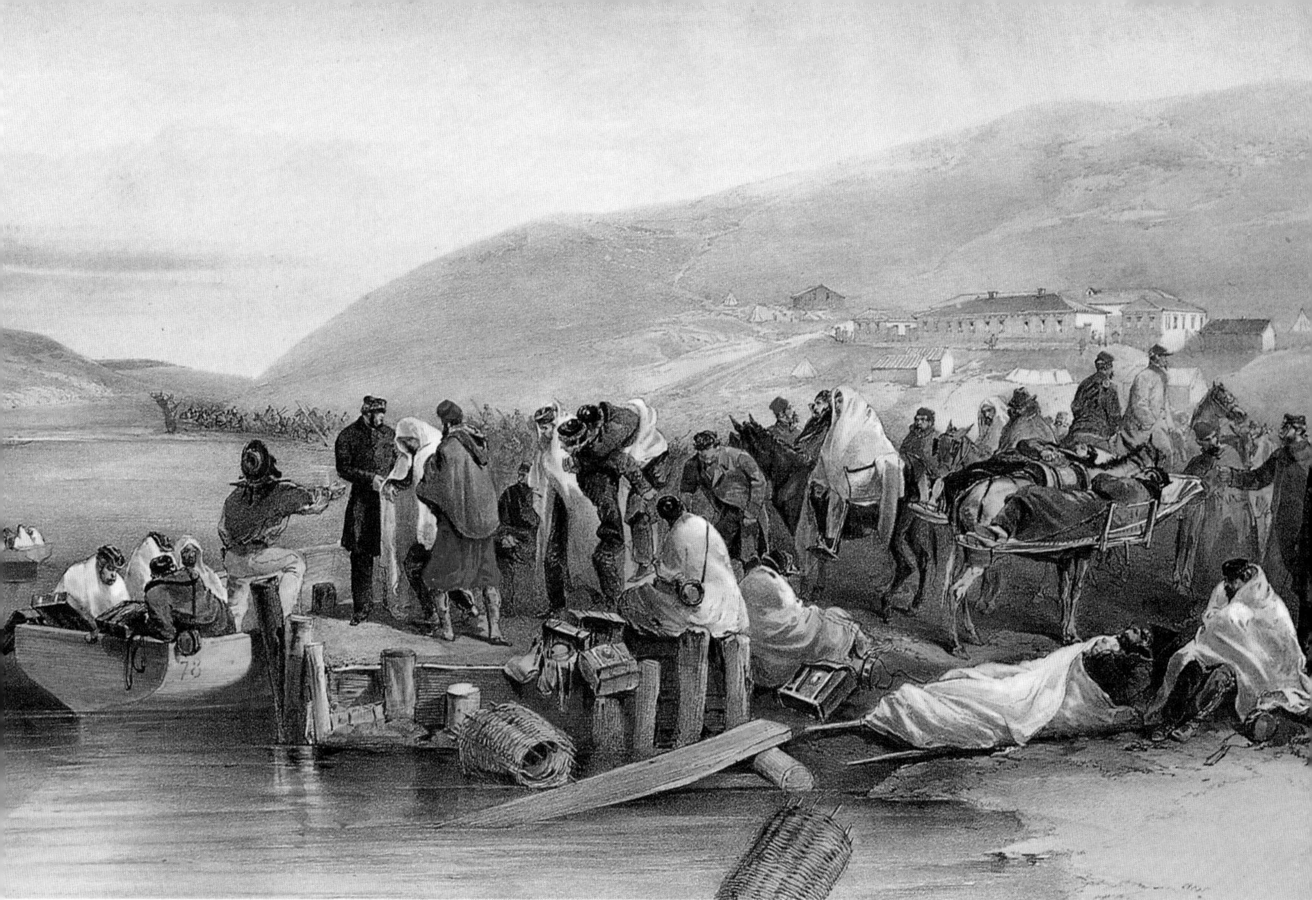

EMBARCATION OF THE SICK AT BALAKLAVA
(WILLIAM SIMPSON).

MANY OF THE SICK HAD TO BE TRANSPORTED FOR SEVERAL DAYS BY BOAT TO THE HOSPITAL AT SCUTARI.

inspired them. One of them was 42-year-old Ekaterina Bakunina:

> **I shall never forget that evening when we received the newspapers with the news that the French and English had landed in the Crimea. I could not imagine that this beautiful corner of our expansive empire could become a theatre of war (we spent 1849 and the summer of 1850 in the Crimea since my sister had been prescribed sea bathing. How nice and peaceful it was there!).**
>
> **I read that French nurses had set off for the military hospitals; then, that Miss Nightingale, with some ladies and sisters, had set off for the English hospitals. And what about us? Surely we weren't going to do nothing?**

Bakunina arrived in Sebastopol in January 1855 and, in fact assumed a far more involved role than that of the nurses by whom she had been inspired. She worked in the operating theatre as hard as the surgeons and for equally long hours. Pirogov wrote of her:

> **When bombs and rockets shot over or fell short and were flying around the Nobles' Assembly, she and her confederates displayed an astonishing spirit that could hardly be associated with feminine nature and which distinguished the sisters till the very end of the siege.**

Unlike the British nurses, the Russians were on duty day and night. She described some of her duties to her sister:

> **They brought in an officer: his whole face was covered in blood. I washed him down, and he got out some money to give to the soldiers who had brought him here; many of them did this. Another one had been wounded in the chest; you kneel down to hold a light for the doctor and in order to find out whether the bullet has**

A wash-house at Balaklava.

Innovations

Isambard Kingdom Brunel's Hospital

In February 1855, the government invited designs for a hospital which could be prefabricated in England and shipped out for assembly on a suitable site. Isambard Kingdom Brunel (1806-1859), who was at the peak of his career as an engineer, was approached. Within a matter of weeks he had designed, prepared and packed off his projected hospital, and by the beginning of August it was up and running. His achievement lay not only in the fantastic speed with which he acted but also in the conception of the hospital.

Brunel realized from the start that fundamental to the undertaking was the problem of organization. What he provided was not just a collection of huts but a highly organized plan of action, right down to the last detail of assembly and transportation. The specifications were far more elaborate than those of the hospital huts already sent out to the Crimea, which were deficient in ventilation, in comfort, and in many other respects. In Brunel's plan there were elaborate systems both for ventilation and the supply of fresh water. There was a separate kitchen unit and an iron building for laundry. Every detail was considered and planned, including basins, invalid baths, and even supplies of toilet paper.

The original intention was to site the hospital at Scutari but there turned out to be no suitable ground there. Instead the hospital was erected at Renkioi, 100 miles from Scutari. It was an absurd distance from the Crimea, and was never used to full capacity, which led to criticism. In many ways, however, it was a major advance in hospital design, and a great improvement on the tented or hutted hospitals originally provided in the Crimea. Indeed, Brunel's design was later adopted by the Federal forces during the American Civil War.

Alexis Soyer's Stove and Teapot

Although Florence Nightingale did much to improve some aspects of the hospital diet, she did not have the time to do much towards the establishment of more efficient general kitchens. In these reforms she would receive unexpected help from the arrival of Alexis Soyer (1809–1858), the philanthropic former chef of the Reform Club, whom she had first met when she attended his lectures to ladies on how to make soup for the 'hungry poors'. He at once became an admirer, close friend and collaborator.

Alexis Soyer was a Frenchman, who had learnt his culinary art in Paris. He had published a book, *The Modern Housewife*, and at the time of the Crimean War it was said, 'officers being compelled to cook for themselves, have with the aid of Soyer's Housewife and their servants, attained a degree of culinary skill which would astonish their friends at home'. After an open letter, from a soldier appealing for his help, appeared in *The Times*, Soyer offered his services without charge and left for the Crimea in February, stopping at Paris to

inspect the cooking arrangements in the French military hospitals.

As soon as he arrived at Scutari, Soyer inspected the outdated cooking arrangements. Meat was issued in the morning, but the patients did not get it until the late afternoon, often overcooked or undercooked. As a result, lots of rations were wasted. Soyer was horrifed that the water in which the meat was boiled was thrown away, so he showed the cooks how to make it into nutritious soup. He put the defects right very quickly. For the first time salt and pepper, at his instigation, were supplied to season the food while cooking it.

Soyer had also been occupied for many years with kitchen arrangements and gadgets. He was aware of the inadequacy of the army cooking stoves and before he set out he designed a portable model for use in camp or hospital, much more efficient and more economical of fuel than the existing types. Rather like an over-sized dustbin, it was essentially a steam boiler with a removable oven on top, and a chimney to take away any smoke.The stoves proved so valuable that the army has used them ever since, still called the Soyer stove. They were in use during the Gulf War, though fired by bottled gas, instead of coal or wood.

Soyer also greatly improved the method of making tea – a real advantage for the British! Previously it was brewed in a copper boiler just emptied of soup. He invented his 'Scutari teapot', a large kettle in which there was a removable filter to hold the tea, enabling less tea to be used to better effect – a great improvement on a dirty teabag.

Alexis Soyer sets up his stove in the French camp.

Charles Dickens' Drying Machine

Charles Dickens' concern was not just limited to making speeches and alluding to the Crimean crisis in his novels. Together with his friend Miss Burdett Coutts, he decided to commission a drying machine which, like Brunel's hospital, could be packaged and sent out to Scutari.

In early January 1855, he wrote to her:

> First, as to the hot Closet. It happens that Mr Traceys being worn out, a new man is now erecting a new successor to it. This man is ingenious in his trade, and his name and style are William Jeakes [Mechanical Engineer], of 51 Great Russell St Bloomsbury. He never has made such a thing to be carried away and put together, but he is positively sure he can... He would undertake that 25 minutes should effectually dry the whole of the closet's contents, so that it might be filled with wet clothes, bandages &c, every five and twenty minutes during the day. He would number all the pieces and component parts, so that any one who could put a gun-carriage together, could put this machine together with perfect ease.

The machine was ready for trial in sixteen days and was then sent in late March 1855 to John Sutherland. Three months later Dr Sutherland could happily report that the machine was still in operation, working well and giving great satisfaction. The machine, he said, did credit to Miss Coutts's 'philandryphy' and Charles Dickens' engineering.

> **gone right through - you put your hand against his back and look for the the exit wound. You can imagine how much blood there is here!.. But enough of this! If I told you about all the awful wounds and torments which I saw during this night, you would not be able to sleep for several nights!**

With a system established for the dressing stations it became possible to help many more wounded in an organized manner. But, as Bakunina observed, the patients also understood the system:

> **It was terribly hard, here at our dressing-station when, after a sick person had been given hope that he would recover, he suddenly begins to get delirious, turns yellow, and the doctor says that he should be sent to the Gushchin House – for a patient this was tantamount to the death sentence. And there was nothing you could do, fully aware that a wounded man who had just been brought in should not be in contact with such a patient and watch him die. At the dressing-station people should not die.**

During one week about four thousand wounded were taken care of by three sisters, one doctor and two doctor's assistants. Nurse Krupskaya wrote home: 'We haven't eaten or drunk for two days, there was no possibility to interrupt the work for a single moment.' Some sisters gave help to the wounded during night attacks and bombardments. One soldier described how...

> **.....a common and uneducated woman, attended our fortifications at her own will and became a heroine. She helped the wounded at the bastion, under the direct fire of the enemy's cannon.**

Being in the front line, many of the Russian nurses suffered concussion and wounds from shells while they were serving. However, from the moment they arrived, the women on all sides were vulnerable to diseases prevalent in the Crimea, and the majority were ill during their time there. To make things worse for both soldiers and nurses, the advent of winter, which coincided with the arrival of Pirogov and Nightingale, would create a medical emergency of its own.

Top left: Zouave and Spahi (Fenton).
Top: An officer with his Nubian servant (Fenton).
Left: Croat Chiefs (Fenton).
Above: Montenegrins (Fenton).

Top left: Turkish infantry (Szathmari).
Top right: 42nd Highlanders (Cundall and Howlett).
Left: French sailors on board the Phlégéton (Durand-Brager and Lassimonne).
Above: A Russian prisoner (Durand-Brager and Lassimonne).

CHAPTER SIX

A REAL RUSSIAN WINTER

After two major battles the Russians had failed to push the Allies back into the sea, and both sides now knew they were destined to spend the next few months where they were. The battle would become one to stay alive. On the night of 14 November 1854, barely a week after the battle of Inkerman, Fanny Duberly was on board the *Sans Pareil* in Balaklava harbour:

> **At seven o'clock, when I looked through the stern cabin windows, the harbour was seething and covered with foam, and the ships swinging terribly. By nine it had increased to a frightful extent, and I could hardly, even when clinging to the ship, keep my footing on deck. The spray, dashing over the cliffs many hundred feet, fell like heavy rain into the harbour. Ships were crushing and crowding together, all adrift, all breaking and grinding each other to pieces... By ten o'clock we heard that the most fearful wrack was going on outside among the ships at anchor, and some of the party started for the rocks to try if by any means they could save life. The next tidings were, that the *Prince* and the *Resolute*, the *Rip van Winkle*, the *Wanderer*, the *Progress* and a foreign barque, had all gone down, and, out of the whole, not a dozen people saved.**

Ships in Balaklava harbour. (Photo by Roger Fenton.)

The Russian reserve army were camped out on the steppes, just like their enemy. Pyotr Alabin described that day in his journal:

> **What a sight! Even in my dreams I have never seen the like! The sea, this time Black not only in name, but in colour, had merged with the black sky. It was as though**

some unfathomable huge monster had opened its bottomless jaw and had flicked into it a multitude of ships of the enemy squadron. Several vessels are already lying on the shore like corpses; amongst the squadron, several ships are beating without masts.

A hurricane was devastating the Crimea. Twenty-one British ships and fourteen French ships went down. The *Prince* had been carrying a large part of the army's warm clothing and medical supplies, all of which were lost.

Destruction and havoc were not confined to the sea. On land the wind was so strong that a French regiment returning from their trench duty were stuck to the spot and had to wait four hours to struggle the final few yards back to camp. Private Harry Blishen woke up to see all the tents and belongings of the Rifle Brigade blowing away. And that was not all:

I saw with my own eyes a man belonging to us blown into the air. The poor horses were blown off the hills... There are at this present time forty or fifty drowned sailors lying on the beach. It is everybody's opinion that if we remain here much longer we cannot live.

As the Allies' lightweight summer tents went 'whirling like leaves in a gale towards Sebastopol' and they realized the fragility of their position, the Russians were busily fortifying the besieged town under Totleben's command.

After the death of his fellow writer Komstadius at Inkerman, Tolstoy had requested a transfer to Sebastopol. He arrived there shortly after the storm,

His fiction echoes his letters home, which celebrate the mood inside Sebastopol:

> **A company of marines almost mutinied because they were to be relieved from a battery where they'd withstood bombardment for 30 days. Soldiers defuse bombs. Women carry water to the bastions for the soldiers. Many are killed and wounded. Priests carrying crosses go to the bastions and read prayers under fire...It's a wonderful time!...it's beautiful in Sebastopol now. The enemy hardly fires at all and everyone is convinced that he won't take the town, that it really is impossible.**

Tolstoy was right. The Allies, and especially the British, were unprepared for the circumstances in which they now found themselves. At first, in spite of the adverse conditions, the morale of men like Private Harry Blishen stayed high:

> **I am happy to state that I am in good health, in spite of being up to my neck in mud in all weathers, and doing my natural sleep every night in a puddle of water. The weather here of late has been very wet; nothing but incessant rain, day and night; for my own part, I have given up all hopes of ever getting dry again. We cannot live in tents; in fact, the tent that I used to live in, has**

ABOVE: THE HURRICANE, 14 NOVEMBER 1854 (ANON).
RIGHT: DESPITE THE HARDSHIP, MANY OFFICERS STILL HAD THEIR 'SOLDIER-SERVANTS'. (PHOTO BY ROGER FENTON.)

although his brigade was then stationed a few miles outside the town. He used this visit as the basis of the first of his *Sebastopol Sketches*:

> **Your first impression is bound to be disagreeable: the strange intermingling of camp and town life, of clean town and dirty bivouac is not only unsightly but gives the sense of complete chaos; it seems that everyone is afraid, that all these people are scurrying about with no idea what to do. But take a closer look at the faces of those around you, and you realise the truth is quite different.**

long since become non-effective. We awoke one morning and found that the wind had made a large back door into it; so we were obliged to take in our canvas, and dig a large hole into the ground to live in; but before we could finish it, the wet weather commenced, so we are living in a well almost.

French infantry officer, Jean-Jules Herbé, was astonished by the lack of basic training of his British counterparts:

> **They have had big tents since the beginning of the siege but they don't know how to put them up! They didn't even know how to dig a little ditch around their tents to prevent the wind and rain from getting in!**

In the French camps senior officers like General Bosquet were often among the men sharing their conditions. The disparity between the conditions of British officers and men, on the other hand, was huge. Many officers, such as Cornet Fisher, sympathized and felt outraged on behalf of their men. But they did not suffer the same degree of hardship in lack of clothing, food and sleep:

> **...the men stand day and night in trenches full of water, holding their muskets in their cramped and half-frozen hands ready to repel the enemy, the rain soaking them through the only clothes they have in the world, which, I speak from experience, once wet will remain damp forever in this climate...you would think that after a night like the last, they would have a good mess of soup**

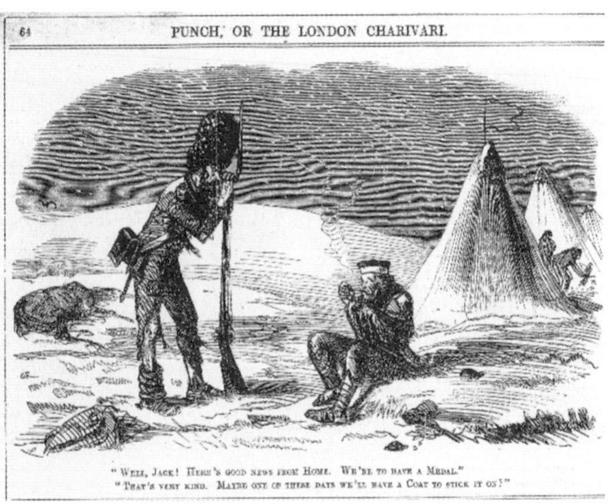

"Well, Jack! Here's good news from Home. We're to have a Medal."
"That's very kind. Maybe one of these days we'll have a Coat to stick it on?"

Appearances

Moustachios and whiskers are to be allowed to grow, but no officer or private will be allowed to wear a beard. Below the mouth there is to be no hair whatsoever, and the whisker is not to be worn more forward on the chin than the corner of the mouth.

'I got .. a paper, which tells pretty well the truth about the Army here ... an Illustrated with pictures of us here only dressed as we ought to be not as we are. I can assure you that to this date, the 12th. Janry. we have neither the huts, fur caps, boots, or anything in the "picture". '

Captain Dallas.

Orders on facial hair such as this one from Lord Lucan were quite stringent during the Crimean War. William Howard Russell, himself bearded, railed against the upper ranks of the army because they would not let the men grow beards. Englishmen were supposed to look like Englishmen, and beards were considered foreign and breeders of vermin. In July 1854, however, Captain Henry Clifford noted that an order was given that moustaches and beards were now to be grown throughout the army:

> This order has given great satisfaction amongst the troops for tho' there are many who like the banishment of the razor because they think its use detrimental to personal beauty, yet there are many who suffer from its use and whose lips and chins after a clean shave look more like raw meat than the mug of a Christian.

The suggestion had been resisted at first on the grounds of cleanliness, but in Varna, the sun 'made inroads on the faces of the men', and, to Sir George Brown's horror, Lord Raglan allowed his army to imitate 'the hairy men amongst our Allies'. No detail of clothing or appearance was too trivial for George Brown. He was a firm believer in the leather stock that soldiers still wore, constricting their throats like a garotte and even a loose button was an acutely painful sight to him. By April 1855, Captain Dallas reported him getting his own back:

> There is a great rumour here that all beards are to be shaved off. It will not affect me, but those who have found the comfort and protection of them, independent of the trouble of shaving in a tent, will feel it much. This order emmanates from 'Sir Brown' whose principal military talent appears to me to be the happy knack

Above: Legacies of the war – when the troops returned both smoking and facial hair proliferated
Right: By the time Roger Fenton got the troops to pose in winter clothing, it was too warm to wear it.

> he has of making everybody about him uncomfortable.

Sir George Brown's strictures became increasingly farcical in the light of practical concerns. Although in Varna the Turkish soldiers had looked on in astonishment at the size and fine clothes of their Allies, the British army landed in the Crimea without a change of clothes and many of them did not take them off for weeks, even sleeping in them. They quickly assumed an odd appearance, as Captain Dallas wrote:

> The French Officers, who are always by the bye most smartly dressed, & always look like soldiers, get on capitally with us, and have got quite accustomed to our extraordinary appearance... It must seem very odd to them, I always think, seeing our officers, for whom at the same time I think they have a great respect, walking about in clothes that no respectable servant could be induced to appear in.

By the end of 1854 much of the army was no longer dressed in what would be recognized as uniform. When the scandal of winter uniforms left to rot in Balaklava harbour was reported in *The Times*, a 'Patriotic Fund' was set up and anxious women started knitting warm clothing for the men, which became known as cardigans and Balaclavas.

and an extra ration of rum. Let's see what they have got... it looks good rich soup, it is not though: it's good rich mud and water. The poor soldier gets his green coffee baked in a shovel, bruised between two stones, and boiled in this water. Fresh meat has not been heard of for a fabulous time in the Army. The pork is awful stuff...It is an infamous shame...

I am thankful to say that mine is quite a different affair – two or three good cups of tea or coffee, some fried beef or pork, French bread and butter; although I may be occasionally content to feed on biscuit and rum and water when no fire can be obtained on account of the rain...

Those British troops who could get away from the trenches would often end up in the French camps trying to find food. The French were more organized, cooking in groups with each man assuming a different task. They were also better supplied by their vivandières, young women who ran cantines for their regiments. Charles Mismer, a young French dragoon, felt pity for his Allies:

Any soldier who has been in the Crimea knows the English words 'bread' and 'boots' from having heard them so often: the English will actually exchange their boots for something to eat. In the absence of bread, which we are lacking in ourselves, we give them what we can, but we never take their money. It's pitiful to see such superb men asking permission to gorge themselves on the dregs in our mess tins.

RUSSIAN CARTOON MOCKING THE ALLIES 'CATCHING A COLD AFTER THEIR FIRST NIGHT IN THE CRIMEA'.

Certain British officers got hold of charcoal stoves, but then proceeded to asphyxiate themselves in their tents. Even the Turks, often criticized by the British for their backward ways, were better organized. Captain Dallas was envious: 'I passed through the Turks' Camp yesterday, and positively they were considerably more comfortable than our men, each tent having a stove smoking away like fun.'

Another discomfort, as Cornet Fisher pointed out, was the fact that the soldiers were still in the same rapidly degenerating uniforms they had arrived in:

Sentries are found dead at their posts. This is not so much owing to the climate as to the want of proper clothing: the men having nothing but what is on their backs, or very little else, which, if it gets wet, dries on them.

The truth was that, in spite of the losses in the hurricane, a great many things for the British, including clothing and wooden huts, had arrived in Balaklava. Most of them, however, were lying in the mud at the harbour, awaiting signatures on bits of paper before they could be released by the commissary general, Filder. Fanny Duberly described this recipe for disaster:

If any body should ever wish to erect a 'Model Balaklava' in England, I will tell him the ingredients necessary. Take a village of ruined houses and hovels in the extremest state of all imaginable dirt; allow the rain to pour into and outside them, until the whole place is a swamp of filth ankle-deep; catch about, on an average, 1000 sick Turks with the plague, and cram them into the houses indiscriminately; kill about 100 a day, and bury them so as to be scarcely covered with earth, leaving them to rot at leisure – taking care to keep up the supply. On to one part of the beach drive all the exhausted bat ponies, dying bullocks and worn-out camels, and leave them to die of starvation. They will generally do so in about three days, when they will soon begin to rot, and smell accordingly. Collect together

Commissariat Difficulties (William Simpson).

from the water of the harbour all the offal of the animals slaughtered for the use of the occupants of above 100 ships, to say nothing of the inhabitants of the town, – which, together with an occasional floating human body, whole or in parts, and the driftwood of the wrecks, pretty well covers the water – and stew them all up together in a narrow harbour, and you will have a tolerable imitation of the real essence of Balaklava.

The British army was bogged down in bureaucracy. Because of over forty years of peace the Commissariat, the branch of the Civil Service responsible for the organization and distribution of military supplies, had been run down and no one was trained to run it in a modern way. This was a crucial weakness. For young officers like Captain Dallas, the situation seemed ludicrous:

What kills us out here is the utter want of system & arrangement in every department. I must give you an instance while I think of it, of the clever way in which everything connected with the Army is done, at home as well as here. We got up at last about 20 pair of boots per company, a great want as the men were all in a wretched state. Would you believe that they are all too small! & except for a very few men useless! How curiously the vein of Incapacity seems to wind about thro' everything, not omitting even the humble boot.

The Russian Commissariat also had problems, but these were not only the result of inefficiency but also of corruption. One of Tolstoy's aims in sending back his *Sebastopol Sketches* was to expose this. Captain Hodasiewicz was also a cynical observer:

> **During the time I was in the town the following occurrence took place. A large quantity of powder was brought up to the 4th Bastion [Flagstaff] already made up into charges for the guns. It was all sorted carefully in the magazine, and afterwards served out to the guns. A gun was loaded with this powder, shotted ready for firing, when it would not go off. A fresh tube was used with no better result, so the gun was left to be unloaded in the evening. When the powder came to be examined it was dyed millet-seed! Things of this kind have frequently happened. Soldiers have found their cartridges made up with sand instead of powder. This was a part of the peculation carried on... In this instance the effect the discovery had on the men was very great, as they began to explain that Menshikov was a traitor, that this was done expressly that they might all be killed, that he had sold the town, etc. Certain it is that the morale of the men fell considerably after this circumstance.**

One of the major difficulties, encountered on both sides, was the problem of transporting supplies. The main road into Sebastopol was from Simferopol, and the Russians used it, on the one hand to bring in ammunition, food and animal fodder and, on the other, to evacuate the sick and wounded to hospitals and burial grounds in the interior. Pyotr Alabin described its worsening condition:

> **Rain, mud, slush. The roads...are an amazing sight. The mud comes up to the horses' bellies; the road is narrow; huge furrows have been formed in it; at night there are frosts, congealing the mud, which, thanks to the clayey soil, makes the road quite impassable. Anyone travelling there has to ride literally over the carcasses of horses and bullocks who have drowned in the mud, and over the debris of carriages which it is impossible to pull out of the mud. It is pitiful to watch the wretched drivers! if one of his horses or bullocks falls in the mud his own exertions to free it from this viscous grave deprive him of his strength even more and push it deeper into the mud; a few drivers gather round and join forces to drag the animal out, themselves standing up to their knees in mud, but in most cases their efforts are in vain and result in them pulling off the horse's mane and tail, they break two or three stakes by using them as levers and go on their way, or swearing and cursing they begin to distribute their comrade's load among the remaining carts. What else can they do? You cannot cast off an official cargo!**

TARTAR LABOURERS. (PHOTO BY ROGER FENTON.)

The Allies were suffering from having lost the Woronzoff Road, the only metalled road that might have helped supply their camps, at the battle of Balaklava. In his reports back to England for *The Times*, William Howard Russell wrote cynically about the dramatic lack of foresight about transport:

> **We were all told that when the bad weather set in, the country roads would be impassable. Still the fine weather was allowed to go by, and the roads were left as the Tartar carts had made them, though the whole face of the country is covered thickly with small stones which seem expressly intended for road metal.**

Omar Pasha, worried that 'the Ottoman troops in the Crimea have lost all consideration owing to their ill conduct at the action of Balaklava' had sent more Turks to besiege Sebastopol. These men had set to work strengthening the positions that had been exposed at Inkerman, and despite the bad reputation

GUARDING THE ADVANCE TRENCH (CAPTAIN HENRY CLIFFORD).

they had gained at Balaklava, the British engineers spoke highly of their working powers, saying that they found them 'as patient and willing as they are manly and strong'. An attempt was now made to employ them in road construction, collecting stones for metalling and digging drains but, underfed to the point of starvation, they could scarcely lift their spades. General Sir Colin Campbell, on being asked by the engineers, on 18 January, for more Turks to work on the lines, answered that 2,000 had died, 2,000 were sick, and the remainder were unfit for work.

The French had more successfully put their engineers to work at metalling, or 'macadamizing', the road from Kamiesch to their camps, so they, of all the armies, encountered the least serious problems with supply as the winter progressed. They had already lent their horses to the British to carry their sick and to drag artillery up to the front, but the situation got so bad that the cavalry itself, both British and French, was reduced to fetching and carrying food and supplies.

The British cavalry had been the pride of the army and the envy of their Allies. But their sleek horses were not able to stand the weather and especially not the hardships of fatigue duty coupled with lack of fodder. The lack of rations even reduced horses to eating each other's manes, tails and covers. In fact, the Arabs were the only horses that could cope with the

***Graves at the head of the harbour* (William Simpson).**

Burying the dead

I witnessed a sight today that would scarcely be credited in England...a corpse stitched in a blanket, carried by two men on a stretcher, and 'canted' into a grave – in fact, buried like a dog... As a further sad proof of the 'moral effect' of war, I may add that crowds of soldiers and others were passing by, and the sight I have mentioned appeared to attract neither notice nor comment.

At first, as Sergeant Mitchell noted, it was the sheer volume of the dead that posed a problem. But it soon became clear that, as death became a mundane reality steps would have to be taken to reduce the morale-sapping psychological effects of witnessing it. One of Florence Nightingale's first measures at Scutari hospital was to introduce a screen to prevent the wounded seeing their comrades die after amputation, and if they did die they were swiftly removed:

> Almost before the breath has left his body, it is sewn up in its blanket and carried away – buried the same day. We have no room for corpses in the wards.

Outside the Allied hospitals and camps, human remains were rolled up in wrappers, as coffins for such a large number became out of the question. At first there was a lack of attention to ritual, as Margaret Goodman noted:

> A nurse having promised a lad that she would follow him to his grave, on the morning after his death she went behind the Turks who were performing the rites of sepultre. A large square hole of no great depth had been dug, and into this the bodies were tossed, until they came up level with the soil: she observed a head protruding beyond the rest, which, when the Turk saw, he jumped in amongst the dead and stamped it down; then a mound of earth was heaped among the whole.

This had a demoralizing effect on the men, however, and it was clear that a proper sentiment of reverence for the dead must be cultivated.

In Sebastopol Yanuari Kobylinsky noticed the disparity between officers and men, even in death:

> Midday...two regimental musicians, accompanying the sad processions along Catherine Street, are playing funeral marches. In each procession one behind the other, several coffins are being carried: it is the funeral of killed officers... And in the distance, without any ceremony, several dozen carts are carrying the bodies of killed soldiers. A plain white blanket with blood stains is thrown over the top. From the sides of some of the carts are sticking out bits of bodies

which have been broken off by shells... And the cannonade batters on without silence; the rumble of weapons is preparing for new victims.

Several times a day a barge would approach Sebastopol, load up with this dead freight and carry it off to the cemetery on the northern side of the town. There, ten to fifteen huge pits dug by prisoners were ready. Up to fifty or more of the dead were lowered into one pit. Then the grave diggers made an embankment and placed a cross made of stones on the ground, and sometimes they stood a wooden cross there. A priest would come and conduct one funeral service for all. Nikolai Berg witnessed the spectacle:

> Here they lay on their backs, in no kind of order, for the most part in their blood-stained clothes: in a shirt or a greatcoat; and others in clean linen, put on them by their comrades, and with a candle in their hand, brought by those very comrades. One could also notice that some had their fingers formed in the sign of the cross... Orthodox believers, soldiers and sailors, approaching the deceased, sadly and silently looked in their faces and crossed themselves. Barely a word was spoken on the promontory of the dead. Yes, and what was there to say when as it was everything could be told by these silent corpses, which accumulated in number with each day that passed...

The war was fought on the same terrain for some time and troops often found themselves going over the ground of old battles. Attempts were made to make the landscape significant, and senior officers on both sides were commemorated at places like Cathcart's Hill or the Kornilov Bastion.

Although there were truces after the most violent actions to bury the dead, there was not always time to find all the bodies. Men would come across corpses 'black as sweeps and shrivelled up'. In the famous 'valley of death' they would find horse skeletons, relics of the famous Balaklava charges. Fanny Duberly described a ghostly trip:

> Rode this evening all over the valley of the Balaklava charge, — 'The valley of death,' as Tennyson calls it; but it reminded me more of another expression of his, 'Oh, death in life!' The ground lay gaudy with flowers, and warm and golden in the rays of the setting sun. It was literally covered with flowers; there was hardly any grass, – in places, none, – nothing but dwarf-roses, mignonette, larkspur, and forget-me-nots. Here and there we passed the carcass of a horse; – we saw five, with 8.H. [her husband's regiment, the 8th Hussars] on the hoof. Six-pound shot lay strewn about thickly enough, and pieces of shell. I did not see it, but was told that a skull had been found quite blanched and clean, with most wonderfully beautiful and regular teeth. We saw today no traces of unburied human bodies, — the horses had all been lightly covered over, but many of them were half exposed.
>
> We gathered handfuls of flowers, and thought, – oh, how sadly! – of the flowers of English chivalry that had there been reaped and mown away.

Left: Officers burial ground (James Robertson).
Below: *Russian burial of the dead* (Vasili Timm).

conditions, and the Chasseurs d'Afrique regiment was the only cavalry to weather the winter and lose very few horses. Even the animals suffered from the bureaucratic nightmare – a situation which particularly infuriated horse-loving Fanny Duberly:

> **No horse is permitted to be destroyed without a special order from Lord Lucan, except in case of glanders, and, I believe, a broken leg. Some horses in our lines have been lying steeped in mud, and in their death agony for three days!**

The French, for all their superior organization, also had their fair share of such absurdities. Charles Mismer, a young French dragoon, recorded:

> **On the days when we went to Kamiesch for fodder we always left several horses en route. Every horse's corpse had its hoof amputated on which a matriculation number was inscribed in order to justify its loss to the Commissariat; because in the middle of all this disaster, routine was still the most important thing. If by accident you forgot to bring back the hoof of an abandoned horse it was 'en route brigadier!' In rain or snow, at the risk of killing one's own horse, it had to be done. I have to say that the dilemma 'hoof or death' more than once drove me to exasperation.**

Eventually it got to the stage where there were literally no horses available to fetch supplies from Balaklava, and the work fell to the men themselves. Colin Frederick Campbell, who had seen the coast of Asia Minor teeming with available horses, but nothing done about it, wrote home:

> **I have seen our men after having come back from the trenches, and having barely time to eat some biscuit and coffee, sent off to Balaclava to bring up rations, warm clothing, blankets, etc. They would return at night after their 14-mile tramp through the mud, and throw themselves down on the floor of their tents as if they were dead, so exhausted, that even if their dinners had been got ready for them, many of them could not have eaten a morsel. Next morning probably a third of them would be in hospital, and the remainder for the trenches the following evening.**

Meanwhile the temperature dropped lower and lower – to the satisfaction of the Russians. Lieutenant-Captain of the Fleet, Pyotr Lesli wrote home:

> **We've got a real Russian winter; there has been such a big snowfall that it comes above the knee; and to add to it, there are frosts at night, though not heavy. There hasn't been such a winter in Sebastopol for a long time. At first we were grumbling that the weather was too warm; but now we don't know how to thank God for such weather. Such weather is very unpleasant for our enemy. Of those who have given themselves up to us there has not been one whose hands or feet haven't been frost-bitten. Our soldiers and sailors are not rejoicing either at the frost, and run around in the snow trying to get warm and saying:– let the Russian winter get its teeth into the English!**

The tsar was said to remark that Lord Raglan might be a very clever general, but that he himself had three generals – January, February and March – any one of whom could beat Raglan's army hollow. Indeed the Allied armies, in particular the British and the Turks, were rapidly disintegrating in the cold. Henry Clifford noted hopelessly that it would be a bold man indeed who dared walk through camp singing 'Cheer Boys Cheer.' When Richard Lluellyn, of the 46th Foot, went to the post office in search of news from home he found:

> **...a ghastly train of sick men from camp...gathered round the building: some had died on the way and being fastened into their saddles were hanging forward in sadly grotesque attitudes. Across them came a regiment of Turks changing quarters, one half carrying the others who were too weak to stand. Out of 1800 of these poor fellows who camped on the hillside 14 days ago, 600 have died and are buried on the hillside and eaten by the dogs who leave their limbs sticking up out of the ground.**

New drafts kept coming out, but old hands like Captain Dallas pitied them, 'I am always sorry to see these miserable drafts arrive, they never live, and look so nice and clean!' Daniel Powell, one of these new arrivals went straight on duty into the snow:

FROSTBITE VICTIMS – WILLIAM YOUNG, HENRY BURLAND AND JOHN CONNERY. (PHOTO BY CUNDALL AND HOWLETT.)

Oh dear me! I think it was the bitterest day as ever I saw after my arrival. Some of the poor fellows who were on fatigue got their ears frost-bitten before they had gone a mile. One poor man had the soles torn from the uppers of his boots, the snow being so deep. For my part, I was one mass of icicles. All my eyebrows, moustachio and the back of my neck was one sheet of ice.

The cavalry in Balaklava had seen suffering, but the experience of the troops at the front was perhaps even worse. Not only did they have to battle to stay alive in camp, but they were still going out digging and guarding trenches. Captain Dallas felt helpless seeing his men's plight without being able to do anything to alleviate their misery:

The Siege goes slowly on. To our unlearned eyes we make no progress but still our accursed trenches have to be occupied. We have (our Division) constantly about 1000 men, I had better call them spectres, sitting 12 hours at a time knee deep in that horrid ditch... Some of our men tell me that they are sometimes 4 or 5 consecutive nights in the trenches! We, the Officers, have to go back 3 nights a week & that with a dry bed to come into & a sufficiency of food, we find quite enough to do.

Many men froze to death and were only discovered by the next shift. Others were bayonetted by the enemy where they had fallen asleep 'fagged out' by their duties. There were incidents of shellshock and suicide. Margaret Goodman, one of Florence Nightingale's nurses at Scutari, was faced with many of these cases:

Several of our younger soldiers became imbecile, and it was believed that this affliction was often caused by fright: not that they were cowards on the field of battle; it was the effect of out-post duty. A young fellow fresh from his own fireside, is taken in his turn by the guard, and left for many hours to pace alone in the gloom three hundred yards in advance of the trench and of his companions; knowing at the same time that he is between them and an enemy whose approach it is difficult to detect until close upon him – as the Russians crawled rather than walked in their grey garments noiselessly over the snow – and whose object was in the first place to despatch him...

Sitting knee deep in mud and snow sometimes for 24-hour stretches more commonly led to horrific cases of frost bite, almost always leading to loss of limbs and often ending in death, as Margaret Goodman described:

The most fearful wounds I witnessed were the frost bites, sufferers from which were generally young lads. The medical men were shocked when the first party of these cases arrived at Scutari. An officer observed, 'It is too hard a fate, that our gallant army, after all they have accomplished, should lie down in ditches to perish in this manner.' Large linseed meal poultices, spread on tow, were placed over the whole foot and ankle, and on being taken off, pieces of decayed flesh, and sometimes toes, were found in them. In one case care was required lest the bones of the leg and foot should drop asunder. Of course, the poor creature thus afflicted died; but at that time he was beyond the severest agony, which is suffered while the flesh is actually rotting. Those who had seen long service affirmed that...the younger

Christmas Day - All that remains of the transport of the Light Division (Captain Henry Clifford).

men...being less disciplined...persisted in lying down in the snow, not resisting, and in some instances even courting death.

The oldest campaigners spoke of those months of night work as having tried their powers of endurance far beyond anything they ever experienced before. They said they would sooner serve six years in the Peninsula War than one month in the Crimea. Later in the campaign the Russians would be rewarded for this severe test of endurance, but despite requests to the British government nothing similar was offered to their British counterparts, much to the annoyance of young officers like Fisher:

I suppose you saw an account in the paper of an Officer in the Russian Army, 23 years old, with 24 years' service, every month in Sebastopol counting a year, better treatment than we get; if the Russians get a year for being inside the town in winter, we ought to have two for living outside without cover.

Many officers had not even stayed to endure the winter. Only days after the battle of Balaklava, Fanny Duberly had noted in her journal: 'Lord George Paget is gone home. Thirty-eight other officers, profiting by his example, have sent in their papers.' For officers who had bought their commissions, euphemistically termed 'Urgent Private Affairs' provided an excuse to get back to England as the situation in the Crimea got steadily more unpleasant. In fact, Paget did not get off so lightly. Snubbed in his London club he returned to the Crimea in the spring. Many of the troops he left behind, however, would not be alive to greet him.

In Sebastopol there was also a stark contrast between the aristocracy and the professionals. While the army had enormous admiration for Totleben and Nakhimov, they were discontented with their aristocratic commander-in-chief, Prince Menshikov. One officer complained:

Commander-in-Chief Prince Menshikov is unfamiliar with everything that is going on in Sebastopol, is the source of all quarrels, intrigues and misunderstandings; all his

free time, and Prince Aleksandr Sergeevich [Menshikov] has much of it, he devotes to inventing what to write to Petersburg. Nobody knows what he is doing, what he is writing, what he receives by way of reply, and what actions he intends to take. Once, the Prince said: 'If my fur hat knew what I was going to do tomorrow, I would throw it into the water immediately.' All this could make sense if the Prince really did something; but months pass with nothing. The despatch of couriers to Petersburg is the sole concern of the Prince. He is loved by no one, and it would be strange to love a man who takes no part in the common deed, and painstakingly tries to say that our troops are not reliable and that with such troops it is impossible to count on success. He never greets the soldiers, has almost never visited the sick and wounded, saying: 'There are so many people looking after them that I am afraid of the proverb, too many cooks spoil the broth!'

The question of who was writing what to whom was also arousing the suspicion of Lord Raglan. In turn, young officers like Fred Dallas were themselves affected:

You will scarcely believe that the mail has been in since Saturday morning, this being Monday night, & except Ld. R's own bag, not a single officer has yet received his letters! The mail has been wandering about & no one knows where or why. The postmaster tells us that every obstacle also has been put in the way of the mails going away from here & it is shrewdly suspected that Ld. Raglan is at the bottom of it as he does not like our accounts getting to England, as soon as his.

Nothing, however, stopped *The Times*' critical accounts getting back to London. The appalling conditions faced by the army and the blatant injustice inherent in its aristocratic structure were laid constantly before the public by William Howard Russell and Thomas Chenery. One of the most scathing reports appeared in *The Times* on 23 December 1854:

...the noblest army ever sent from these shores has been sacrificed to the grossest mismanagement. Incompetence, lethargy, aristocratic hauteur, official indifference, favour, routine, perverseness and stupidity reign, revel and riot in the camp before Sebastopol, in the harbour of Balaklava, in the hospitals of Scutari and how much nearer home we do not venture to say.

Within a short space of time, this sustained criticism would lead to the downfall of the government. On 23 January 1855 John Arthur Roebuck, the Radical MP for Sheffield, proposed a Select Committee to inquire into the condition of the army before Sebastopol. This amounted to a vote of confidence. When the results were read out the government was so soundly beaten that the House of Commons dissolved into nervous laughter. Lord Aberdeen had come to be seen as pro-Russian, and one week later he resigned, to be replaced by Lord Palmerston as Prime Minister of a new government.

On 27 February Tsar Nicholas dismissed Menchikov and replaced him with Prince Gorchakov. The tsar himself died three days later of pneumonia, but Allied hopes of a less belligerent successor were dashed when his son announced, 'I would rather perish than surrender.'

The Allies had thought Sebastopol was doomed, but in three months they had come no closer to taking it. Since the hurricane they had lost thousands of men and had fought for nothing except to stay alive.

THE LANDING PLACE AT BALAKLAVA. (PHOTO BY ROGER FENTON.)

CHAPTER SEVEN

STALEMATE

BY EARLY SPRING, AS the weather and the Allies' morale started to improve, William Howard Russell became more optimistic:

> **If war is a great destroyer, it is also a great creator... The hilltops are adorned with clean wooden huts, the flats have been drained, the watercourses dammed up and deepened, and all this has been done in a few days, by the newly awakened energies of labour.**

THE RAILWAY YARD, BALAKLAVA. (PHOTO BY ROGER FENTON.)

WHILE THE MILITARY ARISTOCRATS WADED THROUGH BUREAUCRACY, MIDDLE CLASS INDUSTRIAL PROFESSIONALS STARTED TO MAKE A DIFFERENCE.

The state of affairs in Balaklava was also getting better:

> **The progress of the railroad is extraordinary. It is already completed out to the entrance of the village of Kadikoi, tomorrow it will have passed through on its way out to the plateau, and on Wednesday it will be, in all probability, used for the transport of a cargo of shot and shell out so far from Balaklava in the intervals of the workmen's labour. The aspect of the town is greatly altered for the better. The wretched hovels in which the Turkish soldiery propagated pestilence and died, have been cleaned out or levelled to the earth, the cesspools and collections of utter abomination in the streets have been filled up, and quicklime has been laid down in the streets and lanes, and around the houses... Indeed the railway, which sweeps right through the main street, very effectually clears away the crowds of stragglers who used to infest the place.**

Neither bureaucracy nor the army had wrought this miraculous improvement. The authors of the change were civilian entrepreneurs. The railway had been conceived very soon after the outbreak of war by Samuel Morton Peto, a prominent railway contractor, and offered to the government at cost price. It was intended to run from the dockside in Balaklava, where supplies could be loaded directly into the wagons, to Kadikoi, and then up to the camps on the plateau

where the Allies were besieging Sebastopol. At first the wagons were drawn by horses or mules, and by stationary steam engines at steep places, although eventually ordinary railway locomotives would run on the tracks.

The railway navvies were regarded as a drunken lot and none of the military authorities knew anything about railways. They would have preferred a new road. However once work started, opinions changed swiftly. Under Chief Engineer James Beatty, the navvies rapidly levelled the remains of the buildings around the harbour and within a few days had actually started laying rails.

Roger Fenton, the pioneering photographer, arrived in March and was struck by the hard work going on:

> **There is great activity with the railway workers; here a stationary engine is being erected to drag bricks up the hill where the road is at present steep, and huts are growing up very fast for the timekeeper and workmen. I found Mr Angel, the Post Master General, who gave me a hearty welcome and promised to give me a hut in a week's time.**

Seven miles of railway were built in only seven weeks and brought huts, medical supplies and belated winter clothing to the base. Fenton persuaded the men he photographed to dress up in the sheepskin coats – ironically now too warm for them. The railway also carried guns and ammunition to the front – and freed those soldiers who had been dragging armaments up themselves. This activity was eagerly observed from the other side by Lieutenant-Captain Pyotr Lesli:

> **We now have two Sebastopols, and there is not much difference between them; the other Sebastopol has even outdone the real Sebastopol, in that, if the newspapers are to be believed, a railway has been built there; but from our heights you cannot see it yet. And how good it will be when we drive them away and the railway and wooden huts will remain in our hands**

The Russians had 'not been yawning either', as Lesli pointed out. In Sebastopol, a careful eye was kept on the Allies' progress. At each bastion an officer was posted to watch the enemy's moves, and report back to Totleben, who then rode through all the batteries of the town, giving orders for what was to be done during

ABOVE: *A HOT DAY IN THE BATTERY* (WILLIAM SIMPSON).
RIGHT: *A HOT NIGHT IN THE BATTERY* (WILLIAM SIMPSON).

the ensuing night. One of the strengths of Sebastopol's earthwork fortifications, as Captain Hodasiewicz observed, was their flexibility:

> **The batteries at Sebastopol were at first nothing but earth, loosely thrown up with the shovel, the embrasures were plastered with moistened clay, but when it was discovered that this was not enough, they were faced with stout wicker work...The batteries were frequently found not to bear upon the required point, or the embrasures were not made so as to enable the guns to be pointed in the right direction. Whenever a discovery of this sort was made the whole was changed during the night. If no changes were required, new and more formidable works were added.**

By swift responses to Allied action and surprising initiatives of his own, Totleben 'brilliantly swindled all the celebrated engineers of Europe'. During the winter neither side had opened a major offensive. However, the French sappers had been digging trenches and tunnels steadily closer and closer to the Flagstaff bastion, one of the major defensive positions covering the town side of Sebastopol. There was little in common between the kind of warfare in which the zouaves were now engaged, and that to which they had been accustomed in Africa, and Colonel Cler described how strange many of them found it to plunge into what they referred to as the 'underground war of moles!':

> **Instead of attacking an enemy they could see, on vast battlefields, where there was room for their intelligence to inform their courage, they were now obliged to burrow, foot by foot, in stony or rocky ground, – or coil themselves up in a hole for twenty-four hours at a time, while watching over the workmen or their works, – and to handle the pick-axe, more often than a musket. Yet this, to them, novel species of fighting – in which an invisible enemy mowed them down with his ceaseless fire, or took advantage of some dark and dismal night, to fall unawares upon the working and covering parties, frequently all benumbed with cold – was never able to depress the elastic spirits of the Zouaves.**

Their spirits may have been up but Totleben had responded with an even more sophisticated network of tunnels and underground quarters. Nikolai Berg described the mines when he went down to visit the defenders of Sebastopol:

> **I went down with an officer, bending over, at first in the half-light, then in complete darkness. When you could**

THE ALLIED CAMP ON THE PLATEAU BEFORE SEBASTOPOL. (PANORAMA BY ROGER FENTON.)

hear that someone was coming towards you, you would shout: keep to the left, or the right, so you wouldn't collide. But it was so narrow that you would always brush against one another. In the end I grew tired and crawled along on my hands and feet. My comrade left me behind and I could only hear his voice: keep to the left, to the right! suddenly, I felt water beneath my hands; it was necessary to stand again. The mine became narrower and narrower. At first I had felt planks and boards along the sides, but then it all came to an end, and there was just a bare earth corridor. The unaccustomed person under these cramped vaults experiences a heavy feeling, something oppressive, suffocating. We went as far as the point in the mine where our gallery meets that of the enemy. Here there is a lamp lit and soldiers are sitting on the floor. I saw the enemy works. Their mines are a bit wider; that is the only difference. They say that when they met us they gave up digging and went away.

The French had got so close that the Russians could hear them cursing. They had then withdrawn into trenches, but were still only 130 yards away from the Flagstaff bastion.

In February the organization of the army outside Sebastopol changed. The French, who had significantly more troops after the winter than the British, divided into two corps. One, the official siege corps, was placed under the command of General Pélissier, a rough diamond who was energetic, ruthless and coarse, and had just arrived from Africa. The other, which was to be an observational corps guarding the rear against an attack from the Russian reserves in the Tchernaya, was placed under General Bosquet.

The French were to continue covering the town, while the English covered the Karabelnaya suburb, protected mainly by the Russian third bastion (known as 'the Redan', or 'big tooth') and more importantly by the Malakoff Tower. However, the British army had been so drastically weakened by the winter that Raglan was only prepared to take on the work of covering the Redan, so the attack against the suburb and the Malakoff devolved on to General Bosquet.

The major initiative of the spring came from the Russians and was to prove fatal to Bosquet's zouaves. It centred on a little hillock known as the Mamelon Vert, which lay about 600 yards in front of the Malakoff Tower. The Mamelon Vert was only weakly defended by the Russians, so it seemed an ideal target for the Allies to capture as a starting point for an approach on the Malakoff. Totleben had foreseen this and the Allies were drawn into a trap. On the night of 22 February, two new redoubts appeared as if from nowhere. Pyotr Alabin, one of the Kamchatka Regiment, took part in this 'exceptionally dangerous enterprise':

In the erection of this redoubt our men were faced with an Egyptian labour: it was raised on stony ground, barely

covered by a thin layer of earth. Practically all the work was carrried out with pick-axes; sparks flew up from our hefty blows on the stony soil, but in spite of this, it was necessary to strike several times with the pick in order to break up a small piece of rock. The soldiers believed in the necessity of this fortification and worked diligently. The night passed successfully. Everyone thought that in the first minutes of dawn the enemy would notice our daring work and would send a whole cloud of lead and iron against it. Not a bit of it.

It was not until well after dawn that Colonel Cler and the zouaves saw the fruits of this Russian daring, 'We were almost stupefied with amazement, when, on the morning of the 23rd, we saw for the first time, right before our eyes, the extent of these works.'

General Canrobert's immediate reaction was to get the 2nd Zouaves and the marines to assault the new redoubts that very night – which was just what Totleben wanted. Even before they went in, Cler realized that this attack was more a question of pride than a realistic offensive:

It appeared that 1,400 resolute men were to pay a visit, and, if we may say so, *leave their cards*, at the enemy's work, – where many of them were certain to perish – for no other purpose in the world, than that of momentarily disquieting the enemy, and giving him to understand that he would not be permitted to remain there, undisturbed.

On the night of 23 February the Russians were continuing their work on the redoubts when the anticipated attack began. Pyotr Alabin noted:

The first to climb over was a staff-officer, the commander of the riflemen, with a long rapier in his hand, but the moment he appeared inside the redoubt he was hoisted up on a bayonet!... Behind him jumped in a young officer, but he barely had time to look around before a nearby soldier welcomed him with a pick-axe round the head. He was laid out flat, the poor wretch!...

In this bloody and futile attack the French lost 200 men. It had been a decisive defeat but the Russians recognized the bravery of their enemy. Baron Osten-Saken, who had taken over the command of the Sebastopol garrison after the death of Kornilov, wrote to Canrobert to assure him that his dead soldiers had been buried with 'the full honours due for their exemplary courage'. Alabin attended this ceremony, which was also watched from the French batteries:

We have now returned from the funeral of those who fell during the nocturnal attack on the redoubt. In one corner of the vast grave lay our soldiers; the remaining space was taken up by the French. Six French officers in oak coffins were lying by a special grave prepared nearby. The funeral prayers for our dead had already been read. A Catholic priest was performing the burial rite. The melancholy sounds of the requiem prayers wrung tears from your heart...

These prayers were soon forgotten, however. Fierce encounters continued every night and one month later Totleben's operation was completed. With similar daring a redoubt appeared on the Mamelon itself, named after Alabin's regiment – the Kamchatka Lunette. The following night the Russians made an even more vicious midnight attack than the previous one, and this time more or less finished the zouaves off. Captain Herbé described it as the Russians' most important sortie since the beginning of the war.

After such carnage it was common for armistices to be declared while both sides collected their wounded and buried their dead. These occasions, in which enmities were momentarily overruled by class etiquette, seemed very peculiar to Henry Clifford:

> **It was a strange and shocking sight. Men talking together, laughing and smoking, who a few minutes before were doing all they could to take each others lives, and who kept turning every now and then an anxious eye to the heap of slain, to see how many yet remained to be carried away, as the removal of the last, would put an end to this unnatural state of things, and the combat of life and death would begin again. The jest and laugh was often interrupted and choked by the passing of the bloody stretcher, in which lay the mangled remains of some poor fellow, who had died the death of a brave soldier.**

Naum Gorbunov, of the Vladimir Regiment, observed one particular curiosity:

ZOUAVES KILLED IN THE ATTACK OF 22 FEBRUARY 1855 (CAPTAIN HENRY CLIFFORD).

> **The French always seemed more sociable than the English. At the demarcation line, the commanders and officers carried on conversations amongst themselves, and in most cases their acquaintance began with the French offering their visiting card... Not because the Russians did not have a similar custom, but rather, because we led such a dirty and hard way of life, and had need of much more vital and essential objects to satisfy our demands, so we, unlike them, did not carry visiting cards.**

During the truce on 23 March, Lieutenant-Colonel Hodge wrote in his diary, there was wry mutual speculation about how the siege was going:

> **The Russian officers chaffed ours, and asked them why they did not take Sebastopol, and whether they passed their time agreeably. Ours said very much so, indeed so much so, they prolonged the siege in consequence.**

The siege was accompanied all this time by vigorous firing on both sides. One assistant surgeon wrote back to his family:

> **As far as imagination filling in the details of a sharp fire of musketry and big guns combined, it is impossible. The booming of the guns, the hissing and whistling of the shot and shell as they travel along on their airy voyage, the popping and pinging of the small arms – these are things that cannot be imagined; and the dread and terrible excitement they inspire are feelings which, happily, you cannot realise.**

The troops had got used to death but this kind of fighting challenged the expectations of men like Lieutenant William Young, who had arrived after the open battles:

> **Last night I stood on top of a hill when it was pitch dark with an Artillery officer looking at the flashes of the guns and the shells flying like flocks of birds through the air and listening to the rattle of musketry. We were saying what wonderful efforts man was making to destroy his fellow man. Really, when you come to look at a town bombarded by night you would think it an awful thing and wonder how anyone could escape; and fellows go down smoking their pipes, talking of their**

Passing the time

The spring weather brought echoes of home, and Fanny Duberly was soon in good spirits again:

> Started on horseback at one o'clock, to attend the 'First Spring Meeting,' the first race of the season. Wonderful, that men who have been starved with cold and hunger, drowned in rain and mud, wounded in action, and torn with sickness, should on the third warm, balmy day start fresh into life like butterflies, and be as eager and fresh for the rare old English sport, as if they were in the ring at Newmarket, or watching the colours coming round 'the corner.'

While the officers were steeplechasing, Captain Dallas noted that the soldiers were having lower-rank fun:

> The men have all sorts of races tomorrow, 'foot', & 'blindfold', & in sacks. An impious Sub. wanted to have a race of General Officers in sacks! These sort of things to the men, are an immensity of good. There is nothing, I am convinced, keeps them from moping and catching fevers &c, like amusing them in some way.

Dallas himself was glad to find civilized English relief when he was off-duty:

> We have got up a cricket club & when not in the trenches play matches, & live luxuriously, in a small way. I cannot describe how pleasant it is out here so far away from home, meeting old cricket antagonists whom one met last time at 'Lords'. By the way, I am going to look up Ewen Macpherson today... We are going to play a Match of Etonians v. Harrovians next week. I think he was at Harrow.

Meanwhile, in the French camp, sport was not the favoured amusement. The talk of the French troops was the zouave theatre at Windmill Camp, to which both officers and soldiers, and frequently even the generals of the neighbouring divisions, used to throng. One of their invented pieces was called *Les Anglais Pour Rire*. Lieutenant William Young paid a visit:

> Where do you think I was a few nights ago? In a Theatre! The zouaves have rigged up a wooden house and made a regular theatre of it, and you never saw devils to act as they are – first rate. I was in the pit which is in the open air, and the band was in a hole in the ground in front of the stage, and used to strike up merrily when the curtain fell. We all gave five or six shillings, or anything you like as the money was for the benefit of the prisoners in Sebastopol. They had dresses, scenery etc as if they were at home, and a Vivandière collected the tin at the door. All the time you could see the shells in the front going about like fun. They played 'Partant pour la Syrie' and 'God Save the Queen' at the reel of the hunt, and we had grand sport.

A day at the races – officers recreate English pastimes

Sometimes performances were interrupted and the next day certain performers would have been 'replaced'. But the show always went on.

The Russians were also amusing themselves. From the trenches the Allied soldiers could see ladies in Sebastopol flying kites, or dancing at parties. Even on the fortifications they had quite elaborate entertainment, as one artillery officer, Ershov, described:

> On the 6th bastion, there was a grand piano...and on some days there would be musical evenings here. The violin and clarinet would be brought from the 4th bastion, and the flute from the 5th. At first, everything would usually go formally, as you would expect; even classical music would be heard all the way through with attention; but, little by little, unnoticeably, suddenly a transition would somehow be made to some sort of mournful national melody. Once, at such an evening, they organised a masked ball. One handsome young officer was dressed in a lady's gown and sung a song very effectively to an instrumental accompaniment.

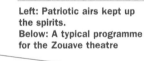

Left: Patriotic airs kept up the spirits.
Below: A typical programme for the Zouave theatre

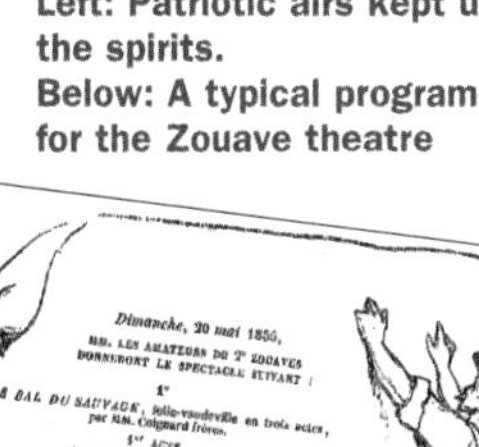

Dimanche, 20 mai 1855,
MM. LES AMATEURS DU 2e ZOUAVES
DONNERONT LE SPECTACLE SUIVANT :
1°
LE BAL DU SAUVAGE, folie-vaudeville en trois actes, par MM. Coignard frères.
1er ACTE.
2e ACTE.
3e ACTE.
LE BAL DU SAUVAGE.
2°
INTERMÈDE COMIQUE.
3°
LES FUREURS DE L'AMOUR, tragédie burlesque en un acte.
4°
INTERMÈDE COMIQUE.
5°
INTERMÈDE COMIQUE,
chanté par un sergent anglais.
ORDRE !
Les Fureurs de l'amour. — Le Bal du Sauvage.

> **horses, of balls at home and one thing or another with an occasional 'Look out for that shell!' or 'By Jingo, that was a close shave!' and that is all about it.**

Tolstoy, in his *Sebastopol Sketches*, describes the effect that the firing was having inside the town:

> **The houses on both sides of the street beyond this barricade are uninhabited; there are no hanging signs, the doorways are boarded up, the windows have been shattered, in one place the corner of a wall has been removed, in another a roof has been smashed in. These buildings look like old soldiers who have experienced every kind of woe and affliction, and they seem to eye you with pride and a certain contempt. Along the way you stumble over cannonballs that lie strewn about in the road here and there, and lose your footing in the water-filled craters dug by shells in the stony soil... every once in a while you encounter a woman or a child – this time, however, it is not a woman in a bonnet but a sailor's wife in an old winter jacket and soldier's boots.**

One such woman trudging the streets in soldier's boots was Ekaterina Bakunina. She was horrified by some of the scenes she encountered:

> **What was awful was to see wounded children, how they, poor little things, were in torment and suffered. There was a boy of about seven with us, who had a broken leg; there was even a little girl who had not been weaned, whose mother was killed while she was feeding her. Another woman was also still nursing her child and took on feeding our wounded little mite, but the child soon died. Lord, how awful and painful all this was!...**

THE DEFENDERS OF SEBASTOPOL (VASILI TIMM).

In Sebastopol enemy bullets which had been collected could be handed in to the Admiralty in return for money. This led to the kind of strange incident that Ershov, an artillery officer, observed:

> **I was struck by the grateful appearance of one boy aged about twelve, who had dragged in four pounds of bullets he had collected in a sack. I began to question him and found out that he was the son of a night-watchman who had been killed by a cannon-ball in the first bombardment on 17 October, that his mother was ill and bed-ridden, and his ten-year old sister was badly injured by a rock when a bomb exploded a week ago and was now bed-ridden too, and finally that, although the Sovereign, as he called him, sent them money through the commanders, this money was not enough for them and that was why he decided to make some more by collecting cannonballs...**
>
> **'Aren't you afraid you'll be killed?' I asked him, since they collect them where most of the shells fall.**
>
> **'No, I'm not afraid,' he replied, with a completely calm, childishly simple-hearted look. 'I'd even go right to the guns; truly, I'm not afraid!' he added.**
>
> **'Yes, and does your mother let you?'**
>
> **'She doesn't know; I don't tell her...'**

In fact, the construction of the Kamchatka Lunette had turned the tables on the Allies and it was decided that no more attacks could be made on the Russian defences until they had been subjected to another heavy bombardment – which would hopefully be more successful than the first one in October.

The major observation point for watching the bombardment of Sebastopol was Cathcart's Hill, named after the general who had been buried there following the battle of Inkerman. Mary Seacole, who had now set herself up as a sutler, selling food and drink to the army at a place she called the British Hotel, was one of the spectators there:

> **I was as assiduous as I could be in my attendance at Cathcart's Hill. I could judge of its severity by the long trains of wounded which passed the British Hotel. I had a stretcher laid near the door, and very often a poor fellow was laid upon it, outwearied by the terrible conveyance from the front.**

'TELL ANNIE THERE ARE TWO RUSSIAN BOYS HERE WHO WOULD BOTH LIKE TO COME TO ENGLAND. ALMA AND INKERMAN SUCH ARE THEIR NAMES... THEY WENT OUT NUTTING LAST AUTUMN AND WERE TAKEN. THEY CRIED SADLY BUT NOW THEY WOULD CRY TO GO BACK.' ROGER FENTON

The bombardment began on 9 April and at first it was difficult to tell who had the upper hand. The Allied fire was heavier, but the Russians, with characteristic energy, repaired the damage with unceasing effort. Naum Gorbunov was in front of the Redan (third bastion):

> **There was a real iron cloud above, – it simply became dark from the mass of shells flying over our heads. In the beginning the reply from our side was rapid, then weaker, and finally by evening quite sparse, since on the 3rd bastion practically all our guns were either hit or overturned, the gun-crews beaten and wounded.**
>
> **All night there was a high pressure of work to repair the parapets from their foundations, to place the guns and repair them, and by the morning the 3rd bastion appeared before the enemy as though nothing had happened... It was the same at the other bastions.**

Colonel Charles Windham had been frustrated by what he saw as the absurdity of the first bombardment. Yet again, he could not believe that the Allies were not getting on with an attack:

> **How true it is that 'War' is usually a series of mistakes. The conduct of the Allies, since we have arrived in this country, has been one continued piece of blundering stupidity; and our opening our batteries on Monday last was, in my opinion, quite unnecessary. We have now fired upon the place for several days, have lost many hundreds of men, and, unless we follow it up with bloody assaults at different places, we shall never take it; and, should we lose a large amount of men in doing so (which is more than probable), we shall have thrown away more life and more money, for a useless object, than was ever done before.**

Over the next ten days the Allies fired almost twice as many rounds as the Russians, and the casualties in Sebastopol far exceeded those of the Allies. But since the Russians continued to repair the damage to their defences each night, no permanent breach was made in their lines and once again the bombardment fizzled out. Lieutenant-Captain Lesli was as puzzled as Windham:

> **No one can understand what their aim was in opening up another bombardment; it seems that experience has shown that it is not all that easy to make our batteries fall silent, and if they want, having knocked out our batteries, to go for a storming, then they've a long wait ahead.**

The last thing the troops wanted was an even longer wait. Sebastopol had been under siege for seven months and still no end was in sight. The main supply road from the interior remained open and the Russians' source of manpower and supplies seemed to be inexhaustible. Morale among the Allied troops was low. Boredom was setting in and there was a feeling that anything, any action, would be better than this interminable game of cat and mouse. In a letter home, Lieutenant William Young wrote:

> **I do not know when we are to get out of this place or take Sebastopol. I am heartily sick of the trenches, new batteries, new mortars and I don't know what else, and the Russians as bad if not worse than ever. There is no honour or glory to be got in the trenches, where you sit**

View of the bombardment of Sebastopol including:
3. Malakoff Tower 4. Quarries 5. Redan
6. Karabelnaya Suburb 16. Fort St. Nicholas (dockyard)

and smoke your pipe and maybe get shot by a Sharpshooter, and if the Russians do come and are licked and driven out – why, that is what you are sent there for! If, on the other hand, you get licked (which we never did yet) you get blamed by everyone, and if you get killed about it is 'Poor so-and-so got killed or wounded', as the case may be, and maybe some fellow would say, 'Confound the Lubber for getting shot – that shortens the roster.' I would ten thousand times sooner take the field and march about with my knapsack on my back, and fight a couple of decent battles in the field, than go shave your head with a miss twice a week and no good done by it, for I say Sebastopol never will be taken until invested, and where are the men to do that?

Ironically, although there were not enough men to invest the town, there were now plenty of visitors in the Crimea. Mary Seacole's British Hotel, located at Spring Hill, two miles from the port of Balaklava, soon became a familiar landmark and the scene of many social gatherings. Using her own resources she had managed to organize an efficient establishment within months, to procure all the necessary provisions and stores, cook nutritious meals, and make refreshing drinks, in addition to dispensing much needed medicines. Her canteen, which was also popular with the ordinary soldier, provided clean and wholesome food, while in the main building officers tried to recreate the atmosphere of an exclusive London club. Seacole wrote:

After (the) unsuccessful bombardment, it seemed to us that there was a sudden lull in the progress of the siege; and other things began to interest us. There were several new arrivals to talk over. Miss Nightingale came to supervise the Balaclava hospitals, and, before long, she had practical experience of Crimean fever. After her, came...the great high priest of the mysteries of cookery, Mons. Alexis Soyer. He was often at Spring Hill, with the most smiling of faces and in the most gorgeous of irregular uniforms, and never failed to praise my soups and dainties.

Having achieved certain improvements in Scutari, Florence Nightingale now saw it as her duty to visit the Crimea, although she had no real authority there, to inspect the hospitals and introduce the new arrangements for laundries and kitchens which had been so successful at base. For a few days she moved about the camps and was received with great enthusiasm by the soldiers, to whom she was now a legend. She visited hospitals, planned nurses' duties, distributed gifts, discussed building new huts and, with Soyer planned new kitchens.

Florence Nightingale's visit was not universally welcome. Dr John Hall was touchy about further inspections. Elizabeth Davis, who already suspected she was being monitored by Nightingale's spies, greeted her with 'I should have as soon expected to see the Queen here as you.' Neither she nor Dr Hall wanted Nightingale exerting her influence over nurses and army organization in Balaklava.

While she was there Nightingale herself came down with 'Crimean Fever,' and nearly collapsed. She had to be nursed for two weeks in a hut near Balaklava, after which she refused to be shipped home and insisted on going back to Scutari. Alexis Soyer remained in the Crimea and introduced reforms to the Allied diet and cooking arrangements.

There were also other less productive visitors. Well-to-do relatives, friends and the plain curious came out in large numbers from England (and even America), some of them on tours advertised by the shipping companies. Among them were acquaintances of Fred Dallas:

> **We have a good many 'amateurs' out here now, one or two acquaintances of mine amongst them. They seem to think it great fun, which of course it is to anyone who comes now in the fine weather, with the immense advantage over the 'professionals' of being able to go away whenever they like. We are all delighted to see them & show them everything. Part of the programme is to go down into the trenches at night & if a shot will only come at the right time they are quite delighted & we always tell them that it went quite close to them, which completely satisfies them & they wisely go home again. Altogether I cannot fancy a pleasanter trip for a man with many acquaintances in the army than a week or two here: everybody only too delighted to see & entertain them & just 'roughing it' enough to be amusing. They do not find champagne at dinner & a bed in a tent in this weather at all disagreeable.**

In one absurd situation a tourist was even given a medal for good conduct in the field. More often, tourists were simply a nuisance. After French complaints, orders were given prohibiting English tourists from wandering about in the trenches. Roger Fenton had special privileges:

> **In the battery I was very comfortable, for the wall sheltered me, only it struck me as a queer sensation to hear the balls thumping into the earth against which one was leaning. Others came topping the ramparts and whistling overhead. I have a pass for the trenches, so was not turned out or put under arrest.**

Men like Harry Blishen, who had been made a Corporal in April, needed no pass to spend days at the trenches. They would happily have traded places with their curious compatriots:

> **I had just returned from the trenches, tired and almost worn out by incessant fatiques, and shocked at the awful spectacles of mutilated human flesh – for there had been three or four fellows literally blown to atoms that day – when a person placed your kind and welcome letter in my hand...until I came into this country, I used to ridicule any person that would designate my native**

Advance Trench (Henry Clifford).

land as 'Happy Old England;' but now I fully appreciate the value of my native land, and have quite altered my mind as regards making [it] my resting place...

The French dispatched regiment after regiment of reinforcements to the Crimea in numbers that the British could not match. Emperor Napoleon III had set his heart on rewarding the army that had placed him on the throne with a great and glorious victory. He was adamant that the French tricolour would fly from the Malakoff Tower before too long!

The British army, unlike the French, did not have the manpower and, as a maritime nation, Britain instead sought ways to exploit the enemy's weaknesses away from the field of battle. From the beginning of the war the navy had seen the Sea of Azov as the key to Russia's hold in the Crimea. If the Allies could sieze control of this sea at Kertch, they would sever the logistics line into Sebastopol. Only with Sebastopol deprived of munitions and food supplies could the siege tactics preferred by the French be guaranteed success.

General Canrobert was persuaded to join forces with the British despite his Emperor's short-sighted preference for a concentration of military might in the Crimean theatre, and an Anglo-French amphibious force was formed. It was the kind of action for which the troops had been waiting. On 5 May, Roger Fenton wrote to his wife:

On our return just before dinner Sir George Brown sent for Hallewell and told him something that made him come home dancing and kicking and emptying a tumbler of champagne, when he grew able to inform us that an expedition was to start off the next day [3 May] by sea somewhere or other,and that he had been chosen to go with it... That night and this morning there has been such a scene of packing and rejoicing among those chosen for the expedition, and sulking and trying to look as if they did not care among those going to stay here, that you would have thought they were all schoolboys. No one knows where they are going.

Just one week before the expedition was to set sail, the electric telegraph from Varna was completed, connecting British and French headquarters to the outside world. What should have been another technological triumph for the Allies, placing their military operations in the modern world of global communications, turned out to be the conduit for unwelcome interference in their strategy on the ground. It gave Emperor Napoleon III, sitting far away in Paris, the opportunity to bombard his commander-in-chief with new and contrary instructions.

Lieutenant Robert Biddulph was on board the transport ship *Magnet*, headed for Kertch:

We steamed away all night, and the next day until sunset, when we became enveloped in a dense fog. We were obliged to go very slowly, all the vessels firing guns to keep company; we were then about 50 miles from Kertch. The fog was so thick we could not see the steamer that was towing us; however it cleared off about midnight, and we made ready for disembarking early in the morning. About 9.0 a.m. the next morning, 5th May, being about 20 miles from Kertch, and just about 4 miles from the entrance to the Straits, land visible on both sides, we saw the French squadron separate from us, and wear round and steam away, at the same time a signal was shown for captains of

ABOVE: THE FRENCH BASE AT KAMIESCH.
(PHOTO BY JAMES ROBERTSON.)
LEFT: A QUIET DAY IN THE MORTAR BATTERY.
(PHOTO BY ROGER FENTON.)

steamers to go on board the flag-ship. We remained lying-to until mid-day, when we also turned round and steamed back as hard as we could. The captain of the Sidon hung out a blackboard to us, having chalked on it the word 'Sold'. Imagine our rage and horror at having been made fools of in this absurd way.

The first Kertch expedition, under the command of Sir George Brown and consisting of French, British and Turkish troops, was within two hours of its destination when it was aborted. General Canrobert had received a telegram from his emperor ordering him to recall the French transports from the Kertch expedition. Although Napoleon III had no authority over the British fleet, it was obviously impossible for them to continue alone.

Canrobert was now being bombarded with almost hourly telegraphic instructions from Emperor Napoleon. On 16 May, debilitated by his own sense of inaction, Canrobert resigned and asked to be demoted to the command of his old division. He was succeeded by Pélissier, who was known to refer to himself as 'that bastard Pélissier'. But he was an ardent supporter of Lord Raglan, and quickly moved to win favour with the British command. Within a week, in defiance of Emperor Napoleon's veto, Pélissier gave the order for the Kertch operation to be resumed.

CHAPTER EIGHT

HOT NIGHTS IN THE BATTERIES

WILLIAM HOWARD RUSSELL EXPRESSED the annoyance of all the British troops when he wrote of the failed expedition to Kertch:

> **Kertch is said to have been the place where Caesar penned his pithy despatch – 'Veni! Vidi! Vici!' We may certainly say we came, and saw, but we cannot complete the sentence.**

THE BURNING OF THE GOVERNMENT BUILDINGS AT KERTCH
(WILLIAM SIMPSON).

When the second Kertch expedition set sail on 22 May 1855, Raglan and General Pélissier were intent on completing the sentence. This time the amphibious operation went without a hitch. A Russian officer, Schultz, passing through Taman on the Sea of Azov on his way to join his regiment in Sebastopol, found himself with a ringside seat as the Allied troops landed on 24 May:

> **As we approached the shore, our eyes were met by a terrifying spectacle of war: on the opposite side at Burun-Kamiesch in the Straits of Kertch stood the entire enemy fleet (more than 60 ships), and they were pelting the coast with bombs. At the same time, troops were**

> **disembarking, forming into columns and heading off to the right in the direction of the Pavlovsk battery. We were soon astonished by an incredible sight: as the enemy approached, the entire battery, suddenly, without a shot being fired, flew into the air. Guns dropped from the steep shore over the precipice. A huge, dense cloud of smoke covered the entire shore, all the way to Kertch itself, and the whole length of it was enveloped in flames, engulfing all the houses, huts, and so on, and concealing the enemy's further movements from our eyes.**

Roger Fenton, the photographer, had accompanied the expedition in the spirit of a jaunt, leaving behind his cumbersome photographic equipment. He was on board the steamer *Bahiana*, from which he could see what the thick smoke had hidden from the Russian officer:

> **What a sight! In the morning, a beautiful beach covered with long rough grass and wild flowers, two or three fishing boats with their nets, a couple of stone cottages with thatched roofs, and a low sandy plain stretching to a ridge of high ground behind, had formed the whole of the picture. Now, the beach was strewn with baggage of every description, horses were splashing through the water to the shore, men dressed in every kind of garment that was ever worn, were walking about, scrambling, swearing, shouting and laughing – a vast deal of the latter. Servants were keeping guard over their masters' baggage horses. My bag and bed were thrown on the shore; I sat down on them and began to calculate my chances of getting any further.**

The Allies had landed. On the opposite shore at Taman, the Russian officer noted what he saw and heard:

> **One battery in Kertch and another in Yenikale opened fire on the enemy troops as they landed, but they soon ceased firing and the enemy entered the town... The alarm was terrible. The inhabitants ran to the hills, and many arrived in boats on our side of the shore... In the mountains to the left of us, near Burun-Kamiesch, you could make out the fires where our troops were bivouacked. They were conducting the defence of Kertch from there. Since Yenikale had held out until the evening, we imagined that our troops would arrive from Feodosia and would be attacking the enemy from dry land at any moment. We spent the whole night in great excitement in expectation of this. Suddenly in the early hours of 25 May, a second explosion shook the air to such a degree that even in Taman the glass in the windows rattled and shattered. This was the powder cellars in Yenikale exploding – the sign that our troops were retreating and that the Sea of Azov was in the hands of the enemy.**

The Sea of Azov was indeed in the hands of the enemy. This time, like Caesar, the Allies had conquered, with only one fatality on the British side.

Lieutenant Biddulph, who had been so dejected after the first Kertch expedition had been recalled, was among those who now entered the town on the morning of 25 May:

> **We arrived at Kertch about 8 o'clock. We found there a large foundry and bullet factory (Minié and round bullets, the latter were made with machinery exactly the same as we use at Woolwich); we destroyed the machinery and burnt the buildings. When we got into the town we found that none of the inhabitants had left, consequently sentries were placed on all the houses and no plundering allowed. The inhabitants all thronged the streets to gaze at us, and were very civil giving wine etc. to all who wanted it; the fact being that they were in a horrid fright for fear of their houses being sacked.**

Biddulph passed quickly through the town and marched on to Yenikale, whose inhabitants had all fled. Roger Fenton, at first impressed by the beauty of the coastal road, after the 'bare barren red earth of the camp before Sebastopol', was also on his way to Yenikale when he was brought up short:

> **On each side and in front as far as we could see, the country was covered with stragglers, Turkish and French, but principally the latter, intent on plunder. We could see the French rushing through the plantations into the houses and coming out again laden with fowls, geese, looking-glasses, chairs, ladies' dresses and everything useful or useless that they could lay their**

hands on. As they got the contents of wine casks they got more outrageous, discharging their muskets right and left at fowls, pigs and birds...

The army halted on some heights on the other side of which was said to be the town of Yenikale, though nothing was to be seen of it from where we were except some Tartar cottages, whose inhabitants had to look on quietly while the soldiers – French, Turks and English – went in and helped themselves to everything they wanted.

The honour of victory had been tarnished by rampant looting and pillaging, by no means limited to the French and Turks. William Howard Russell never imagined he would witness such scenes of destruction when he had intoned Ceasar's heroic words, just weeks before. In a despatch from Kertch on 28 May, Russell spared no details of the barbaric and cruel behaviour of the Turks, noted in many contemporary accounts, but it was something else that really offended: the wanton destruction by representatives of 'civilized' nations, of a unique collection of monuments housed in the museum at Kertch:

On coming close to the building, it is observed that the doors have been forced open, and that some of the ancient Greek marbles and tablets which stood against the walls outside have been overturned. On the white panel of the door some indignant Frenchman or Russian has written in pencil the following admonition, which was only too much needed, whoever were the perpetrators of the ruin within:-

En entrant dans cette temple, où repose les (souvenirs?) d'un siècle passé, j'ai reconnu les traces d'une invasion des Vandales. Hélas! Français ou Anglais, faites la guerre à la (posterité?), mais ne la faites pas à l'histoire. Si vous avez la prétention d'être nations civilisés, ne faites pas la guerre des barbares!

[Coming into the temple, where the relics of a bygone century lie, I found the traces of an invasion by Vandals. Alas! Frenchmen and Englishmen, make war for posterity, but do not make war on history. If you aspire to being civilised nations, do not make war like barbarians!]

Most shaming of all, it transpired that the looters included soldiers in the British army. The flower of civilization was behaving like barbarians! At the very time that Lord Elgin was actively promoting the idea of British custodianship of classical antiquities in the British Museum, his fellow-countrymen in Kertch, ancient capital of the Bosporan kingdom, were behaving like vandals. Russell continued:

The floor of the museum is covered for several inches in depth with the débris of broken glass, of vases, urns, statuary, the precious dust of their contents, and charred bits of wood and bone, mingled with the fresh splinters of the shelves, desks, and cases in which they had been preserved. Not a single bit of anything that could be broken or burnt any smaller had been exempt from reduction by hammer or fire.

After the war, when classical scholars protested, they were informed that the British consul's wife had bought a number of items of Greek jewellery, coins and architectural fragments from local dealers during her stay in Kertch; when war had been declared she had shipped her collection back to London as a donation to the British Museum. Small consolation!

News of the success of the Allied operation in the Sea of Azov had travelled fast. Inside Sebastopol, Lieutenant-Captain of the Fleet, Pyotr Lesli, was quick to spell out the consequences for the Russians, in a letter home dated 29 May 1855:

Yesterday we received some bad news: it seems the French have taken Kertch. This is a most unpleasant thing because then, having cleaned up in the Straits of Kertch, they will have free passage through the Sea of Azov, and as a result can reach Berdiansk, where, according to recent letters sent to our officers, 2,000,000 quarters of wheat have been prepared [a quarter was equivalent to 2.10 litres dry measure]. Of course, this wealth will not get into the hands of the enemy; either they will manage to take it out or they will order it to be burnt. Besides this, the enemy can make their way to Taganrog or to Rostov; from there it is not far to the Lugansky works, from where we get all our

ABOVE: *THE DISEMBARKATION OF THE ALLIED TROOPS AT KERTCH* (WILLIAM SIMPSON).
LEFT: *KERTCH - THE RUSSIANS FLEE* (MAX BEEGER AND GUÉRARD).

shells at the moment; having taken control of the Arabat spit, they have stopped communication with the eastern region of the Crimea from Russia.

For the Allies, the strategic advantage of capturing Kertch was indisputable. By taking the town of Yenikale on the other side of the straits, their command of the Sea of Azov was complete. Russian logistics depended entirely on the use of boats to link Rostov and the Don basin with the Crimea, on the forage depots around the sea, on the fisheries, and on the flour mills of Kertch. What was not destroyed by the enemy, the Russians destroyed themselves. William Howard Russell could see no fun in that:

Off Yenikale, 11th June 1855

The mode of defence adopted by the Russians has left one nothing to write about. Corn ricks blazing, batteries and forts blown up, and stores and magazines gutted and burnt, offer but little variety of detail. We have inflicted great ruin on the enemy, but they have emulated our best efforts in destroying their own settlements. Our haste to attack has not exceeded their precipitation to retreat.

Despite the Allied victory at Kertch, Russell was itching to get back to camp. Sebastopol was the place for true heroics, and true heroics made better copy.

With morale high among the Allied troops, plans were now underway to capitalize on the advantage gained at Kertch. Now that Sebastopol was cut off from its main supply route, it was just a matter of time before the Russians would be forced out. The Allied commanders set to work to achieve that end. The key to Sebastopol was the Malakoff Tower, protecting the Karabelnaya suburb and the dockyard. Once that had fallen, the Redan and the rest of Sebastopol would follow.

Between the Redan and the British positions some diggings known as the 'Quarries' had been fortified by the Russians and the foreground peppered with fougasses, the Crimean predecessor of the land mine. The Quarries gave the Russians a vantage point from which to harass the British trenches and batteries, as well as serving as a buffer to the Redan. Between the Quarries and the Mamelon, which the Russians had siezed under the very eyes of the French, the Russians had an effective defence for the Redan and the Malakoff. They were putting all their efforts into fortifying this area. This had been evident as early as 14 May 1855, when Major Colin Frederick Campbell of the 46th had written to his brother Archibald in England:

> **The mass of the batteries that they are now building do not command the town, but the land between the Malakhoff Tower and the harbour. A great part of the defences round and about the Flagstaff and Garden batteries is in ruins, yet there are very few men employed in repairing them; whilst on the north side men are working in tens of thousands; it really resembles an ant-hill.**

By the end of May, Generals Raglan and Pélissier had agreed to combine forces to capture the Quarries and the Mamelon Vert as a first step toward the grand assault on Sebastopol itself. The prelude to the assault was another vigorous bombardment of the town. Pyotr Alabin was sitting with some fellow Russian officers some distance from Sebastopol when the bombardment began:

> **First smoke rises from the mortar guns in an enormous ring, next it bursts in a huge puff from a siege gun, then it twists slowly upwards in a beautiful spiral, it issues from the fiery-smoky column which forms when a rocket falls, and the sky is scattered with the traces of exploded bombs, like white roses, and draped with light clouds of powder smoke, swiftly blown away into the distance...**
>
> **But suddenly with horror and a trembling in the heart we noticed that the Allied fire against the left half of our line of defence had almost completely stopped, and instead rifle shots were pouring out furiously.**

Alabin knew what that signalled – an enemy assault. Lieutenant William Young of the 49th Foot, who had been bored witless by the general inaction before Sebastopol two months earlier, had at last got what he wanted. In a letter home dated 8 June 1855, he wrote:

> **Well, yesterday about 2 o'clock we heard that 200 of our men were to take the pits in front of the Redan, and so we ordered our dinners as we had to fall in at 4 o'clock. At the same time the French were to storm the Mamelon and the Round Tower. Well, down we went. Our party was divided into 4 divisions, one of which I had given me.**

Council of War between Lord Raglan, Omar Pasha and General Pélissier. (photo by Roger Fenton.)

Roger Fenton was drinking claret with his friends of the 88th in Captain Corbett's tent when they too received orders to be ready at four o'clock:

> **It was nearly four and there was no time to get dinner, so each one snatched up what he could. I made Edmund take something, and did my best to see that all should go out in a fit state of body to encounter fatigue.**
>
> **Corbett said when we were alone, 'Now Roger, my boy, we could not breakfast with you today, but if we come out all right Edmund and I will brush you up tomorrow at six, and you shall take our likenesses.' He ordered dinner to be got ready for me; I was too anxious to wait for it, so took part of an omelette that was ready and prepared to march a little way with them...**

Roger Fenton never did photograph Corbett. Of his drinking companions of the previous night, three were killed outright, including Corbett who was shot through the head while leading up the reserve; Edmund Maynard and one other were badly wounded. Lieutenant Young, meanwhile, finished the letter he had begun on 8 June two days later from his hospital bed, recovering from a bayonet wound to the knee:

> **It was the first time I had ever been under fire without a trench in front of me. There we were right under the guns of the Redan that were blazing grape and canister at us like mad, infernal machines exploding under our feet, round shot, bullets, shells and everything you can think of whistling through us.**
>
> **I never once thought of being killed or wounded and paid no more attention to the bullets than if they had been flies. The excitement and desire to get forward was all one thought of. But on our right where the French stormed the Mamelon was the sight: from one end of the Quarries to the very Mamelon was one sheet of fire and a continual rattle of musketry. The French were beaten back at first but then up came their reserves etc., drums and bugles playing a rub-a-dub-dub you could hear a mile off, and they actually walked through the Mamelon. Not content with that, they must needs go on to attack the Malakoff or Round Tower, and then after a desperate fight they were driven back. However, they are now in the Mamelon and have turned Master Ruskie's guns against himself, besides which they have taken some redoubts on the north side, and 60 guns and 400 prisoners, but bear in mind they had 30,000 men attacking that night and we had only 400 men and we took the Quarries splendidly. Where we would send 1,200 men the French would send 5,000 and lose a good lot of them. The sight of a red coat and a good British 'Hurrah' has a most wholesome effect on Ruski.**

The Quarries were taken, but Lieutenant Young and his fellow soldiers would never again boast of how few British compared to Frenchmen it took to hold a position. In the months leading up to the final crescendo, the British army command would allocate pitifully few troops to carry out the assaults opposite their positions, with tragic consequences for the brave men who attempted them.

Despite the enthusiasm of Lieutenant Young, happy to be in action at last, the operation had left much to be desired in the planning and execution. Orders had been garbled and sometimes contradictory, reserves had been too few and too distant, the proportion of experienced Crimean soldiers was very low and the percentage of officers killed was higher than ever before. The Quarries had been fought for and won, but it could all so easily have ended in disaster. A ripple of optimism went through the Allied camp, and in the general mood of elation, the valuable lessons to be learnt were overlooked.

For the Russians, it had been a terrible blow. At the truce for burying the dead two days later, Colin Frederick Campbell was struck by:

> **...how much worse the Russians looked than they did on March 22. This time they looked both ill-fed and overworked; even the officers looked so. Many of the officers were quite boys, and looked very sad and downcast; the older ones tried to look cheerful, and were liberal with their cigars to us.**

The Russians had fought tenaciously and lost heavily, but although they had still managed to repair their defences during the short night, they had not managed to replenish their batteries with ammunition. The

ENTENTE CORDIALE. (PHOTO BY ROGER FENTON.)

Allied assault on Kertch was beginning to reap benefits. Lieutenant-Captain of the Fleet, Pyotr Lesli, wrote to his family from Sebastopol:

> **The saddest thing of all was that to every one of our shots, they would answer with ten. Our factories could not keep up with manufacturing the amount of ammunition that we required in order to do at least some harm to the enemy; and moreover, transport on carts was much more cumbersome than by steamship which is the method the Allies used to bring them everything.**

The Allied command set to work on the next stage in the plan to capture the key to Sebastopol – this was the Malakoff Tower. A French assault on the Malakoff was planned to coincide with a British attack on the Redan; being opposite the British positions, the Redan presented the British army with a challenge which honour dictated could not be ignored – after so long, the British were not going to stand by as the French collected all the military plaudits for the fall of Sebastopol. But, to capture the Redan without the Malakoff was a futile waste of lives – it simply could not be held alone. For the assault on the Redan to succeed, the Malakoff had to be in French hands, by which time, however, such an assault would be redundant.

The Redan bristled with guns, sometimes in two tiers, behind embrasures protected by rope mantelets which shielded the gunners from rifle fire. A wide road led up towards it, concealing a battery in which troops could be collected and rushed forward to defend it. About fifty yards in front of the ditch a rampart had been made of brush and branches to impede the advance of enemy troops. It was many feet high and several more deep.

The simultaneous assault on the Malakoff and the Redan was to commence at 8am after a heavy bombardment against the Russian defences. The date was to be 18 June, the fortieth anniversary of the battle of Waterloo. It was hoped that the success of the coming offensive would cancel out any uncomfortable memories which cast a shadow over the Anglo-French alliance in the Crimea. Perhaps this was tempting fate too far, since the Russians were also well aware of the significance of this date.

Lieutenant-Captain Pyotr Lesli was stationed in a battery which made up the forward façade of the Malakoff Tower. The bombardment which had commenced the previous day kept them very busy:

> **Our work was terrible. At least 2000 men crowded into that small space to dig up earth to remake what had been destroyed by the bombardment during the day, and throughout this time, there was literally not a minute when a shot was not being fired... I don't remember any of the preceding bombardments having been even a little bit like this one. This time it was pure hell. It was clear that they had prepared themselves for something out of the ordinary.**

'...THAT BASTARD PÉLISSIER'. (PHOTO BY ROGER FENTON.)

Many Russians, beleaguered inside Sebastopol, found their domestic arrangements profoundly altered after that night. One inhabitant of the town wrote to his relatives, about his newly reduced circumstances, almost a month later:

> **My silence has probably led you to imagine that I am too lazy to write to you; but it has come about not as a result of laziness, but from circumstances entirely beyond my control, namely my sudden move from my usual abode to one underground, or, to be more precise, to a cellar... In mid-June, two bombs fell on my house, one in the kitchen, the other in the pantry, and they destroyed everything there down to the foundations... After that it was no longer possible nor wise to remain in the house...**
>
> **Allow me to describe my underground dwelling. It is a cellar, dug into a natural cliff, without windows and with one door; my improvised furniture consists of a small, upturned empty barrel with two wooden handles, which serves me for a chair; another barrel, a bit larger, with a wooden board across it, takes the place of a table; my ink-well is a broken cup and my bed consists of some hay laid out on the floor with a covering of sacking.**

From his position inside the Malakoff Tower, Lieutenant-Captain Lesli witnessed what the Allies had been preparing themselves for:

> **Finally, before dawn, from our former Kamchatsky Redoubt [Mamelon Vert], one after another three rockets were launched like a cascade – a spectacular sight – and then a few moments later rifle crossfire belted out on the left flank of our tower. At first, you could not see a thing, but then, as the smoke cleared, we saw large enemy columns advancing on the first and second bastions. But our men did not miss a trick over there and opened fire on the enemy with bullets and grape-shot, and forced their retreat... Believe me my friends, in comparison to a bombardment, an assault is a jolly affair, or**

COLLECTING THE DEAD (CAPTAIN HENRY CLIFFORD).

at least an interesting one, and more than once we all burst into laughter when a column of French, cheerfully advancing, suddenly turned around like rabbits and made a run for the ravine... It is impossible to calculate exactly how great were the losses of the French and the English, but they must have been enormous to judge by the number of dead bodies in front of our fortifications. And how many did they remove during the night before the armistice, and how many wounded?

It had all gone horribly wrong. Allied losses that day were enormous, a futile waste of life. An assistant surgeon with the Rifle Brigade wrote to his family in Edinburgh that very evening:

This has been a sad anniversary of the great victory which restored to Europe the blessings of a long peace. The Allied armies met with a reverse to-day as disastrous as it was unexpected. It was determined to assault the Malakhoff Tower and the Redan, and arrangements were made for the attack to be delivered this morning at day-break. As an assistant-surgeon had to go with each regiment, we drew lots, and the lot fell upon me. I did not esteem the privilege very highly, but marched off with our men at 12 o'clock last night. I am sorry I cannot give you the plan of attack as everything was changed at the eleventh hour, and caused no little confusion.

Pélissier had decided at the last moment to bring the attack forward by two hours, to dawn. He did not consult Raglan over this but presented him with a *fait accompli*. Raglan gave way and was too much of a gentleman to play a game of wait-and-see with the French, even though he knew that the Redan was untenable if the French could not hold the Malakoff.

Captain Fred Dallas of the 46th Foot was in one of the supports for the attack, and was lying waiting in a trench, enveloped in smoke. He wrote home on the evening of 18 June:

> **When the proposed assault took place the result was that the French failed at the Malakoff, and by some misunderstanding, our Stormers (whose attack on the Redan was supposed to depend on the success of the French at the Malakoff) went on to the Redan under the most terrific fire of every description of missile. It was utterly impossible for them to get on as they were literally mowed down. It was almost a good thing that comparatively few faced it, or the slaughter would have been only more horrid. The Russians must have had information of the whole affair for they were prepared at all points. Our loss is not yet known, but the proportion of Officers (who, in some cases, were not followed by their men) was immense. Sir John Campbell, who led the Stormers instead of commanding and directing the Supports as was his duty, paid with his life for his reckless gallantry, and fell one of the first. Poor Colonel Yea of the 7th was killed. Colonel Shadforth was killed & his Regiment, the 57th, suffered awfully, and hosts of others whose names I don't know, & many whom I did and liked, poor fellows...**

The truce for burying the dead took place the next day at four o'clock in the afternoon. Captain Henry Clifford of the Rifle Brigade described the scene in a letter to his parents:

> **The sun was so hot that it was impossible to recognise the dead, their bodies were swollen to an enormous size and their faces and hands quite black, and so dreadful was the stench that the men who were taking them off the field often vomited.**
>
> **Some, Sir John Campbell amongst others, had already begun to decompose and worms and maggots were eating away the flesh. I saw as I thought a dead rifleman on the ground partly hid by the grass. I went to the spot. It was the backbone of one with part of his bowels and a lump or two of flesh with part of his jacket and head by it; all the rest had been blown away by a shell.**

From the safety of the frigate where he lodged in Sebastopol harbour, Nikolai Berg described the relief felt by everyone inside Sebastopol as daylight made it clear that they had once more been spared the awful humiliation of defeat :

> **The town and everything began to look different for us. The fires on the southern side went out. There was only one place where smoke was still burning, rising in a thin streak... It was pleasant to watch how the troops marched across the hills and how their bayonets were iridescent and sparkled in the early morning rays of sunlight... A fresh wind blew away the cloud of smoke, and we saw the retreating, disorderly columns of the enemy... It was seven o'clock. I drank my fill of tea and set off for camp...**
>
> **We were joyful for a long time. The June days could be counted as the best days of the whole siege. It seemed that we had repulsed all future assaults. There appeared an inevitable and all too human sense of self-assurance, especially when we saw masses of new bayonets which kept on arriving. In a word, we experienced exactly the same feelings as the French had done not so long before this.**

In Asia Minor, the Allies received another blow to morale on the morning of 18 June. General Muraviev, the new commander of the Russian Caucasus army was marching towards Kars. General Williams, in charge of the Turkish garrisons at Kars and Erzerum, had made repeated appeals for help but was palmed off with reassuring platitudes from an Allied command too preoccupied in the Crimea to spare much thought for remote Turkish fortresses. On 18 June, Muraviev's army arrived at its destination, watched by Dr Humphry Sandwith, the chief medical officer at Kars:

> **About 10 o'clock the whole Russian army comes in sight, and a magnificent spectacle it is. About 40,000 men are in march towards our position; their cavalry, numbering 10,000, are in advance and on each wing. Vast grey bodies of infantry, whose arms gleam and flash in the rays of a morning sun, form the main body,**

while a powerful artillery is discovered in the intervals of the masses. In the rear of the army are carts and horses innumerable, covering miles of country, and laden with the necessaries to be consumed by so vast a host.

Muraviev's army had brought plenty of provisions. They were here for the duration, intent on recapturing the fortresses which would give them the advantage in Asia Minor and allow them to control the region and access to the East. Inside the Kars garrison, provisions for the army and civilian population were paltry. General Williams managed to get extra supplies from Erzerum, but by mid-July the Russians' blockade of Kars was complete and Williams was forced to take strong measures, as Dr Sandwith noted in his diary:

The General causes the state of our provisions to be rigorously investigated and the most careful lists to be made of all who are receiving rations; he also orders the men to be put on two-fifths rations of bread, and fed regularly with animal food... It is found that we have still provisions to last until the end of August, and we hope by that time to have aid from the Central Government.

PRINCE GORCHAKOV

The British and Turkish army officers inside the besieged fortress of Kars fed on that hope for another four months. In the end it was of as little sustenance as their exhausted rations.

The Russian commander in-chief in the Crimea, Prince Gorchakov, was not of the same mettle as General Muraviev. In the aftermath of the Russians' first major triumph of the siege on 18 June, Gorchakov planned the construction of the bridge to be used for the eventual evacuation of Russian troops and civilians from the south to the north side of Sebastopol.

Lord Raglan, although not killed in battle, was himself to prove the most famous victim of the British defeat at the Redan. Even before this terrible reversal, he had declared that he dared not go home for fear he would be stoned to death before he reached his town house in Stanhope Street. Now, his health began to decline rapidly and he showed signs of weariness beyond the mere physical. During this time, cholera had once again scourged the camp, and Raglan had neither the will nor the strength to resist it. On 28 June, just ten days after his humiliating defeat, Lord Raglan died.

After the death of Raglan, the British army in the Crimea came under the command of General Sir James Simpson. On the day of his promotion he is supposed to have said: 'They must indeed be hard up when they appointed an old man like me.' Like Raglan, Simpson was a veteran of the Peninsular War (1809-14), but his strategy was even more lackadaisical. The heart had gone out of the campaign, and apart from a few bombardments and sorties, there was little decisive action. The men were beginning to wonder whether they were in for another Crimean winter. Lieutenant Young expressed everyone's disappointment when he wrote, one day after Raglan's death:

I am afraid I will have to eat my Christmas Pudding in the Crimea in place of home as I thought last Xmas, for out of this we can't go till either we lick the Russians or they lick us.

THE BATTLE OF THE TCHERNAYA (WILLIAM SIMPSON).

In St Petersburg, Tsar Alexander II was looking for a way to lick the Allies. It was his aim to put all his strength behind a final battle which he hoped would inflict such a blow that France and England would be prepared to come to the negotiating table on terms more favourable to Russia. Prince Gorchakov was pessimistic about Russia's prospects and dragged his heels. He regarded the whole situation as hopeless, and his pessimism was filtering down to his men. Lieutenant-Captain Lesli wrote from Sebastopol at this time:

> **A kind of apathy has set in with all our commanders and seeing this all your energy disappears too. In general it's time to finish this terrible blood-letting war. Because of it, many things have now turned out in a completely different aspect than when first we saw them, and much time is needed to correct them.**

Schultz, the Russian officer who had seen the Allied landing at Kertch on his way to Sebastopol in May, was now in charge of a line of defence of Sebastopol. In his diary entry for 6 August, he corroborates Lesli's frustration at the Russian commanders' passivity, while the enemy became more and more entrenched on Russian soil:

> **This entire, unsurpassed army of ours watches quite calmly as the enemy, before our very eyes, digs itself deeper and deeper into our land, even cultivating its own vegetable gardens, cutting hay in the Baidar valley, chopping down forests and grazing cattle (while we pay twice the normal price for forage); it is even building barracks, and has taken command of Kertch, Yenikale and other coastal towns wielding its power there at will. While we, on the other hand, blow up our own batteries and powder-stores, destroy our reserves and sink our own ships.**

The main headquarters of the Russian army was on the Inkerman Heights, in view of the Allies, at a distance of about two miles and still closer to the place where the River Tchernaya flows into Sebastopol harbour. To the left of the main quarters, in the direction of the Mackenzie Heights, were the camps of Russian

LORD RAGLAN'S FUNERAL (DE MORAINE).

army regiments, all the way to Mackenzie Hill itself. Between this hill and the Fediukhin Heights flowed the River Tchernaya. This was the boundary between the Russian army and the Allies.

The tsar's idea was to cross the Tchernaya, and to recapture the Fediukhin Heights as a base for further operations against Balaklava and the Allied camps. The river had an arched bridge in the centre, known as the Traktir Bridge. This, the extreme left flank, was defended by the French. On their right were some fresh troops from Sardinia, who had joined over the summer under General della Marmora. The Sardinians hoped that being on the winning side would help their struggle for a united Italy.

The new Russian offensive was confirmed for first light on 16 August. After a prolonged and unsatisfactory correspondence with the tsar in St Petersburg, Prince Gorchakov had agreed to go ahead. He had been reluctant to stake his reputation on an attack against well-defended positions occupied by an enemy superior in numbers and armaments. To the tsar's letters urging decisive action, Gorchakov replied in defeatist tones. He did not refuse outright but stressed that such a plan would not save Sebastopol, merely delay its eventual fall. He even ended one letter with the words: 'But one should not deceive oneself, for there is little hope of success in such an attack.' With such little confidence, the Russian commander-in-chief planned a last offensive fling – the battle of the Tchernaya.

Prince Sviatopolk-Mirsky arrived in Sebastopol from the Caucasus on 30 July. He had decided to join the Crimean army because his Caucasus army battalion had been left behind in Tiflis when General Muraviev marched on Kars. He wanted to see action and had come to Sebastopol to find it. On 15 August, he was assigned to the Odessa Chasseurs Regiment and went to join them at their position on the Mackenzie Heights. That night, the eve of battle, he and the other battalion commanders were dining with their regimental commander, Colonel Skyuderi:

> **The subject of conversation was naturally the forthcoming battle. I was amazed by the gloomy disposition of my**

commander and of my new comrades. It was evident that they were prepared to die and had doomed themselves to sacrifice, but without any hope not only of success, but even of bringing some benefit to bear on the general cause...

After dinner we began to get ready for the attack – towards evening, there were prayers before the assembled regiment, and as night fell the battalions, in columns of six rows, set off down the road into the valley of the Tchernaya... At nine o'clock, there was an order to stop and rest. Each one lay down where he was standing... I was awoken by the voices of the men – the soldiers were crossing themselves, rubbing their eyes – it was growing light.

The Russians were well prepared. Provision had even been made to increase the nursing staff at the nearby field-hospitals and dressing-stations set up in preparation. Nurse Alexandra Krupskaya went by cart with eleven other nurses to the battlefield:

The night of our journey was dark; a dead silence reigned everywhere, the road was nasty, deep drops and pot-holes at every step, so that we constantly caught hold of one another so as not to fall off, and we filled the air with gasps of fear because we couldn't make a noise.

Having travelled like this as far as Inkerman, six of us remained there and the rest of us, including me, set off for the Mackenzie Heights, near the Tchernaya River, where dressing-stations and places for the wounded had already been prepared. This was at five o'clock in the morning, there were no wounded men there yet and we went to have a look at our new bivouacs...

Over in the French camp, the movement of Russian troops and nurses went unnoticed. That night was one of national celebration in France. Lieutenant Octave Cullet of the French 95th described the mood among his regiment as, unsuspecting, they drank the health of Napoleon III:

On 15 August, we were merrily celebrating the Emperor's birthday. It was a happy evening – several bottles of champagne bought in Kamiesch helped us to forget our past misery, to close our eyes to our comrades' empty shoes and to nurse our sweet hopes of coming home.

Day had scarcely broken...we scoured the plain to no avail, it was buried in a thick mist and we could make nothing out.

André of the 3rd Zouaves was also carousing that night, when:

...we were woken up by some quite lively firing. It rattled not far from us, and echoed resoundingly on our extreme right, in the direction of Mount Hasfort which was occupied by the Sardinians. That night had been very black, not a star had shone in the sky and it seemed as if day didn't want to break at all, so thick was the mist over the plain...our commanders didn't quite know what to do with us, since the enemy was invisible...

Over in the camp of the Sardinians, Sub-Lieutenant Ricci was sleeping off the previous night's excesses:

Everyone was asleep in the Allied camps when a burst of shooting surprised us about an hour before dawn. It was the Russians who, having marched and manoeuvred for a good part of the night, were starting battle with a furious attack on the Piedmont advance guard. The combat was short, but very lively: we fought with bayonets, with the stocks of our guns, finally even with stones. This was enough to alert those in the camps behind us, and they got into a defensive position in good time.

Suddenly André could see what had been invisible to him only moments before:

We saw a whole army on the plain. Its right wing was made up of two or three regiments of Uhlans and Cossacks, whose horses were stamping and snorting, waving the little black and yellow pennants of their veritable forest of lances. Behind this curtain a whole infantry division was swarming, a big black mass lit up by the glistening of eight to ten thousand bayonets.

Prince Sviatopolk-Mirsky was behind those glistening bayonets as they advanced on the French positions. He was glad no longer to be locked in combat with Shamil and his wild Caucasian tribesmen:

> **My heart was light and easy, here there were no God-forsaken mountain slums and precipices, no dense forests filled with wild mountain people, driven by their fanaticism to acts of savagery, no grasping Kurds and base Bashi-Bazouks, who cut up the wretched wounded and curse the dead. Facing us were people of the same ideas as us, prone to the same feelings, observing the same rules. It seemed that all of Europe was watching us and that this was more a tournament than a war. I will go straight up to them, I thought, and exclaim: 'Messieurs, voulez-vous croiser la bayonette?' We drew closer and closer – you could see the expression on their faces, it was possible to distinguish the smallest movement. Suddenly the French halted, the order was heard, they turned around and at the same time scattered in a line which immediately opened fire... I decided to open up the battalion and in this way turn it round into a line, which would have served as a reserve of troop units behind me. I took a position a bit to the left, in order to give the command, but at that very moment, as I was about to utter some words of command, I felt a terrible, familiar blow in the left side of my chest, which stopped my voice and movement in a flash...**

The prince had felt the stab of a bullet wound. André and his fellow zouaves had been quick off the mark:

> **The Russians had crossed en masse by way of flying footbridges and yoked beams. But we bore down on them at an athletic pace and, By God! from that moment on I couldn't quite say what happened. Just like at Inkerman and at the Mamelon Vert we had to dig in, advancing and retreating in turns, climbing over wounded and dead bodies, closing our eyes sometimes, so as not to see what we were striking, or out of fear of a bad strike that only with luck would fate or a companion steer us clear of. How anyone got out of there safe and sound is impossible to explain. We can only thank God... Finally however we managed to push the Russian columns back down to the river, where many unfortunates, tied up in their long cloaks, drowned.**

Sub-Lieutenant Ricci and the Sardinians caught the Russians in a pincer movment:

> **While the French were reacting head-on, we Piedmonts went from the defensive to the offensive and assailed the Russians on their flank, so that caught between two lots of fire they were obliged to retreat a second time, leaving the field covered with dead and wounded.**

As he was helped on to a cart for the wounded, Prince Sviatopolk-Mirsky heard the beating of the Russian retreat:

> **The cart stopped at one of the turns in the road, I turned my head and saw nothing but smoke in the valley.**
>
> **'It seems our men are retreating,' said the bugler, indifferently, 'it must have been that they weren't strong enough.' Indeed, that's how it was.**

The prince was brought to the main dressing-station on the Mackenzie Heights:

> **They cut my clothes off me, placed me face down on a high bed covered with an oilcloth, something was handed to the doctor, I felt it sharp and cold on my back, once, twice, and again, then I could hear the doctor rinsing something in water.**
>
> **'Here it is,' he said cheerfully, and showed me a large conical-shaped bullet of the Belgian type, which had just been extracted from my body... A nurse gave me some tea, and then I began to suffer a great deal. I was twice treated with a cupping-glass to suck the blood to the surface; the blood was cupped twice and I felt better.**

It was the first time that Alexandra Krupskaya had been so close to a battlefield. She and the other Russian nurses soon witnessed the most terrible sights as the wounded men began to make their way to the field dressing-stations:

> **Suddenly we saw the artillery returning; one soldier was astride a cannon, reins wound around his hands, and, oh, horror! – he had no head!... Soon they began to convey the wounded. I say 'convey' because they carried them, and they brought them, and some even crawled themselves. There were thirty-five doctors and as many**

Ten Russians killed by one cannonball at the battle of the Tchernaya (Captain Henry Clifford).

medical assistants, but there were only six nurses. Throughout the course of several hours the whole of the Mackenzie Heights was crammed full of wounded men. It was a terrible sight: one was shouting, 'Cut me, don't let me suffer any more'; another, 'Save me, for God's sake, save me, I have a wife and children at home! I don't want to die yet!'; a third, dying, muttered some incoherent words; a fourth was just crying out with all his strength...

For the Russians, the battle of the Tchernaya had been a massacre. Mary Seacole went down onto the battlefield as soon as it was thought safe to do so:

I derived no little gratification from being able to dress the wounds of several Russians; indeed, they were as kindly treated as the others. One of them was badly shot in the lower jaw, and was beyond my or any human skill. Incautiously I inserted my finger into his mouth to feel where the ball had lodged, and his teeth closed upon it, in the agonies of death, so tightly that I had to call to those around to release it, which was not done until it had been bitten so deeply that I shall carry the scar with me to my grave. Poor fellow, he meant me no harm, for, as the near approach of death softened his features, a smile spread over his rough inexpressive face, and so he died.

This Russian died in battle with the enemy. Others met their death less gloriously. The Russians added to their fatalities by firing at their own wounded. William Howard Russell described this folly in a long reports written that night from the camp on the Tchernaya:

The French made every possible despatch to collect the

wounded. They were laid on the open space about the bridge until the ambulances arrived. While there, the Russians, who could plainly see that the French were engaged in bringing help to their own wretched countrymen, suddenly began to open with their guns upon them, repeating the barbarous practice which they had already often previously shown to the troops. A gentleman who was with me at the moment, and who speaks Russian, asked one of the poor fellows who was trying to trudge along with deep flesh wounds on both his thighs, what he thought of the behaviour of the Russians in firing among their own wounded? He answered, 'They are accustomed to beat us when we are with them, and there is no wonder that they should try to ill-treat us when we are on the point of escaping out of their power.'

In the cool light of day on 17 August, André looked down on the battlefield:

Oh! I once praised the grace of this valley. Now it is covered with corpses for which the nurses are fighting the vultures, with the birds of prey being more active in their voracity than the men in their pious work...it must be recognised that glory is dearly won.

The glory of that day at the Tchernaya River had been won by the French and the Sardinians. The British were minor players, as Lieutenant Robert Biddulph reassured his mother when he wrote to her from Balaklava:

I send you this line to tell you that I am all right, as you have doubtless heard of the battle yesterday. It was all fought by the French and Sardinians. We were in reserve, and consequently inactive spectators of the whole... The Russians had a tremendous lot of very heavy guns; and to answer them, one of our heavy Batteries went up and opened with good effect, a troop of Horse Artillery had a few shots, and those were the only English troops engaged...

Lieutenant Biddulph, not yet twenty at the time, then described what he had seen when the battle was over:

As soon as I had brought the Battery home and had some breakfast, I rode off to view the field; at the bridge where all the fighting was, the dead lay so thick I could hardly avoid treading on them. The ditch of the tête-de-pont was filled with dead and wounded, and I saw, what I have frequently considered to be a 'façon de parler', the river dyed with blood.

The French had fought a great defensive battle but the price had been high. Cullet's regiment, the 95th, had been more than halved. Out of 500 men who had turned out that morning, 256 were *hors de combat*. Captain Jean-Jules Herbé, also of the 95th, was moved to philosophize:

In the room which I am occupying at the moment there are two captains lying side by side, both hit by a bullet in the middle of the chest – they were the commanders of two batteries – one French, one Russian – opposed one against the other. They are now as good friends as if they had fought together in the same ranks...

It's my belief that this is the penultimate bloody act of our operations in the Crimea. The final one will be the taking of Sebastopol.

Captain Herbé's prediction was to be borne out, but it was an Allied offensive a thousand miles away in the Baltic Sea which was to weaken the Russians' resolve. When it came to bringing Russia to its knees, it was naval warfare that proved decisive.

COSSACK BIVOUAC (NIKOLAI BERG).

15
14
9
11
10
6
8
5
3
7
4
1

CHAPTER NINE

THE FALL

IN THE SPRING OF 1855, the Allies relaunched their Baltic campaign. Sir Charles Napier had been scapegoated for the previous season's failures and was replaced by Rear-Admiral Sir Richard Dundas. The fleet set sail in March with the aim of re-establishing the blockade of the Russian Baltic ports and carrying out reconnaissances of Revel, the Åland Islands, Hangö, Sveaborg and Kronstadt, with a view to a possible naval attack against Sveaborg and Kronstadt.

THE BLOCKADE OF KRONSTADT BY THE ALLIED FLEET (MAX BEEGER).

IN 1855, ONCE THE ICE HAD THAWED IN THE BALTIC, ST. PETERSBURG, THE HEART OF THE RUSSIAN EMPIRE, WAS AGAIN THREATENED BY THE ALLIES.

It was largely for his failure to attack Sveaborg that Sir Charles Napier had been dismissed. Together with Kronstadt, Sveaborg was one of a pair of key naval fortresses for the defence of the Russian capital. But the fortress had fallen into disrepair, and it was only in the summer of 1854 that the tsar had sent an inspector to look into it. He had found it unserviceable and the defences in poor condition, with batteries where they were not needed and no batteries where they were. Rear-Admiral Matyushkin wrote to the commander-in-chief of the Russian fleet in 1854:

> **Materially and in the art of using our artillery we belong to the last century...if the enemy knew that we have at our disposal only nine guns firing shell and how few other guns we have and the weakness of the wall they would be able to destroy everything this autumn... But Sveaborg's undeserved reputation has led the enemy to postpone their attack until they receive more reliable information... Very few of our projectiles will reach the enemy, but on our side a good deal will be burned and destroyed.**

Had Rear-Admiral Napier been privy to such information, he might not have suffered the ignominy

PANORAMA OF HELSINGFORS AND THE FORTRESS OF SVEABORG (ANON).

of a failure that was not of his making.

When the Allied Baltic campaign resumed in 1855, the planning of the operation was passed to Captain Bartholomew Sulivan, the fleet hydrographer. He was asked to submit a written report on his proposals for the bombardment and possible destruction of Sveaborg and Kronstadt. As far as Sveaborg was concerned, Sulivan suggested an attack from the northern side, by mortar vessels and armoured floating batteries, protected from attack by a fleet of gunboats. He saw no need for an amphibious force, and anyway all the British land troops were detailed for the Crimea. After the awful news of the Crimean winter and its effect on public opinion at home, the new Prime Minister, Lord Palmerston, was reluctant to incur disfavour by redeploying troops and transports away from Sebastopol, where the pressure to force the Russians out was overwhelming.

Sulivan was sanguine about this decision and felt sure that a naval bombardment of Sveaborg would be sufficient to scare the tsar and his ministers sitting across the gulf in St Petersburg. He based this confidence on two major additions to the Anglo-French naval arsenal. These were the steam-screw battle fleet and the armoured floating batteries. The floating batteries, a French invention, solved the problem of wooden ships and stone-walled fortresses. These new steam warships were built of wood protected by wrought-iron plates, four inches thick, with a heavy gun battery. They could withstand bombardment by explosive shells and could get close enough to inflict damage themselves. In the event, neither steam-screw ships nor armoured floating batteries were brought into action in the Baltic in 1855. The main naval effort was still concentrated on the Black Sea and, as a result, the British and French armoured floating batteries, ready for action by the summer of 1855, were redirected there. But their presence in the Allied arsenal acted as a deterrent and had the desired effect on the Russians.

The Baltic Fleet began its campaign by reconnoitring Revel, where it found the defences strengthened, and worked its way round to Kronstadt by early June. The more serious business of reconnoitring Kronstadt led Sulivan to conclude that they dare not attempt anything with only a portion of

the force originally intended for the operation:

> **The enemy have not been idle, and out of the thirty-four steam-crew gunboats we heard they were preparing, fifteen showed yesterday, all ready and manned, and they have a much heavier flotilla than we can bring against them. Besides, all their steamers were able to act inside, whilst ours cannot get near to help our gunboats. I can see the admiral is very doubtful, and I dare not urge him on to try it, unless with a force sufficient to give every probability of success. We may perhaps have a chance of a distant bombardment of Sveaborg; and if managed well with the necessary means sent out, we may do great injury to the enemy without the loss of a man to us: that we can do even with the smaller force said to be coming out.**

During the winter of 1854-55, the Russians had made considerable improvements to their naval and land defences in the Gulf of Finland. When the British fleet was sighted off Kronstadt, Alexander II wrote to Prince Gorchakov in the Crimea:

> **The British fleet has approached us and anchored off Krasnaya Gorka presumably to await the arrival of the French vessels. In Kronstadt, where I was a few days ago, everything is ready for their reception; both land and marine troops are burning with a desire to show themselves worthy of their comrades of Sebastopol. With the exception of isolated minor bombardments of coastal telegraph stations, the enemy fleet has still not done anything and lies sometimes in view of Kronstadt, sometimes in sight of Tallinn.**

A few days later, Sulivan's *Merlin* was to be the first-ever warship to feel the effects of an exploding mine – a new weapon which the Russians had placed by the score in the main sea approaches to their naval defences. Up until now the Allies had not taken mines seriously. On board *Merlin* was an artist from *The Illustrated London News*, J.W. Carmichael. Sulivan felt the need to keep a tight rein on his artistic licence:

> **His great delight seemed to be in the engineers' mess-place, with all the smashed crockery and mess-things; and I expect you'll see a sketch of it in all its glory. He is going to show me the drawings. I want to prevent any exaggeration. The smash in the store-room, where the real damage was done, and the heavy tank thrown away, he could not he said, make a point of – , that is, I suppose, it was not picturesque enough; but the smashed crockery seemed to have a great charm for him. He kept some fragments of cups and glasses as**

The explosion on board HMS *Merlin* (drawing by J. W. Carmichael for *The Illustrated London News*).

relics of it, and I think you may see a wonderful sketch of broken teacups.

On the advice of Sulivan that Kronstadt was an unwinnable battle, Rear-Admiral Dundas was persuaded to turn his fleet's attention to Sveaborg. Substantial effort had been made on the part of the Russians to strengthen Sveaborg's defensive works, but it was a huge task and the precaution was taken there, too, of placing almost 1,000 mines in the immediate vicinity. Sulivan and his small flotilla now spent three days and nights in an intensive survey of the rocks and skerries so that the possibility of their obstructing the operation could be eliminated. The work was a success and the bombardment of Sveaborg began on the morning of 9 August. It was watched by the Reverend Mr Hughes from his yacht *Wee Pet*, and by an anonymous correspondent who provided *The Times* newspaper in London with its Baltic coverage:

Off Sweaborg, Aug 9
A glorious morning, and all hearts beating quick with anticipation of to-day's work...
7.30 a.m. - Signal made, 'Mortar vessel open fire with shell.' The bombardment will last 48 hours.
8. a.m. First shell fired; nine gunboats commenced firing, and the action became general along to the eastward as far as the eye could see; and to the westward as far as a gun could reach; every rock and garden, and house seems full of guns.
10 a.m. we set fire to Fort Vargon, and at 11.05 the magazine blew up with an awful explosion, and for a few minutes the Russian fire slackened. The enemy's fire is very good when once they get the range; to prevent their doing this, the gun-boats kept moving in circles formed of four or five in each, and as each brings the bow gun to bear upon its object, it is fired, then turning as sharply round as possible, the broadside gun pointed and fired, and they proceed to complete their circle while doing which they have time to load.
12 noon (exactly). A monster explosion took place, which lasted without interruption for more than two minutes; it was like a volcano in a state of eruption, vomiting forth light, shells, roofs of houses, and beams of timber following this, in the course of half an hour, three other explosions took place, which set fire to the barracks and town in four places.

The enemy's fire has been very slack since 7 o'clock, and there are so many fires on the islands of Swartoe, Vargon, Gustavsvaard, on which the town and its hitherto formidable fortress is built, that it is one continuous sheet of red flame and smoke. Our men behave nobly, and if this war has done us no other service it is an unanimous opinion in the fleet that it has taught us the immense use of steam gun-boats, of which too much cannot be said in praise.

Up to the time I close this (8 p.m.) I am not aware of a single casualty happening to our whole squadron.

On the Russian side, Finnish Governor-General Berg was required to make a detailed report on the bombardment of Sveaborg. It was inevitable that he would cast his own contribution to the defence of the fortress in a positive light and play down the effects of the 'monster explosion' that had so impressed the man from *The Times*:

The powder cellars, despite the endless bombs falling

> **on them, held up to the last, with the exception of four small reserves of old bombs kept in some ancient storehouses of Swedish construction on the island of Gustavsvaard. On 9 August at 12 noon, the explosion of an enemy incendiary bomb set fire to one of these storehouses; this spread instantly to the others which were situated nearby, and in such a way all four storehouses almost simultaneously flew into the air. By God's mercy, the harm caused by these explosions consisted only in one death and three wounded among the lower ranks...**
>
> **As night fell, the action did not cease but, on the contrary, under cover of darkness, the enemy armed the mortar battery it had erected the previous night on the small, rocky island of Langorn (located within their position), and on the night of 9 August they opened fire from it, at the same time stepping up the fire from their ships. As a result of this action, the port buildings in the fortification of Stura-Oster-Swartoe with all their outlying workshops and stores were burnt.**

Neverthess, Governor-General Berg still felt able to conclude:

> **...apart from a few fires which it was not possible to contain, the damage sustained by the fortress and the batteries during the two-day heavy bombardment was generally insignificant.**

In spite of Berg's reassurances, as soon as the bombardment ceased the people of Helsingfors were convinced a landing was about to be made. Panic spread and long lines of carts, loaded with people and their belongings, left for the countryside. When after a few days nothing had happened, they slowly made their way home again.

PANORAMIC VIEW OF THE GULF OF FINLAND, FROM ST. PETERSBURG.

The Allied bombardment of Sebastopol eventually began to have an effect. (Photo by James Robertson.)

For the Allies, the object of the exercise had been achieved. The bombardment of Sveaborg boosted public spirits at home and demonstrated to the Russians that if so much could be achieved there, with only a fraction of the naval power and land forces that could be brought to bear in the Gulf of Finland, then the security of St Petersburg itself was threatened. As *The Times* correspondent wrote when the operation was over:

> **...the blow, however, which we have so successfully given, and which, I believe, was more successful than ever was anticipated, will be severely felt by Russia. It shakes her confidence in her stone walls, and makes her tremble for every town along her coasts, when she sees that a few small boats, some of them actually old dockyard lighters, after having a gun or a mortar put into them, are able to destroy stores, public buildings, and property worth millions, and defended by between 500 and 600 guns, without the slightest accident or casualty...**

Captain Sulivan's meticulous planning and organization had been vindicated. Now, the focus of attention once again returned to the Crimea where the Allied army was determined to lay the ghost of Sebastopol once and for all.

The day after the battle of the Tchernaya, on 17 August, the Allied bombardment of Sebastopol had recommenced. Under cover of fire, the French sappers dug their trenches closer and closer to the Malakoff Tower. From the camp before Sebastopol, William Howard Russell sent this despatch on 20 August:

> **The fire which opened at daybreak on Friday continued the whole of Saturday and yesterday, but slackened this morning by order. I should not wonder if it were to be again increased to-night, in order to favour the progress of the French works. This has already been**

considerable, and the French seem duly sensible of the service our cannonade has rendered them. It has enabled them, I heard a French officer say on Saturday evening, to do in four hours what they previously could not have done in fifteen days. I believe that the three days' fire has enabled them to do what they otherwise would probably never have done.

The British army in the Crimea was now only a fraction of the size of its French ally. Since it lacked manpower it concentrated on the cannonade rather than digging trenches, which was much more labour-intensive. Ironically, this understandable decision was to inflate British casualties of the assault out of all proportion.

It was clear that Sebastopol could not withstand enemy attack for much longer. With every bombardment, the Russians were finding it harder and harder to keep up the pace of repairs. On Wednesday evening, 22 August, Lieutenant William Young wrote in a letter home:

The town is a great deal knocked about now. I was looking at some of the buildings the other day through a telescope, and in some of the large ones you might drive a coach and four with ease. The other day we were firing some rockets into the town and we set a house on fire. So the old bloak [*sic*] inside got a couple of carts and horses and set about removing his furniture, and when he had his two carts nicely packed some of our guns fired a shell slap into them and knocked furniture, carts and all to pot.

From inside Sebastopol, Lieutenant-Captain Lesli wrote to his relatives:

With every hour that passes it gets harder and harder. Everything has become so loathsome that, oh, oh, – there's no strength left! And I would be prepared to leave for Siberia at once to do hard labour, even for a lifetime, if only it meant I could get out of Sebastopol...

In his despatch of 20 August, Russell even described Allied strategy for all his readers at home and, as it turned out, abroad:

Opinions are divided as to the plan of attack that will be observed. Some think that without pushing their works beyond the point at which they have now arrived, the French will give the assault; and a report is prevalent in our camp that a British division (the Light, it is rumoured) will share with them the peril and honour...the distance is now so greatly reduced – is, indeed, so very short – between the French trenches and the Russian defences, that a vigorous assault ought to succeed, unless, indeed, the more desponding anticipations that I have heard indulged in, as to the impregnability of the internal defences of the Malakhoff, should be even more than realized.

It is little wonder that Russell's despatches to *The Times* found their way back to Russia as part of intelligence reports compiled by Russian agents in London for the tsar in St Petersburg.

On 26 August, the Russian pontoon bridge linking the south to the north side of Sebastopol was completed, and it was ceremoniously opened the following day. Nikolai Berg recorded the event:

On 27 August, after the mass to mark the Feast of the Dormition, the bridge was opened and blessed – and whole crowds of people walked and rode along it. It was strange to hear the clatter of horses' hoofs and the thunder of carts in the middle of the harbour, over the ripple of the waves, which had never had such a girdle across it. The huge logs, sticking out from under the rafts, were soon covered in long, pale green strands of underwater grasses, and in these strands, which looked like a handsome beard, parted on two sides, tiny fish swam in and out, as though through a forest, playing in the sunshine like flashing blades.

Berg's *Sebastopol Album* includes his own drawing from life of this remarkable feat of construction. The Russians were preparing for the final act. It began, as it had done at the dress-rehearsal on 18 June, with a heavy bombardment, only this time, there were to be no last minute changes of plan to send the whole affair off course. Nikolai Berg was at the Russian main camp on the Inkerman Heights:

On the morning of 5 September, the last, terrible bombardment began, the like of which there had never

The Pontoon bridge, the Russians' escape route from Sebastopol (Nikolai Berg).

been before. The whole of Sebastopol (the southern side and the Karabelnaya) was drowned in smoke, which at the beginning rose up in sparse white columns but then merged into one grey, dense cloud, and for three days in a row, this cloud hung over the town. You couldn't see the sun on the southern side at all, although it was shining in the sky. Sometimes, in the midst of the ceaseless, steady roar, there resounded the stupendous volley of many guns. These were such thunderous roars that we, who you would think were already rather accustomed to such things, could not contain ourselves and would jump out of our tents to see what it was: was the earth opening up? And that was at camp, several miles away from Sebastopol! What could it have been like there?

Company commander Yanuari Kobylynsky of the Zhitomir Chasseurs was inside Sebastopol, bearing the brunt of the enemy fire:

Bombs, shot, shells, various kinds of grape-shot and

> bullets poured as though through a sieve and fell, exploding as they hit the ground and with a furious wickedness breaking and destroying all that crossed their path. Before noon and in the evening the firing stopped for fifteen or twenty minutes. During this interval of heavenly silence, the enemy was, in all probability, checking their gun-sights and re-aiming their guns; and on our side their was an extraordinary flurry of domestic activity: everyone was clearing away the rocks, pieces of wood and gun-carriage strewn all over by the enemy's shells, levelling out the pits made by the bombs, heaping and piling up anew... The work was not yet completed, only half-finished when, suddenly – a terrible thunderous boom and a whole mass of iron was flying at us again, tearing up the ground, scattering masses of stones, hitting people, guns...

After two days' of the heaviest bombardment by the Allies, Nikolai Berg noted:

> By the morning of the 7th, the Malakoff Tower was in a worse state than it had been the day before. This was the *first* such morning in the whole siege. Usually by morning all the damage was repaired and the batteries looked fresher than they had done the previous evening.

The Russians were running out of time. On 7 September the plan of attack, until now a closely guarded secret, was made known in the British camp. Major Colin Frederick Campbell of the 46th noted the details in a letter home:

> On Friday afternoon we were informed that a general assault would take place at 12 o'clock next day. My post was with a working party, who, as soon as the Union Jack was hoisted on the parapet of the Redan, were to go forward and make an entrenchment in the interior. My party of 200 men was posted in the quarries and I myself went forward to the advanced trench to look out for the signal. It had been agreed previously that the French were to assault the Malakoff at 12 o'clock and that we were not to go at the Redan until the French had gained *un succès sérieux*.

One lesson from 18 June had been learnt: there was to be no British assault unless the French were successful.

The morning of 8 September broke, cold and wintry. Sergeant Timothy Gowing of the 7th Fusiliers wrote of that morning:

> We fell in at 9 a.m. A dram of rum was issued to each man as he stood in the ranks; all hands had previously been served out with two days' rations. There were in our ranks a great number of very young men, who had not much idea of the terrible work that lay before them; but there were others who knew only too well, having had near twelve months' hard wrestling with the foe...
>
> After remaining for a short time under arms, we

View of the ruined interior of the Redan.
(Photo by James Robertson.)

Inside Sebastopol

For so long seen only through a glass, the defences of Sebastopol were a source of immediate fascination to the Allied soldiers. The Redan, which had taken the lives of so many brave young men, was inspected in its every detail by Frederick Robinson:

> In the walls of the parapet there were little apartments admirably constructed, roofed in with sacks of earth. These, resembling the cabins of a ship, in size, appeared to be constructed for various purposes – temporary hospitals, officers on duty, commandant etc. Some of the furniture, broken up already, remained. One apartment towards the rear, exactly resembling the sick room of a man-of-war, had a fine grate and chimney, complete. In the embrasures were excavations, to admit of men sleeping or resting with tolerable safety... It communicated with the Malakoff by a series of trenches, and, from the commanding position of the former, it was quite evident the work would be untenable after the capture of the stronger fort.

The town itself was off-limits to the British until the Sunday following the fall, much to the consternation of Fanny Duberly:

> The English until to-day have been denied admission to the town, except with a pass provided by Sir R. Airey. The French, on the contrary, have been plundering and destroying everything they saw. The town was mined, and these mines, going off perpetually, made it very unsafe for amateurs. Nothing, however, deters the French. Five officers were blown up to-day; and a zouave came out driving a pig, carrying a dead sheep, a cloak, and a samovar, and wearing a helmet.

But when permission was no longer required, Mary Seacole won a bet she had made long before:

> For weeks past I had been offering bets to every one that I would not only be the first woman to enter Sebastopol from the English lines, but that I would be the first to carry refreshments into the fallen city. And now the time I had longed for had come...
>
> I was often stopped to give refreshments to officers and men, who had been fasting for hours. Some, on the other hand, had found their way to Russian cellars; and one body of men were most ingloriously drunk, and playing the wildest pranks. They were dancing, yelling, singing – some of them with Russian women's dresses fastened round their waists, and old bonnets stuck upon their heads.

The Zouaves leave their mark in Sebastopol.

Fanny Duberly went first with her husband Henry to look at the Redan:

> The Redan is a succcession of little batteries, each containing two or three guns... and hidden away under gabions, sand-bags, and earth, are little huts in which the officers and men used to live. Walking down amongst these...we found that tradesmen had lived in some of them. Henry picked up a pair of lady's lasts the precise size of my own foot. Coats, caps, bayonets lay about, with black bread and broken guns.

They then made their way into the town itself:

> Actually in Sebastopol! No longer looking at it through a glass, or even going down to it, but riding amongst its ruins and through its streets. We had fancied the town was almost uninjured – so calm, and white, and fair did it look from a distance; but the ruined walls, the

Above: *Church in the Rear of the Redan showing the effects of shot and shell* (William Simpson).

riddled roofs, the green cupola of the church, split and splintered to ribands, told a very different tale.

After the initial shock of seeing the extent of damage to the buildings of Sebastopol, Captain Dallas found himself full of admiration:

> The Public Buildings are so beautifully situated and are themselves so handsome, I don't think that there is a single house that is not completely destroyed, excepting the mere outward shell, and most of them with great shot holes through them. Menshikoff's Palace must have been a charming house, now quite gutted, but not much so injured by shot, as it was a long way from our Batteries. I saw the French packing up some beautiful marble 'Sphynxes' I suppose to send to Paris from Menshikoff's house.

Venturing further afield, Henry Clifford had gone in search of two young soldiers of the 90th who had been taken prisoner and were said to be in one of Sebastopol's hospitals:

> ...Every possible attitude of agony was there depicted, and I did not see one that looked like he had died quietly and without great pain. They were almost all naked and had crawled about the room. Some had been dead for days, and their flesh was falling off them, some looked like negroes, so black, and almost all were swollen to an enormous size. Three large houses were full of these dead bodies, and one vault had evidently been set aside for wounded Officers. In it we found two hundred dead, none alive, and some had been placed in coffins ready to be taken out, but the tremendous fire kept up on the town during the last bombardment no doubt prevented these poor creatures being looked after.
>
> These awful sights gave me a better idea than anything else of what the Russians must have suffered in Sebastopol. Fancy the sufferings, the horrors, of those houses devoted to the wounded, with shot and shell every now and then falling in through the roof. We have been three days with carts carrying these bodies out of the Town.

Left: French soliders stand proud in Sebastopol (Photo by Durand-Brager and Lassimonne).

marched off about 9.30 a.m. There was no pomp or martial music, no boasting; but all in that mighty throng moved with solemn tread to the places that had been assigned them.

In the French camp, too, positions were being taken up, but not before the troops had been read a stirring speech from General Bosquet, wounded the previous afternoon. André of the zouaves described how they set off:

> **Our march got under way in a gust of wind, which sent all the dust from the Chersonese whirling about our heads and which whistled through the trenches like the winter wind in a chimney. On top of that we had to stumble over a pile of the previous night's cannonballs – a parting gift from the Russians – until between 10 and 11 we finally reached our waiting post, on the left of the Mamelon, almost the same point from which we**

TOP: *THE LAST DEFENDERS OF THE MALAKOFF TOWER* (V. TSEKHOMSKY).
ABOVE: THE GENERALS WATCH THE ASSAULT (*ILLUSTRATED LONDON TIMES*).

had set off to take the place last time. The bombardment was still going on – intermittently furious and then with calculated lulls before suddenly starting up again. This iron storm passed far above our heads. The flight of murderous flies, which we could hear but not see, was our only distraction: our brief was to keep hidden until the very last minute, in order to surprise the enemy, whom our artillery with its disjointed game was trying to force away from the ramparts.

At a distance from the Allied positions, onlookers, including the British generals, assembled to view the assault. William Howard Russell entertained his readers with a description of this motley crew:

The Commander-in-Chief, General Simpson, sat in the trench, with his nose and eyes just facing the cold and dust, and a great coat drawn up about his head to protect him against both. General Jones wore a red nightcap, and reclined on a litter, muffled up in clothes, and Sir Richard Airey, the Quartermaster-General, had a white pocket-handkerchief ˚tied over his cap and ears, and fastened under his neck, which detracted from a martial and belligerent aspect... All the amateurs and travelling gentlemen, who rather abound here just now, were in a state of great excitement, and dotted the plain in eccentric attire, which revived olden memories of Cowes, and yachting, and seabathing. They were, moreover, engaged in a series of subtle manoeuvres down in the ravines, to turn the flank of unwary sentries, in order to get to the front, and their success was most creditable to their enterprise and ingenuity.

The indefatigable Fanny Duberly was characteristically contemptuous of the sentries' efforts to safeguard the interests of amateurs:

...we were advancing on the batteries so we turned our horses' heads across the ravine, and rode up to the front of Cathcart's Hill, where we found the Cavalry at their usual ungracious work of special constables, to prevent amateurs from getting within shot. Now, in the first place, amateurs have no business within range; and in the next place, their heads are their own; and if they like to get them shot off, it is clearly nobody's business but theirs.

For André, waiting for zero hour seemed like an eternity:

The hour which preceeded the assault on the Malakoff must count amongst the longest ever. Midday arrived, however, and at the same time, the signal for the attack. Our hearts were fit to burst, whilst our batteries kept their admirable and frightening silence, when we heard on our right an immense cry of 'Vive l'Empereur.'

The bugles and drums struck up their own racket... Everyone hauled themselves up in the ravine, so that they could at least see their brave comrades at their duty. Away they went, racing like hares, the 1st Zouaves: some of them fell, but most of them just stumbled or slipped in the holes: they got up and carried on all the faster. They dashed off, leaning forward so as to run better. All that could be seen of them were their huge red pantaloons, which grazed the ground like balls of fire. One by one, ten by ten, they disappeared behind the overhang of the bastion which flanked the tower. It was impossible to see any more, but then a regiment of the line arrived; they too went forward proudly...under the rifle shot of those big devils in the white caps who showed their heads through the embrasures. Sappers and infantrymen intermingled; they carried flying bridges, planks, and ladders, like the Russians at Tchernaya.

Up on the Inkerman Heights, Nikolai Berg woke up on the morning of 8 September to find that:

...it was as though the destructive thunder grew even stronger, but at twelve mid-day everything grew quiet. Our camp sprang to life: here and there horses were being saddled. A few horsemen were already flying along the road into town. The enemy had made the assault ...

I went down, into the bushes, and began to watch. Directly opposite me, across the bay, you could see the First and Second bastions and the Malakoff Tower — for

---

OVERLEAF: *THE ATTACK ON THE MALAKOFF* (WILLIAM SIMPSON).

those who don't know the place: hills, dissected by trenches and crammed with the earthern walls of the batteries. Further on stretched the plain, covered in stones and bushes, and across it, at a quick march, slightly bent forward, came the columns of French, marching magnificently. The wind was blowing in their faces, the skirts of their frock-coats fanning out, which gave them an air of even greater speed. Our bombs were falling among their ranks, causing the dust to rise, but they carried on coming, superb – the brave Frenchmen.

Russian naval officer Vladimir Kolchak was second-in-command at the Glasis Battery of the Malakoff Tower when the assault began:

A shout rang out, 'The French!' Rear-Admiral Karpov, passing the Tower on the way to his dug-out, ordered the alarm to be sounded; but the drummer had been killed and the alarm was sounded by the bugler standing by. Rapid crossfire could be heard, like dried peas poured from a sack... Naturally, a few shots could not hold back the advance of an animated mass. The French just kept on advancing and advancing towards the Tower. I picked up the first linstock with a smoking fuse that came to hand, grabbed a hand-grenade and ran to the right face of the battery. The guns were already covered in earth, or put out of action; they stood on broken platforms. The French, having jumped the ditch, were swiftly clambering across the embrasures and parapets with the help of ladders, and onto the battery. Hand-to-hand fighting began. In the open spaces of the Tower our soldiers were fighting in separate groups with the overwhelming mass of the French. They fought with bitterness – using anything that came to hand: bayonets, the butts of their fire-arms, cleaning-rods, pick-axes, spades, even stones.

André wrote to his mother, telling her how it felt to be a zouave that day:

I'm not exaggerating when I tell you that the ground was covered by at least 4000 men, as many Russian as French, some of whom were already no longer breathing, and many of whom were moaning, groaning, writhing with the pain of atrocious wounds, in the midst of a confused pile of abandoned sabres, overturned cannons, fallen rock, planks tied to ropes in which our feet got caught up... In the midst of all these horrors, General MacMahon, calmly circulated, stepping carefully, but without looking, over the wounded and the dead...

I could see his sparkling golden *képi* [cap], and nearby our three colours flying, being waved by a Zouave. What can I say, Mother, it may be childish, but in spite of that, it makes you proud and happy to resemble a hero, even if it is just because of your uniform. After all, our corps has exerted itself enough since the beginning of the campaign, to make it fair that the honour of planting the flag in the most dangerous and glorious spot should be ours...

The French had taken the Malakoff Tower in a matter of minutes. A British officer raced in to ask MacMahon if the position was secure, to which he replied, 'J'y suis, j'y reste', and the signal for the British assault was given. Colin Frederick Campbell saw the British advance from his working party in the Quarries:

Nothing could exceed the manner in which they went out, and in spite of the showers of grape and canister they pushed steadily on over about 200 yards of ground, planted the ladders, and scaled the parapet. In the Redan there were not more than 200 Russians ready to receive them, and even these were siezed with a panic. Nevertheless, the mass of our men, instead of going boldly into the Redan, remained clinging to the outside of the parapet and shooting over at the Russians, who ensconced themselves in shell-holes and behind a small entrenchment. Brigadier-General Wyndham [*sic*], with about 100 men, entered the Redan, and after remaining there about ten minutes under a pretty sharp fire had to retire on account of the Russian reinforcements arriving.

General Windham kept a diary of his Crimean campaign. The entry for 8 September explains why he was forced to retire:

The assault took place at one, and I went over the Parallel at the head of the 41st. The Grenadiers followed

FINAL ASSAULT OF THE GREAT REDAN LED BY COLONEL (NOW GENERAL) WINDHAM, WITH A HANDFUL OF HEROES ON THE 8TH SEPTEMBER, 1855 (ANON).

me pretty well, but not in the best order. I went straight at the ditch, and did all that man could do to get them into the centre of the battery, but it was no go. I ran out into the middle of the battery with my sword over my head, but it was useless. They would stick to their gabions and to firing, and not come to the bayonet...

If I could have got the men of the storming-party to make a rush, I should have carried it; but I never could. They were all in disorder, and each looking out for himself. The officers behaved well, and so did the men as individuals, but not collectively.

The men could not be induced to follow their officers. Colin Frederick Campbell was appalled by their behaviour:

...the plain truth is, that from the time they reached the parapet they showed the most arrant cowardice. On mounting the parapet of the Redan, you see before you a large open space, and the sight of this appeared to paralyze the men.

...No one can deny the fact that, in spite of all the exertions of the officers, the men clung to the outside of the salient angle in hundreds, declining to go in, although they were swept down by the flanking fire in scores. The officers, as usual, behaved as well as possible: I saw many of them – mere boys just from school, who had not been a month in the Crimea – standing on the parapet, and endeavouring to get their men on in the most gallant manner. This sort of thing lasted for about an hour, when the Russians at length

mounted on the parapet, and, with bayonets, muskets, and even stones, beat our men down into the ditch, and they had to fly back into the advanced trench.

Captain Henry Clifford showed more compassion, reserving his criticism for the British army command:

Was it prudent to send these two Divisions (the 97th and the 90th), that have never been a moment out of the trenches, to take the Redan? Second, was it right to send any men two hundred yards in the open against a place like the Redan, with guns vomiting forth grape, and when hundreds of their comrades fell long before they ever got to the Ditch? The French, with older and more tried troops, would not assault the Malakoff again till they had silenced the fire of the guns and brought their trenches within twenty yards of the Ditch from which the sharpshooters could keep down the fire from the parapet.

Thirdly, as it was certain the Malakoff would command the Redan, when the former was in the hands of the French, was it right to sacrifice thousands of lives in attacking the Redan, only because the French went at the Malakoff? Why were not our trenches pushed on within twenty yards of the Redan?

The French managed to hold the Malakoff, although they were severely routed at their other two points of assault, the 'little Redan' and the Flagstaff. British honour was at stake at the Redan. They beat a retreat on 8 September, but to save face, General Simpson ordered a fresh assault on the Redan for the following morning.

What neither the French nor the British knew was that inside Sebastopol the Russian commander-in-chief, Prince Gorchakov, had visited the second line of defence behind the Malakoff Tower and, seeing that it could not be retaken without enormous human sacrifice, had decided to activate his plan for evacuating the south side of Sebastopol. General Semyakin received the instruction to evacuate at six o'clock that evening:

I had been instructed to begin the retreat at 6.30 and to finish at 10; to leave the riflemen and some of the gun crews at the line of defence in order to maintain the firing; when all the troops had left, at a given signal, to blow up the bastions, batteries and all the powder-cellars, numbering 35 in the first division, 28 on the shore-side batteries and No. 7 and 8 bastions. There was no time to think, one had to act; orders received and executed.

RIGHT: RUSSIANS SET FIRE TO THEIR TOWN AND FLEE. BELOW: *PUBLIC LIBRARY AND TEMPLE OF THE WINDS IN SEBASTOPOL* (WILLIAM SIMPSON).

Nikolai Berg described the mayhem that ensued:

> **It is impossible to describe what was happening on the bridge. A wave of carts, horses, people flooded over it for six or seven hours in a row. Sometimes it seemed to those crossing that the bridge had collapsed and was sinking to the bottom. Crowds, shouting and screaming, ran back; the crossing was held up... in the meantime, the sky flared with shots and bomb after bomb burst over those retreating. Then the town burst into flames...**

Leo Tolstoy ended his *Sebastopol Sketches* on the northern side, at the same moment:

Each man, on getting across the bridge, took off his cap and crossed himself. But this feeling concealed another, infinitely more draining, agonising and profound: a mixture of remorse, shame and intense hatred. Nearly every man, as he looked across from the North Side at abandoned Sebastopol, sighed with a bitterness that could find no voice, and made threatening gestures at the enemy forces.

ABOVE: *CAPTURE OF SEBASTOPOL* (GUSTAVE DORÉ).
ABOVE RIGHT: *THE TRENCH IN FRONT OF THE REDAN THE MORNING AFTER THE ATTACK* (CAPTAIN HENRY CLIFFORD).

Retreating, the Russians had spiked all their guns, mined all the bastions with explosives, and detonated all the powder-stores. Sergeant Gowing was back at British camp, trying to get a decent night's rest before the next morning's renewed assault on the Redan:

Our camp was startled by a series of terrible explosions, and we could not make out what was up; but at length discovered that the enemy were retiring under cover of the blowing up of their vast forts and magazines.

Oh, what a night! It baffles all description. Many of our poor fellows were then lying on the ground, having been wounded in all sorts of ways, with the burning fortress all around them. The Redan was blown up, and a number of our men went up with it, or were buried alive. Imagine the position of the wounded lying just outside the Redan!

When Henry Clifford was awoken by a huge explosion, he jumped onto his horse and, seeing Sebastopol all in flames, he rode on, past the empty trenches, so recently crowded with troops, past the batteries, where everything was now still as death, and a few yards on, into the Redan itself. He expected to feel the elation of victory, but what he saw there put him in a very different mood:

If a few days before I had been told 'on the morning of

the 9th of September at five o'clock Sebastopol will be in the hands of the Allies and you will stand in the Redan held by the English,' I should have said, 'Oh, that will be a proud and happy moment, that will repay us for all we have gone through, even the loss of so many lives, so much suffering and hardship will not have been thrown away in vain!' But no, I stood in the Redan more humble, more dejected and with a heavier heart than I have yet felt since I left home.

I looked towards the Malakoff and there was the French Flag, the 'Tricolor' planted on its parapet. Yes, the French had taken the Malakoff, but the English had not taken the Redan. No flag floated on the Parapet on which I stood and if it had, I could have siezed it, and dashed it into the ditch which we could not pass, or hid it in the bosom of the young officer, dead at my feet inside the Redan. I could not stand it long. The Redan was ours because the French had taken the Malakoff which commanded it, and we have lost a great number of our brave Officers, and some brave men and some that were not so, two thousand at least and to no purpose.

One of those lost at the Redan was Corporal Harry Blishen, whose naked body was found covered in bayonet wounds in Sebastopol.

That prized possession, Sebastopol, had at long last been won; but it was a hollow victory. The empty shell of a town had merely been scorched and evacuated, while the Russians had retreated to a commanding position in the Star Fort on the north side. It was almost one year since the Allies had landed at Kalamita Bay. Another six months were to pass before the war was brought to a successful conclusion. The decisive blow once again came from the Allied fleet, with a display of naval superiority which was to silence Russia for a long time to come. It took more than the fall of Sebastopol to wrest a peace from Russia that would satisfy all her enemies.

CHAPTER TEN

WAR AND PEACE

WHEN NEWS OF SEBASTOPOL'S fall on 8 September 1855 reached France, Paris was lit up in celebration. French national honour had been satisfied with the capture of the Malakoff, and the fall of Sebastopol surely signified that peace was close at hand. Influential court circles in France felt that the war had been going on for long enough and that it was now time to curry favour with the tsar in the hope of securing patronage for French commercial ventures.

BASTION DU MAT (THE FLAGSTAFF BASTION) (WILLIAM SIMPSON).

THE NEW OCCUPANTS OF THE RUSSIAN EARTHWORKS IN FRONT OF SEBASTOPOL.

In Turkey, Sultan Abdul Medjid hoped to gain more from continuing the war. The Turks had little chance of recovering the Crimea, but Asia Minor was another matter. General Williams, in charge of the Turkish garrison at the fortress of Kars, was running short of supplies and, anticipating Russian strategy to force the Turks out by starvation, had sent a plea to the British Foreign Secretary, Lord Clarendon, for assistance as early as June 1855:

> **I have now four months' provisions in the garrison of Kars, and I trust the central Government and the Allies will soon prove to this remnant of an army that it is not entirely forgotten by them.**

For much of July and August, Omar Pasha had been trying to get the Allies' consent to release Turkish units from the Crimea in order to reassign them to Erzerum and Kars in the Caucasus, where Allied forces were making little headway against the Russians. As early as 31 July 1855, Fuad Pasha, the Minister of

Foreign Affairs at Constantinople, had written to the British ambassador urging him to convey the significance of this offensive to London:

> **The position of Kars is so to speak, the key of the frontiers of Asia; so that if (which God forbid!) it were to fall into the power of the Russians, in the first place Erzeroom would be in danger, and then the whole of Anatolia would be threatened – of that there is no doubt. If Anatolia were to become the theatre of war, and the enemy were to make an advance in that quarter, great evils would result, not only to the Sublime Porte, but also to the whole alliance. Moreover, the success of the Russians at Kars would be a defeat which would create through the whole world a bad impression with regard to the alliance.**

The Sultan was hoping that an Allied victory would give him the opportunity to move his borders northwards, and once Sebastopol had fallen there was no longer anything to stop the Turks from an offensive to relieve Erzerum and Kars. The British supported the Sultan in this; they wanted to keep Ottoman interest in the war alive because it suited their own aims. But time was running out. In early September, a more desperate note had arrived on Clarendon's desk:

> **KARS, September 1, 1855.– The most is made of our provisions; the soldiers are reduced to half allowances of bread and meat or rice-butter. Sometimes 100 drachmas of biscuit instead of bread; nothing besides. No money. Mussulman population, 3,000 rifles, will soon be reduced to starvation. Armenians are ordered to quit the town to-morrow. No barley, scarcely any forage. Cavalry reduced to walking skeletons, and sent out of garrison; artillery horses soon the same. How will the field pieces be moved after that? What is being done for the relief of this army?**
>
> **(signed) WILLIAMS**

Although Sebastopol fell on 8 September, it took until 29 September for a conference of the Allied generals in the Crimea to release Omar Pasha's contingent to go to the Caucasus and another contingent to set off for Trebizond under the command of Selim Pasha.

News of the fall of Sebastopol was brought to Kars on 23 September by a Georgian Muslim who talked his way past the Russian sentries and entered the city at night. The feeling of relief and joy inside the walled city was overwhelming. It was widely believed that Muraviev would now raise the siege; only General

Kméty, known as Ismail Pasha, persisted in the belief that an attack would be made before the Russians left. Six days later, Kméty was proved right:

> **About three o'clock on the morning of 29th September, messengers from advanced posts on three different sides came to my tent almost at the same moment, breathless with haste, and reported, 'The enemy is advancing'...**
>
> **The night, now drawing to its close, was clear, almost cloudless, and the moon high. By its light, at first, I could only see in the valley before me that some parts of the ground were darker than others, not unlike the contrast of ploughed and pasture lands lying in a distant plain.**
>
> **As, however, the darker parts were seen alternately to move and then to remain stationary, as the valley became continually more and more full of these fields of shadow, as, with my ear upon the ground, I was able to distinguish the noise of wheels moving quietly through the valley, I was soon convinced that the enemy was before me in great force, and was preparing to storm ...**

The Turks were prepared and and were the first to start firing. A Russian officer with the Vilensky Regiment heard that first shot:

> **The nocturnal silence was broken by the roar of a large-calibre gun. A shell, tracing a fiery curve, ricocheted across our heads and burst among the ranks of the Dragoons. In its wake, a blaze of shots began to flare up at many points on the heights, and shells, criss-crossing the sky in every direction, were now bursting among our ranks, now ricocheting across our columns. The roar of enemy fire, the doleful scream of shells and sound of them exploding, merged with the roar of firing from our battery guns. We were enveloped in smoke... At our first shot being fired, a loud voice bellowed: 'Stand! March!' The soldiers jumped up, the columns moved forward at an assault march, the drummers beat the attack... Through the smoke we could distinguish the dark mass of the parapets, crowned with a fiery crest; in places the bright blaze of cannon fire was exploding from it. Grape-shot screamed and pranced through our ranks, ricocheting on the stoney soil. We fell under the fiercest**

IN JANUARY 1856, THE ALLIES FINALLY DESTROYED THE DOCKYARDS AT FORT ST NICHOLAS IN SEBASTOPOL. (PHOTO BY DURAND-BRAGER AND LASSIMONNE.)

After the fall of Sebastopol

After the fall of Sebastopol, the Allied troops amused themselves with sightseeing and visits, theatres and dances, wining and dining. It was another ten months before they had all set sail for home shores, and many of the officers and men were determined to make life more agreeable than it had been for the previous ten months.

On 20 September 1855, the Allies had their first excuse for a celebration, as Lieutenant Young recounts:

> We all dined together in the Mess Hut. Everyone brought his mite and we had a jolly dinner, lots of everything, and one fellow good-naturedly stood loads of Champagne. We had no end of fun in honour of the Battle of Alma, in fact, a good many bottles went in drinking the health of the Heroes of said battle. We are going to have an awful blow-out on the 5th of November.

Lieutenant Young and his fellow-soldiers had more to remember than Guy Fawkes on the 5th of November:

> I must now tell you about the anniversary of the Battle of Inkerman. We had a very nice dinner in our Mess hut, and the band was in a little covered-in place outside the door, where they performed whilst we were at dinner. After dinner we adjourned to the Sergeants' Mess, where we found a great many French Sous Lieutenants and Sous Officiers. There was no end of lush there: Champagne, Claret, Punch and I do not know what besides. The band played 'Partant pour la Syrie' and a number of other airs and the French fellows appeared highly delighted and cheered loudly for the Queen whereupon we cheered loudly for the Emperor and Empress and lushed away. I do not know how I would have fared if I had not bolted about 12 o'clock as the Sergeants were insisting on our bolting huge bumpers of Champagne and Punch every minute as if we were made of iron. When we got out the scene beat all descriptions. In some places French and English were lying about in every direction just as if there had been an action, which plainly showed that the Battle of Inkerman was kept up by both parties. The whole English camp was in a blaze as tar barrels and bonfires were kept going like fun, to the great danger (as I thought) of the numerous wooden houses in the vicinity.
>
> ...The Sergeants had their large Hut very handsomely decorated and the Colours crossed on the end wall with 'Alma,' 'Inkerman,' 'Balaklava,' 'Sebastopol' all over the walls, with 'Success to the Allies' and I don't know what else besides. Everything passed off very well indeed, barring that I think some of our men and the Allies had a little too much *water.*

Christmas Day in the Crimea, 1855.

The Monastery of St George, a favourite picnic spot for officers. (Photo by James Robertson.)

An assistant-surgeon with the Rifle Brigade found another form of entertainment in the French camp, but the absence of ladies dampened his enthusiasm:

> ...The French have established a village of shops and restaurants a short distance off on the Woronzoff Road, which intersects the camp. Here they have a dancing-saloon in which balls take place, chiefly on Sunday evenings. It is an objectionable practice, and I never go

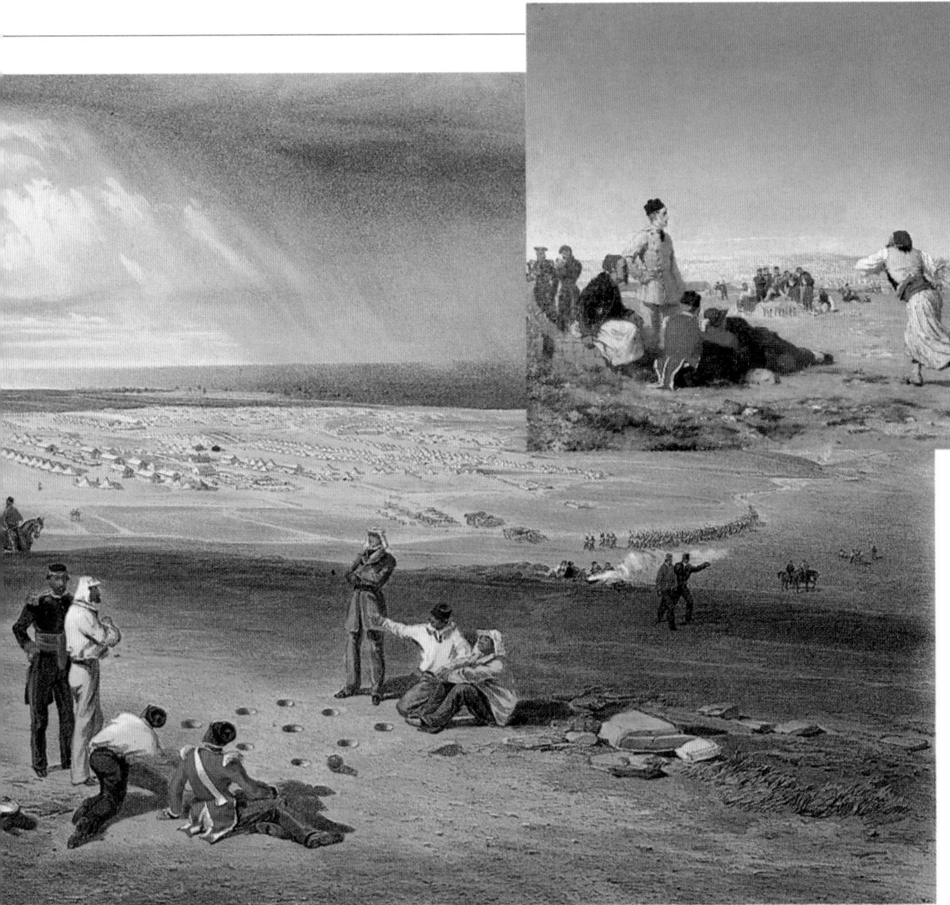

Shot flying a little more gently
Above: ***Boules Game*** **(Protais).**
Left: ***Camp of the 3rd Division*** **(William Simpson).**

even on week-days. There are no ladies to dance with, only vivandières, who are generally the wives of the restaurant-keepers. On a recent occasion a young English officer, with a face as smooth as a baby, had himself arrayed in female attire, and went to the ball with several brother officers. The French officers were delighted to welcome *la belle Anglaise*, and several of them had the supreme felicity of dancing with her. The English party was discreet enough to leave early, to the regret of the Frenchmen. But when the secret transpired afterwards, their regret was transformed into fury, and they declared that if they could discover who it was that had insulted them so grossly, they should demand satisfaction, or have him tried by court-martial.

When the armistice was declared, the armies visited one another's camps. The Russian camp made an indelible impression on the assistant-surgeon:

> Their camps are very dirty, and the stalls in their bazaar displayed an array of vegetables, black bread, dried fish, skins of leather, and nails: they seem to have few luxuries, and to incline to Spartan simplicity in their manners. Passed by two enormous burying-places, compared to which any of ours is as nothing. The graves are not made singly, but huge pits are dug, where probably hundreds of men are entombed together. These graveyards alone are visible proofs of the havoc that has been made in the Russian army...

Two days later, he visited the Russian camp on the Mackenzie Heights:

> The camp, for the most part, is a miserable array of mud-huts, nearly all of which are in a ruinous condition, and so dirty, it is no wonder the men suffer so much from disease. Went into the camp church, a long mud-building; but it struck me that the beautiful paintings and the gaudy appointments used in the Greek form of worship were worthy of a better shrine... The soldier who is in charge had about a dozen crosses and medals on his breast. I have often wondered at the lavish display of decorations in the Russian army, but now I have the key to the mystery,– they are given alike for victories and defeats! Thus a medal was given for our repulse at the Redan on the 18th of last June, and a cross to those engaged at the siege of Silistria, where the Russian army was beaten... When the large crowds of Russian soldiers who come to our camp contrast its comfort with the dirt and wretchedness of theirs, I imagine they will not be particularly satisfied with their condition. Yet who knows? They have such blind confidence in their little father, the Czar, that they would suffer martyrdom for him, as indeed many thousands have already done in this part of his dominions. The black bread they have to eat would alone suffice to make me renounce allegiance to such a father.

cross-fire and...were pelted with a hail of grape-shot and bullets.

General Kméty was behind the parapets, observing the Russian column as it drew closer:

As soon as it arrived within 150 paces' distance from us, the head of the column opened its fire, but without for an instant giving any sign of either halting or turning. The slowness and feebleness, however, which now began to show itself in the advance and the opening of the fire, now led me to suppose that the officers, who, as in all gallant armies, had placed themselves in great numbers at the head of the storming columns, had fallen, otherwise the men would now have been firing upon their own officers.

Panic had set in amongst the Russians; they were firing at their own officers:

At that fatal moment, they began to fire from behind us, and this finally put an end to the whole affair. The soldiers, falling between two lines of fire, threw themselves at the ground, lay down behind rocks, behind piles of their comrades' corpses, behind dead horses, and, in answer to the enemy's shots, opened rapid fire, but soon, seeing that no help was at hand and sensing that all was lost, they stopped firing and under a veil of thick smoke, began to retreat, silently, bending low and covering the whole slope of the mountain with their bodies. The path of their retreat rang out with the muffled groans of the wounded...

The Turks had carried the day and by eleven o'clock the next morning, the Russians had abandoned the field at all points. It was now that the deprivations endured by the Turkish army at Kars really told on the situation. Dr Humphry Sandwith, chief of the medical staff at Kars, wrote in his diary that evening:

About midday the Russian columns were seen running down the hill, their cavalry and artillery steadily protecting their retreat. A confused mass of citizens, horse and foot, followed them with the utmost temerity, firing into their retreating ranks. But where was our cavalry? where were the fierce Turkish horsemen who once overran the east of Europe? Two thousand of these horsemen would now destroy the Russian army: as it is we are forced to keep to our entrenchments – we have no cavalry and no horse-artillery; and, with deep chagrin, we see the enemy gradually, re-form, and march off unmolested.

The truth was that the Turkish cavalry horses had been dying in their hundreds from starvation. To prevent an outbreak of disease, in early September General Williams had issued orders for all horses in desperate condition to be led a considerable distance from the encampment, and there have their throats cut. There was nothing left now but to wait for relief from the Allied armies.

When news of the fall of Sebastopol had reached London, the Prime Minister, Lord Palmerston, sent a letter to the Archbishop of Canterbury, stating that the surrender of the Russian naval base should be observed not by a weekday service of thanksgiving, as had been the case with Waterloo, but by special services on a Sunday; it was not to be assumed that this victory had been so decisive that peace was imminent. When the full story of the British assault on the Redan was made known in England, pressure was brought to bear on General Simpson, as commander-in-chief, to take the initiative in another offensive action to redeem Britain's lost honour. Simpson crumpled under the strain and tendered his resignation on 3 October. He remained at his post for another five weeks because of doubts as to the abilities of his designated successor, Sir William Codrington. Codrington nevertheless took over the command on 11 November. There were no more heroes with untarnished reputations from which to choose.

On the ground in the Crimea, the Russians' position on the northern heights above the bay of Sebastopol seemed impregnable and the Allied command suspected that they were planning for reinforcements to join them and draw the enemy further and further into the interior of Russia where the Russians would have the advantage. The tsar's proclamations to his subjects after the fall of Sebastopol were littered with allusions to an anniversary of another war with France, and he urged them to remember 1812 and not to lose

Bodies of a Zouave and a Russian soldier – amongst those left behind in the Crimea (Captain Henry Clifford).

heart. He wrote to Prince Gorchakov in the Crimea:

> **Sebastopol is not Moscow, the Crimea is not Russia. Two years after we set fire to Moscow, our troops marched in the streets of Paris. We are still the same Russians, and God is still with us.**

On 29 September, at the same conference which released the troops to relieve Kars, attended by Generals Pélissier and Simpson, by Rear-Admiral Lyons and, for the French, Admiral Bruat, Pélissier gave in to Lyons' proposal to launch an amphibious operation to capture the Russian fortress at Kinburn situated in a commanding position over the confluence of the rivers Dniepr and Bug. The success of the operation would redeem Britain's honour after the ignominy of defeat at the Redan. Its strategic importance lay in Kinburn's role as guardian of the entrance to the Russian naval base of Nikolaev, ten miles upriver. Odessa, at the mouth of the Dniepr, and Kherson, capital of the province, would also be threatened by this action, and supplies from these commercial centres to the Russian camp outside Sebastopol would be cut off.

Kinburn, despite its important position, was not well defended and was in a vulnerable position. Built of sand, at sea level, the fort was armed with obsolete 24-pounder guns, which were situated in two batteries at the end of a long spit where they could easily be isolated. After many false starts, 10,000 troops were despatched on ten transports, escorted by ten battleships, twenty frigates and a number of gunboats, with a special detachment of mortar boats and, the jewel in the Allied crown, three French floating armoured batteries. The land forces were set ashore across the spit of land three miles up from the fort itself; this was to prevent the garrison from retreating and reinforcements from coming to the rescue. Their job was all but over then, for the navy would do the rest. Daniel William Powell was with the British army contingent:

> **On the 13th we steamed out, very slowly. Our fleet was a most magnificent one, a terror to any enemy that saw it. We dropped anchor about 25 miles from Odessa, at a place called Kinburn, having a fort which counted about 150 guns and commanded the rivers Dnieper and Bug. We anchored some distance from it and remained a day and night to allow our boats to go sounding.**
>
> **On the morning of the 16th we got orders to make a landing. We got three days' provisions and loaded our pieces. We fully, one and all, expected a warm reception, this being the first army that landed in Russia, and I can say that our colours were the first on Russian soil, for I planted them after wading to my middle in the sea: our boats couldn't get nearer to land us dry. We met with no opposition. I saw a Cossack riding in great speed along the beach. We fully expected that an army was in rear of him: but no – they were all in the fort. If there had been, our gun boats would have**

LEFT: FORT KINBURN. (PHOTO BY DURAND-BRAGER AND LASSIMONNE.)
BELOW: A FRENCH SHIP STUCK IN THE ICE AT KINBURN. (PHOTO BY DURAND-BRAGER AND LASSIMONNE.)

swept them from the face of the earth.

Russell of *The Times* was still in the Crimea. He accompanied the fleet to Kinburn and sent the following despatch on 17 October at 5pm:

> **Kinburn has fallen, after a short but most desperate defence. The floating batteries opened with a magnificent crash, at 9.30 a.m., and one in particular distinguished itself for the regularity, precision and weight of its fire throughout the day. The enemy replied with alacrity, and the batteries must have been put to a severe test, for the water was splashed into pillars by shot all over them. At 10.10 the bombs opened fire. At 11.10 a fire broke out in the long barrack, and speedily spread from end to end of the fort, driving the artillerymen from their guns. Small explosions of supply and ammunition took place inside.**
>
> **Two hundred are said to be killed, and four or five hundred wounded; but admittance to the town is denied by the French, as it is reported that the governor, inflamed to madness, is in the powder magazine, watching for the victors to enter, in order to fire the mine, which is well stored with powder. We shall know more tomorrow.**

Readers of *The Times* were reliably informed the next day that the governor did not fire the mine, but in surrendering,

> **...was moved to tears, and as he left the fort turned round and uttered some passionate exclamation in Russian, of which the interpreter could only make out, 'Oh! Kinburn! Kinburn! Glory of Suwaroff and my shame, I abandon you,'...**

The tsar's evocations of 1812, and of its legendary hero General Suvorov, had left the governor of Kinburn feeling all the more crushed in defeat.

Unfortunately for the British, the French were not interested in advancing on Nikolaev, the Black Sea Fleet shipyards, and Odessa was left untouched because Napoleon III wanted it as a base for the

French campaign in 1856. The fleet and most of the troops returned to Sebastopol at the end of October. The season for active campaigning was almost at an end, and the Allies were left to anticipate another winter in the Crimea.

At the camp before Sebastopol, the British were far better prepared to face the coming winter than they had been the previous year. Lieutenant Young wrote home with news that:

> **Our men are all turned to navvies now, and are employed in making roads and railways from the Camp to Balaklava, so that there may be no difficulty in getting provisions and forage up in the winter...**
>
> **We are all building great stables for our horses now, and I have not been out riding for the last 2 days having sent my pony each day to town for wood. I have sent him and my servant down today to get wood to make a cooking house, so that I will take no excuse for not having as good a dinner in winter as in summer...**

Nevertheless, living under canvas was not the best protection against another Crimean winter. It was not long before Lieutenant Young turned his attention to solving that problem:

> **I am present very busy building a hut for myself and another fellow to live in during the winter... I think we will have it built for about £5 between us as nails, canvass and other things are very dear here. I am now at a standstill for want of a window. I have a frame, and if I can get a couple of panes of glass I can get a man to put it in all right. Sometimes I could get one for about 10 shillings from a Frenchman but they are very scarce now as every window has been taken out of the town.**

The French were the ones to suffer in the winter of 1855. The British had overcome their earlier problems of disease and transportation, but the French system, which had worked so well for them when it had been a small-scale, mobile campaign, finally disintegrated as their support systems broke under the strain of increased numbers in static formation. Typhus and cholera tore through their camp, and in the first three months of 1856, 53,000 patients were admitted to French hospitals in the Bosphorus; 10,000 died, the overriding majority from typhus.

At Kars too, the cold was beginning to bite, and the hospitals were stretched to the limit with patients dying from cholera, exhaustion and hunger. As food supplies dwindled, mutiny and desertion increased. General Muraviev, basing his strategy on information from spies, intensified his strategy of close blockade and starvation against the garrison. To further this aim, all deserters from Kars were sent back; the greater the strain on rations the better for the Russians. Dr Sandwith's diary entry on 14 November describes the suffering:

> **All the mosques, khans, and large houses are full of invalids. The citizens nobly furnish us with beds, which, however, scarce suffice for our numbers. Women are seen gathering the dust from the flour-depôts to eat, mixed as it is with flour. I observe people lying at the corners of streets, groaning and crying out that they are dying of hunger.**

Although the garrison of Kars had welcomed the news of Selim Pasha's arrival with a reinforcement army of 20,000 on 22 October, Selim had since marched from Trebizond, where he landed, only as far as Erzerum, where he had called a halt. In late October, Omar Pasha's force disembarked eighty miles further to the north than he had originally intended. His progress towards Kars was proving to be circuitous and dilatory. General Williams was now sending messengers from Kars nearly every night, and the following despatch in cipher, dated 19 November, reached Mr Brant, the British Consul in Erzerum, on 23 November:

> **Tell Lords Clarendon and Redcliffe that the Russian army is hutted and takes no notice of either Omer or Selim Pashas. They cannot have acted as they ought to have done.**
>
> **We divide our bread with the starving townspeople. No animal food for seven weeks. I kill horses in my stable secretly and send the meat to the hospital, which is now very crowded.**

On 22 November, as Dr Sandwith records, another despatch arrived which sealed the fate of General Williams and the Turkish garrison inside Kars:

> **At 6 a.m. a messenger comes in with a despatch from Selim Pasha to the Mushir [Turkish governor of Kars]. He was to have left Erzeroom for Kars on the 16th, and would hasten on. Besides this veracious Turkish document there is a little note in cipher from Mr. Brant; it is as follows:- 'Selim Pasha will not advance, although Major Stuart is doing his utmost to make him. Omer Pasha has not advanced far from Soukhum Kale. I fear you have no hope but in yourselves; you can depend on no help in this quarter.'**

With barely any food left in the garrison and no pack-animals with which to attempt a retreat, General Williams had no option but to capitulate. Kars was surrendered on 25 November. From the Russian camp near Kars, Major Teesdale, one of the British officers at Kars who had fought so bravely alongside General Kméty, wrote in a letter home:

> **The game has been played out and we are prisoners...Still, even in our degradation, I cannot help feeling that the disgrace lies with those whose duty it was to help us; and not with us, who, I believe in my heart, have done what men could do...**
>
> **Have the Allies ever thought, I wonder, how much it would have cost them to redeem all this ground, or what they will have to pay, even for what we have lost? The whole business passes my comprehension, and I cannot scarcely yet believe that all our trials have ended thus; that six months of endless toil, misery, privation, and, at last, moral agony, should have such a termination.**

This was the first military success of Tsar Alexander II's reign since 18 June. But the length of the siege had meant that the Russians were in no position to make capital of their victory. Colonel Lake, the engineer in charge of the fortifications at Kars, found consolation in that fact:

> **Had we abandoned Kars, and fallen back on Erzeroom, as, shortly after the victory of the 29th of September, we could so easily have done, we should have yielded to the enemy so strong a spot, at a time of the year when there was still some opportunity for further operations, that Asia Minor must have been almost entirely in his power. As it was, we held the place until the season was too advanced to permit of doing more than keeping the position he had won.**

Rather than using the victory to obtain better terms for Russia, the tsar merely confirmed his conviction that the Allies were more in need of peace than Russia. In this climate of stand-off, with each side jostling for position, it was Austria that took the initiative for peace. After consultation with London and Paris, the Austrian government gave St Petersburg an ultimatum: unless Russia accepts the Allies' demands, Austria will enter the war. The four main demands of the Allies were:

1. Freedom of the Danubian Principalities
2. Freedom of the River Danube
3. Neutralization of the Black Sea
4. Guarantee of the rights of the Christian subjects of Turkey

On 16 January 1856, the tsar accepted the Austrian ultimatum. His hand had no doubt been forced by the fact that simultaneous negotiations by the Allies to form a Northern Alliance with Sweden had been ratified in a Treaty of Alliance signed by Sweden, France and Britain the previous November. Russia was weak, militarily and financially. It was unlikely that the imperial regime could hold out for better peace terms than were now being offered.

On 28 February, news from the Paris Peace Conference of the declaration of an armistice until 31 March arrived in the Crimea by telegraph. Parties from both the Russian and Allied sides met at the Traktir Bridge to discuss the terms of the armistice. They arranged reviews of each other's troops. The Treaty of Paris was finally ratified on 27 April 1856, and the war was officially over. Four days previously, the British Fleet had organised a spectacular display of strength – the Great Armament at Spithead. If the Russians were in a mind to hesitate over the terms of the peace, newspaper reports of the royal review on St George's

Russian Prisoners of War (GUSTAVE DORÉ).

Day, 23 April, would have banished any such thoughts. The next day's *Times*' leader would have reached St Petersburg by telegraph within 24 hours:

> **Not three years have elapsed since the last great naval review at Spithead, yet no one could witness the magnificent spectacle of yesterday without feeling that in naval matters we have gone through a whole century of progress... We have now the means of waging a really offensive war, not only against fleets, but harbours, fortresses and rivers – not merely of blockading, but of invading, and carrying the warfare of the sea to the very heart of the land.**

Next time the Allies would do more than merely reconnoitre Kronstadt.

Preparations were soon under way for transporting the Crimean regiments home, but not before both sides had fraternized and paid extensive visits to one another's camps. On 2 May, Lieutenant Young got a parting gift from the Crimea:

> **I was in a Russian village the other day with one of ours and we saw a small cottage with the door open and 3 or 4 girls inside.**
>
> **'Bedad,' say I, 'I'll go in if you do!'**
>
> **So we tied up our animals and walked bang in, and they were very civil till one of the young ladies began to pull my beard and I could not make head or tail of a word she was saying. She offered us some soup made of some very greasy-looking stuff, and vermicelli and some beef, but we declined, and having given the young ladies a cigar each we went away, but not until my young lady had given as fine a kiss as I ever got which I thought only proper to return.**

By the end of July, the last Allied ship had taken the last Allied soldier home, leaving 'beneath the sod of the grim Chersonese peninsula' the many thousands of their comrades who had perished.

AFTERMATH

EVEN AS SEBASTOPOL WAS about to fall, Lieutenant-Captain Pyotr Lesli was thinking of the conflict he had lived through as a watershed:

> **Sebastopol has had to experience so much, more than any other town in the world will ever have to go through; because with time there will be no war; the means of destruction of people are getting stronger with each day; and it would be no wonder if they invented some sort of machine which will kill a thousand people in one go.**

The Crimean War presaged a new era of warfare. Several weapons proposed but never deployed in the Crimea would go on, in a developed technological form, to help define twentieth century conflict. Plans for chemical warfare against Kronstadt were rejected by Aberdeen's government as inhumane. Aberdeen's successor, Lord Palmerston, was more receptive to such suggestions and also expressed interest in a military 'submarine vessel' and a kind of prototype tank, a 'locomotive land battery fitted with scythes to mow down infantry' – though nothing came of either proposal. In the 1850s such ideas seemed grotesque.

In human terms, the Crimean War was nevertheless the costliest conflict between the major Western powers in the century from Waterloo to the Somme, including the American Civil War, which lasted twice as long. Estimates vary considerably but, by the time the peace was signed in early 1856, probably 500,000 Russians had died – of disease, wounds, starvation, and cold. The number of French dead is equally uncertain but may have reached close to 100,000. The latter had suffered terribly from disease during the first summer at Varna and the second Crimean winter, as their previously successful support systems simply collapsed under the weight of numbers. On the British side 22,000 died – almost as many as had been sent out in the original army two

ABOVE: CLEMENCE BROPHY, 34TH REGIMENT, AT CHATHAM HOSPITAL.
RIGHT: THE FRONTISPIECE OF SIMPSON'S COLLECTED DRAWINGS.
OPPOSITE: 13-YEAR OLD WILLIAM LANG RETURNS WITH TROPHIES FROM SEBASTOPOL.

CORPORAL MURPHY AND TWO OTHER SOLDIERS OF THE ROYAL ARTILLERY WITH A GUN CAPTURED AT SEBASTOPOL.

years earlier. The huge disparity between French and British casualties points to the former's far larger force in the Crimea. As many as 2000 Italians also died in the Crimea, despite their only having arrived at the front in May 1855. Numbers of Ottoman dead are most difficult to estimate – no reliable figures exist but casualties were certainly very high and at least as many Ottoman soldiers died as Frenchmen. Most of the fatalities on all sides were due to disease.

In March 1855 Queen Victoria and Prince Albert travelled to Fort Pitt Hospital at Chatham to visit convalescent soldiers. Each patient stood, or sat if disabled, at the foot of his bed holding a card showing his name, rank, regiment, age, service record, wound and action in which it had been received. Her conversation with the servicemen there was a turning point in the royal family's previously rather distant relationship with its subjects. Later that year Victoria would also speak publicly to such men for the first time. In January 1856 she approved the design and inscription of the Victoria Cross, the first ever medal open to all ranks of both services. These crosses were made from Russian guns captured at Sebastopol and awarded 'for valour'. On 26 June the Queen awarded the first VCs in Hyde Park. The earliest action of the war to be so rewarded was that of Charles David Lucas, Mate of the *Hecla*, who had thrown a live Russian shell overboard during the bombardment of Bomarsund. Six crosses were won for actions at the Alma, another six awarded to those who had ridden in

Survivors

Some survivors of the war lived well into the twentieth century. One Crimean midshipman, Colonel Rookes Compton, was even alive when the Second World War began, and could remember not only the trenches of 1914, but also those in front of the Redan in 1855.

Among those who had found themselves in the Crimea, some went on to become famous for other reasons. Charles Gordon arrived as a sapper in January 1855. Thirty years later he gained renown as Gordon of Khartoum. General MacMahon, hero of the Malakoff, later became president of the French Republic. One of the visitors in the Crimea had been an American, Captain George B. McLellan. He was there to observe Allied – and Russian – strategy, and report back to the US army. Less than a decade later during the American Civil War much of the Federal strategy resembled that of the Crimea: Lincoln's army was for some time commanded by that same Captain, now General McLellan.

In the late summer of 1855 William Howard Russell had been visited in the Crimea by a certain Azimullah Khan. He even slept in Russell's tent. Khan had a letter requesting Russell to assist him visiting the trenches. In fact, the purpose of his visit was to witness British military failure at first hand and bring the news back to India. He was 'much struck by the wretched state of both armies in front of Sebastopol' and it was then he and a companion 'formed the resolution of attempting to overthrow the [East India] Company's Government'. Azimullah Khan turned out to be a spy for the ringleaders of the Indian Mutiny in 1857.

William Howard Russell, the first war correspondent, went on to cover the Indian Mutiny, the American Civil War, and the Zulu War among many others. He received a knighthood in 1895 and died in 1907.

Fanny Duberly's *Journal Kept During the Russian War*

the charge of the Light Brigade, and nineteen to survivors of Inkerman.

Despite the bravery of Britain's ordinary soldiers and sailors, the Crimean War dealt a huge blow to the self-confidence of its military and political leaders. The government which had brought the country into the war and the aristocrats who had commanded the army and navy had been discredited. When the purchase of commissions was finally abolished in 1871, it was a decisive moment in the transformation of Victorian society – from a system based on aristocratic privilege to one based on meritocracy and professionalism.

One of the professionals who went on to have the most profound impact was Florence Nightingale. She called the war :

> **...the finest experiment modern history has seen upon a large scale – viz. as to what given number may be put to death at will by the sole agency of bad food and bad air.**

Her own experiment, into the number of lives that could be saved by sensible sanitation and hygiene in hospitals, had far-reaching consequences. The foundation of the Nightingale Training School for Nurses at St Thomas' Hospital in London and the dozens of reports she contributed on the better running of hospitals are monuments to her achievement. She was determined such medical mismanagement would never happen again, declaring: 'I stand at the Altar of the murdered men and while I live I fight their cause.'

Nightingale became a powerful and prodigious figurehead in Britain for medical reform, a cause that was also being increasingly recognized internationally. In 1861 this reform would be furthered by the

---

was published before she left Sebastopol. She felt snubbed when her dedication of the book to Queen Victoria was not accepted. After only a few months back home Fanny and her husband Henry Duberly also set off to India, where the 8th Hussars were among the regiments ordered to put down the mutiny, and where Fanny herself set to work on a new journal. During her stay she had the satisfaction of hearing herself referred to as 'the Crimean heroine'. She remained in India until 1864. Fanny Duberly died in 1903.

Within a month of returning to England, **Fred Dallas** was on foreign service again. He served briefly in China and then in India after the Mutiny. He eventually became a Lieutenant-Colonel and retired from the army in 1876, aged 49. During the war **Henry Clifford** had considered a vocation as a priest. In February 1857 he was awarded with a Victoria Cross for his bravery at Inkerman. The following month he was married, but by summer he was on a new military expedition – this time to China, which he once again captured in watercolours (unfortunately now lost). He also served in South Africa. He died in 1883. **Timothy Gowing** served for another twenty-two years (eighteen of them in India). He fathered nineteen children, seven of whom died in one day of cholera in 1867. At the end of his days he travelled around offices and factories in Lancashire trying to make money by selling copies of *A Voice From the Ranks*, his account of life in the Crimea.

After the war **Roger Fenton** resumed his work as photographer for the British Museum. He also built on his reputation as the British master of both landscape and still life photography. In 1862, at the height of his fame, Roger Fenton announced his retirement from photography. It seems he was depressed by the fading of his prints and the low status given to the new art form at that year's International Exhibition (at which photography was relegated into the category of 'Machinery'); he sold off his equipment and returned to his previous career as a solicitor. He died suddenly in 1869 aged 50.

When **Florence Nightingale** returned from the Crimea she was exhausted. She cut herself off from the world, dictating her pamphlets from a couch and being carried around on visits in a special chair. She nevertheless wrote and campaigned ceaselessly until the age of 90, dying in 1910. She had been offered, but declined, a national funeral and burial in Westminster Abbey.

Alexis Soyer never really recovered from his exertions during the Crimean War and died two years later. His 'Soyer Stove' was used by army cooks a century later, and even during the Gulf War a modified version was still in use.

When the war ended **Mary Seacole** was left with considerable unsold stock and returned impoverished to England. By November she was in the London Bankruptcy Court, but both *The Times* and *Punch* set up funds to reimburse her losses. In December 1856 *Punch* published a poem in her honour. In 1857 a gala benefit was held on her behalf at the Royal Surrey Gardens, attracting audiences of 10,000 a night. Queen Victoria joined those who praised her, and Mary Seacole became the masseuse of the Princess of Wales. She died on 14 April 1881.

Captain Hodasiewicz deserted the Russian army before the fall of Sebastopol. For his bravery at the battle of the Tchernaya **Leo Tolstoy** was promoted to the rank of Lieutenant just as peace was signed. But he took a year's leave and then resigned his commission in order to devote all his time to writing. *War and Peace*, which was published in 1868, is set during the 1810s. The battle scenes, however, are based not on the Napoleonic War, but on the author's experiences in the Crimea. Tolstoy died in 1910.

foundation of the Red Cross.

Both the Russian and Ottoman Empires were practically bankrupted by the war, and this accentuated their need for modernization. Russia's underdeveloped economy, dependent on a virtually feudal serf-based labour force, proved too inflexible for staffing modern armies or industries. When Tsar Alexander II accepted the peace terms in January 1856 he also agreed to abolish serfdom, but he was unable to avert the stirrings of revolution. In spite of his reforms he was assassinated in 1881. In the Ottoman Empire too, as soon as peace was declared, the sultan issued a decree forbidding discrimination against any of his subjects on grounds of class, religion or race. The war also encouraged the Ottomans to push ahead with other reforms, including improvements in communication, inspired by the telegraph and railways introduced by their Allies.

The effect of the war on France's Second Empire was ambivalent. Paris had been restored to its former role at the centre of European politics. At the beginning of the conflict, negotiations took place in Vienna; by the end of the war it seemed natural that the peace should be signed in Paris. Similarly, in 1851 the Great Exhibition had taken place in London; in 1855 the Exposition Universelle took place in Paris. When in 1854 an 'Emperor' was mentioned it was assumed the speaker meant the tsar; by 1856 the Emperor on everyone's lips was Napoleon III. He had regained some of the glory of his uncle.

In the longer term however, Napoleon III's ambition to reduce the power of the two absolutist monarchies, Russia and Austria, worked against him. Although the defeat of Russia put an end to the latter's influence as a major power over central Europe (a role it was not to play again until after the Second World War), a weakened Austria helped unleash the forces of Prussian militarism, which first led to the creation of a unified Germany and later destroyed the French Second Empire.

Another significant result of this changing balance of power was its effect on emergent nationalist

LEFT: *THE GUARDS RETURN TO PARIS FROM THE CRIMEA* (DE MORAINE).
ABOVE: THE VALLEY OF THE SHADOW OF DEATH. (PHOTO BY ROGER FENTON.)

movements. Despite requests for help to Queen Victoria herself, the Allies failed to support the Chechen rebel, Shamil, and the rebellion in the Caucasus collapsed in 1864 with Shamil himself captured by tsarist forces in 1859. However, when a place at the peace conference was won by Sardinia, Italian unification as a sovereign state followed swiftly. The Danubian Principalities of Moldavia and Wallachia also won their independence, becoming Rumania in 1862.

Of the three great international empires involved in the Crimean War none survives today. The Ottoman Empire is long gone, the British Empire withered away in the second half of this century and and the Russian Empire collapsed in 1917. And yet the current explosiveness at flashpoints from the Holy Places to the Balkans is in large part the result of conflicts which the Crimean campaign failed to defuse.

In late 1991 the collapsing Soviet Union became the latest sick man of Europe. When it finally died, the Crimea became part of Ukraine, one of many newly independent states to rise out of its ashes. One of Tolstoy's diary entries, written shortly after the battle of Inkerman, still resonates today:

> **The feeling of ardent patriotism that has arisen and issued forth from Russia's misfortunes will long leave its traces on her. These people who are now sacrificing their lives will be citizens of Russia and will not forget their sacrifice.**

In 1997, after protracted negotiations, Russia and the Ukraine finally agreed to a deal over the Black Sea Fleet. Nevertheless, Sebastopol remains a place, not only of strategic importance but also of patriotic emotion for the Russians. Let us hope there continues to be peace in the Crimea.

BIBLIOGRAPHY

FURTHER READING

Adkin, Mark: *The Charge* (Leo Cooper/London, 1996)

Baring Pemberton, W.: *Battles of the Crimean War* (Pan Books/London, 1962)

Chesney, K.: *Crimean War Reader* (Frederick Müller Ltd/London, 1960)

Compton, Piers: *Colonel's Lady and Camp Follower* (Robert Hale & Co/London, 1970)

Cooke, Brian: *The Grand Crimean Central Railway* (Cavalier House/Cheshire, 1997)

french Blake, R.L.V.: *The Crimean War* (Sphere Books/Buckinghamshire, 1971)

Gammer, Moshe: *Muslim Resistance to the Tsar* (Portland/London, 1994)

Goldfrank, David: *The Origins of the Crimean War* (Longman/New York, 1994)

Gooch, B.D.: *The New Bonapartist Generals in the Crimean War* (Martinus Nijhoff/The Hague, 1959)

Gouttman, Alain: *La Guerre de Crimée* (Editions S.P.M./Paris, 1996)

Greenhill, Basil & Giffard, Ann: *The British Assault on Finland* (London, 1988)

Hibbert, Christopher: *The Destruction of Lord Raglan* (Longman/London, 1961)

Lambert, Andrew: *The Crimean War: British grand strategy against Russia, 1853-56* (Manchester University Press/NewYork, 1990)

Lambert, Andrew, and Badsey, Stephen: *The War Correspondents: The Crimean War* (Alan Sutton Publishing/Avon, 1994)

Palmer, Alan: *The Banner of Battle* (Weidenfeld & Nicolson/London, 1987)
The Decline and Fall of the Ottoman Empire (John Murray/London, 1992)

Seaton, Albert: *The Crimean War: A Russian Chronicle* (B.T. Batsford/London, 1977)

Shepherd, John: *The Crimean Doctors* (Liverpool University Press/Liverpool, 1991)

Sweetman, John: *Balaklava 1854* (Osprey Military/London, 1990)

Thomas, R.H.G., and Scollins, R.: *The Russian Army of the Crimean War* (Osprey Military/London, 1991)

Woodham-Smith, Cecil: *The Reason Why* (Penguin/London, 1958)
Florence Nightingale (Constable/London, 1950)

The War Correspondent (Journal of the Crimean War Research Society)

CONTEMPORARY WITNESSES

Alabin, Pyotr: *Pokhodnyie zapiski v voiny 1853,1854,1855 i 1856 godov.* (Vyatka, 1861)

Alexander, Ziggi & Dewjee, Audrey (ed): *Wonderful Adventures of Mary Seacole in Many Lands* (Falling Wall Press/Bristol, 1984)

Anglesey, The Marquess of: *Little Hodge* (Leo Cooper/London, 1971)

Bazancourt, *César de: L'expédition de Crimée jusqu'à la prise de Sebastopol. Chroniques de la guerre d'Orient.* (Paris, 1856)

Berg, Nikolai: *Zapiski ob osadye Sevastopolya* (2 vols, Moscow, 1858)

Blackwood, Alicia: *A Narrative of Personal Experiences and Impressions during a Residence on the Bosphorus during the Crimean War* (Hatchard/London, 1881)

Blishen, Harry: *Letters from the Crimea* (Emily Faithfull/London, 1863)

Bonham-Carter, Victor (ed): *George Lawson: Surgeon in the Crimea* (Military Book Society/London, 1968)

Calthorpe, Lt. Col. S.J.G.: *Cadogan's Crimea* (Book Club Associates/London, 1979)

Campbell, Colin Frederick: *Letters from Camp to his Relatives during the Siege of Sebastopol* (Bentley/London, 1894)

Clifford, Henry V.C.: *His Letters and Sketches From the Crimea* (Michael Joseph/London, 1956)

Collection: *Sbornik rukopisei predstavlennykh ego imperatorskomy vysochestvu Gosudaryu nasledniku tsesarevichu o sevastopolískoi oboronye sevastopolítsami* (3 vols, St Petersburg, 1872)

Cler, Colonel Jean Joseph Gustave: *Souvenirs d'un*

officier du 2e Zouaves (Paris, 1859)

Dallas, Lt. Col. George Frederick (sometime Captain): *A Soldier's Duty* (unpublished – courtesy of Michael Hargreave Mawson, Crimean War Research Society)

Delorme, Amédée: *Lettres d'un Zouave (Paris, 1896)*

Duberly, Fanny: *Journal Kept During the Russian War* (Longman, 1856)

Fisher-Rowe, Cornet E.R.: *Extracts from Letters written during the Crimean War* (R.D. Stedman/Godalming, 1907)

Fenwick, K.(ed): *Voice from the Ranks: A Sergeant-Major's Account* (Gowing) (Folio Society/London, 1954)

Goldie, Sue (ed): *'I have done my duty': The Selected Letters of Florence Nightingale* (Manchester University Press/Manchester, 1987)

Goodman, Margaret: *Experiences of an English Sister of Mercy* (Smith, Elder & Co./London, 1862)

Herbé, Jean-Jules: *Français et Russes en Crimée. Lettres d'un officier français à sa famille pendant la campagne d'Orient* (Paris, 1892)

Hodasiewitcz, Captain R.: *A Voice from within the walls of Sebastopol (London, 1856)*

Hughes, Reverend R.E.: *Two Summer Cruises with the Baltic Fleet (London, 1855)*

Kinglake, A.W.: *The Invasion of the Crimea* (8 vols, Blackwood, 1863-87)

Marx, Karl: *The Eastern Question* (Swan Sonnenschein & Co./London, 1897)

Mismer, Charles: *Souvenirs d'un dragon de l'armée de Crimée* (Paris, 1887)

Mitchell, Sergeant Albert: *Recollections of the Light Brigade* (N. Ginder Canterbury, 1885)

Paget, Lord George: *The Light Cavalry Brigade in the Crimea* (John Murray/London, 1881)

Peron, Guy: *Les Derniers Invalides. Memoires, souvenirs, récits et épisodes* (Paris, 1904)

Pirogov, N.I.: *Sevastopol'skie pis'ma* (St Petersburg, 1899)

Robins, Major Colin (ed): *The Murder of a Regiment: A Crimean War Officer's Journal* (Withycut Press/Bowden, 1994)

Robinson, Assistant Surgeon Frederick: *Diary of the Crimean War* (Bentley/London, 1856)

Russell, William Howard: *The British Expedition to the Crimea* (Routledge/London, 1858)
The Great War with Russia (Routledge/London, 1895)

Sandwith, Humphry: *A Narrative of the Siege of Kars* (London, 1856)

Slade, Adolphus: *Turkey and the Crimean War* (Smith, Elder & Co./London, 1867)

Soyer, Alexis: *A Culinary Campaign* (Southover Press/Lewes, 1995)

Tolstoy, Leo: *Sebastopol Sketches* (Penguin/London, 1986)
Tolstoy's Diaries (Edited and translated by R.F. Christian) (Flamingo/London, 1984)
Tolstoy's Letters. Volume I, 1828-1879 (R.F. Christian, ed) (London, 1978)

Tyrell, Henry: *The History of the War with Russia* (3 vols, London, 1857)

Williams, Jane (ed): *An Autobiography of Elizabeth Davis, a Balaklava Nurse* (London, 1857)

Young, William: *Sodgering in Earnest: The Crimean War Experiences of an Irish Infantry Subaltern* (unpublished – courtesy of Andrew Sewell, Crimean War Research Society)

The Illustrated London News
L'Illustration, journal universel
Sovremennik, vols. 1855–1858

BOOKS ABOUT VISUAL MATERIAL

Gernsheim, Helmut and Alison (ed): *Roger Fenton: Photographer of the Crimea: His Photographs and his Letters from The Crimea* (London/Secker and Warburg, 1954)

Hannavy, John: *The Camera goes to War* (The Scottish Arts Council, 1974)

Harrington, Peter: *British Artists and War* (Greenhill Books/London, 1993)

James, Lawrence: *Crimea: The War with Russia from Contemporary Photos* (Hayes Kennedy/Thame, 1981)

Lalumia, M.P.: *Realism and Politics in Victorian Art*

of the Crimean War (Ann Arbor/ Michigan, 1984)

Öztuncay, Bahattin: *James Robertson: Pioneer of Photography in the Ottoman Empire* (Eren/Istanbul, 1992)

Robichon, F. and Rouillé, A.: *Jean Charles Langlois. La photographie, la peinture, la guerre. Correspondance inédite de Crimée* (Nîmes, 1992)

Simpson, William: *The Seat of War in the East* (Colnaghi/London, 1856)

Smith, Karen W.: *Guys, Constantin: Crimean War Drawings 1854-1856* (The Cleveland Museum of Art, 1978)

Crimée: premiers reportages de guerre (Catalogue of an exhibition at the musée de l'Armée, Paris, 1994)

ACKNOWLEDGEMENTS

This book is a collaborative effort in several senses. It is a collaboration between five authors and a collaboration between television and publishing. It is also a collaboration between the authors and the many individuals who - and institutions which - helped us along the way. There are too many of these to name all of them but we would like to thank a number of people without whom this book undoubtedly wouldn't exist: first of all, our commissioning editors Peter Moore and Alan Hayling at Channel Four and our co-funders, The Learning Channel and *La Cinquieme*. Secondly, Susanna Yager and Sandy Holton at C4 Publishing. At Mentorn Barraclough Carey thanks to George Carey, our executive producer, and a special thank you to Amanda Quaile, Anna Dìs Òlafsdòttir and Karla Bryan, who not only turned a blind eye to our moonlighting but were a positive help. At Boxtree, many thanks to our commissioning editor Charlie Carman and to Susie Jenkins. Thanks also to copy-editor Miranda Stonor.

In the making of the series and the book we have consulted a number of specialists including Andrew Lambert, William Blair at Princeton University, Major Colin Robins OBE, Andrew Sewell, Michael Hargreave Mawson and other members of the Crimean War Research Society, including Brian Cooke. Special thanks to Andrew for permission to quote extracts from the letters of William Young and to Michael for permission to reproduce extracts from the letters of his ancestor, Fred Dallas. Thanks also to Peter Harrington, curator of the Anne S.K. Brown Military Collection at Brown University, and Oliver Hughes at the Slavonic Section of the British Library. We have relied on the co-operation and courtesy of a number of military museums including The National Army Museum and Regimental Museums too numerous to mention.

Marianne Ellingworth and Jonathan Sugden translated the few Turkish eye-witness accounts we came across; Teresa Cherfas translated all the Russian and Georgina Pye translated the French accounts.

We would like to thank Michael Hargreave Mawson again since he kindly agreed to read the entire manuscript and did his best to correct the most obvious howlers Any mistakes which remain are, of course, our own.

Finally, and most importantly, two special thank yous: to Sally Brien, who not only found all the pictures but also read the entire manuscript and made many invaluable suggestions; and to Georgina Pye, who saw the book through from our first meetings with Channel Four publishing through the redrafting of individual chapters, the copy-editing and proofing stages right down to writing all the picture captions.

PICTURE ACKNOWLEDGEMENTS

The Publisher wishes to thank the following: **Anne S.K. Brown Military Collection, Brown University Library** 14 bottom, 27, 38-9, 62, 90, 139, 161, 164, 182; **Bahattin Öztuncay** 8-9, 32 top; **Bibliothèque Nationale de France** 95 bottom left, 95 bottom right, 155 bottom, 168-9, 174 left, 174 right; **Birmingham Central Library** 18 top, 25, 36 top, 37 bottom, 45 middle, 50, 52 top, 53, 58-9, 68, 70 left, 76, 80 left, 94 top left, 94 top right, 94 bottom left, 94 bottom right, 99 bottom, 101 bottom, 104, 111, 112-3, 116-7, 121, 131, 133, 134, 183; **Border and King's Own Royal Border Regimental Museum, The Castle, Carlisle** 171 top right; **Brian Borthwick/The Animation People** 12, 29; **Centre Canadien D'Architecture** 10-11; **Constantin Savulescu** 19, 20 top left; **George Eastman House** 20 bottom; **Illustrated Times** 156 bottom; **L'Illustration** 52 bottom, 119 bottom right; **The Illustrated London News** 23 middle, 85, 92 top, 92 bottom, 100 top, 148, 170 top; **Imperial War Museum** 44, 54 bottom, 87, 88, 95 top right, 96-7, 101 top, 107 top, 109, 124-5, 150, 154 top, 170 bottom, 178 left, 180; **The Julia Margaret Cameron Trust, Dimbola Lodge, Freshwater Bay** 71; **Musée de L'Armée, Paris** title page, 45 top; **National Library of Jamaica** 89; **National Museum of Finland** 31, 34, 35, 146-7, 149; **The National Trust** 22, 63, 66-7, 75, 91, 103, 106, 114, 115, 126-7, 130 top, 138, 155 top, 158-9, 162-3, 166-7, 170-1, 178 right; **Nicholas Fitzherbert** 26, 42-3, 46, 54 top, 55, 67, 74, 77, 78-9, 83, 105, 110, 118, 123, 135, 142, 165, 173; **Orr's Circle of Sciences, London** 45 bottom; **Punch** 100 bottom; **R.A.M.C. Historical Museum** 81 bottom; **The Royal Archives © Her Majesty The Queen** 20 top right, 20 middle, 24, 32-3, 37 top, 86, 95 top left, 125 bottom; **Royal Engineers Library, Chatham** 61; **Russian Historical Museum, Moscow** 14-15, 16-17, 18 middle, 23 top, 36 bottom, 51, 80 right, 84, 98-9, 102, 107 bottom, 119 top, 119 bottom left, 120, 122, 130 bottom, 137, 143, 144-5, 152-3, 154 bottom, 156 top, 163 top, 177; **Sally Brien** 70 right; **Wellcome** 81 top; Whilst every effort has been made to trace copyright holders for photos featured in this book, we would like to apologise should there have been any errors or omissions.

INDEX